MY LIFE WITH

MICHAEL

10 YEARS OF **THRILLER** *Live*

About the Author

Photograph: Michael Wharley

Gary Lloyd has been directing and choreographing for over twenty years and has won many awards in recognition of his work on television and in the theatre.

Born in Leeds, England, he spent his childhood as a dancer, competing in Ballroom and Latin-American dance with his sister Joanne, moving on to the musical theatre stage as a teenager, later establishing a successful performing career internationally and in London's West End.

The opportunities to direct and choreograph came quite early on around age twenty-one when Gary was working in the United States.

Gary has been the director and choreographer of *Thriller Live!* since 2008.

Twitter: @garylloyd1
Instagram: @garylloydme
www.garylloyd.me

MY LIFE WITH
MICHAEL

10 YEARS OF **THRILLER** *Live*

GARY LLOYD

The Book Guild Ltd

First published in Great Britain in 2019 by
The Book Guild Ltd
9 Priory Business Park
Wistow Road, Kibworth
Leicestershire, LE8 0RX
Freephone: 0800 999 2982
www.bookguild.co.uk
Email: info@bookguild.co.uk
Twitter: @bookguild

Cover photo courtesy of ©Flying Music Image: Michael Duke

Photo credits
© Colin Panter ‰ The Press Association Limited © Kevin Wilson © Adrian Grant
© Betty Zapala © Bonnie Britain © Gary Lloyd © Edson Cabrera Junior
© Dan Wooller © Flying Music © Kevin Wilson © Gary Lloyd

Every effort has been made to trace copyright holders and to obtain their permission for the
use of copyright material. The author apologises for any errors or omissions in the above list
and would be grateful if notified of any corrections that should be incorporated in future reprints
or editions of this book.

Typeset in 12pt Minion Pro

Printed and bound by CPI Group (UK) Ltd, Croydon, CR0 4YY

ISBN 978 1912881 666

British Library Cataloguing in Publication Data.
A catalogue record for this book is available from the British Library.

This book is dedicated to my mother Judy,
whose eternal love gave me the gift of freedom
and the wings I needed to fly.

Mum, I miss you…

Contents

Preface

I never got to meet Michael Jackson. In fact, I was just weeks away from meeting him at the O2 as a guest at his *This Is It* show. This of course, devastatingly, did not happen.

So, it may seem strange that I would endeavour to write a memoir called *My Life with Michael*, when our paths never crossed in person. Yet seven days of my week, both day and night, is filled with all that Michael Jackson created. The sights, sounds and all he stood for and what he gave his whole life to are part of my daily routine.

When it comes to entertainment, I have been given the gift to inspire and educate young people and their families who come to my show with all the things Michael and the Jackson family gave us.

I cannot claim to know anything about Michael's personal life, nor wish to comment on the media perspective or the constant speculation that continues, sadly even after his death. But I have been immersed in all that he created for almost forty years. I have experienced first-hand the spirit and commitment he put into his work and seen how his music has fascinated and thrilled fans around the world for decades.

Some would rather focus only on the propaganda, the (unproven) allegations, and the bizarre and headline-worthy tabloid junk that follows and haunts anyone with such high profile, none more so than

MJ. Working so closely on *Thriller Live!* keeps that ugly world pushed outside. Perhaps a little protected by the bubble of theatre but with a deep-rooted connection to this work since childhood, I am able to focus on what I believe in and what I do best.

This book focuses on the truth. My truth, the truth surrounding me, and the truth that has kept my heart pounding and my feet moving for over forty years.

And for the last ten years I have had the privilege to call it home.

When starting on the journey to turn these stories into a book, wading through all my notes, emails and transcripts while interviewing my fellow passengers, I made a wonderful discovery. That this group of people I am involved with is more than a band of brothers and sisters, much more than a company of performers or gang of Michael Jackson fans.

We are a large family of ambassadors who, in some beautiful twist of fate have, at one time or other, been called upon to study and perfect (or as close as is humanly possible) Michael Jackson's work.

His work that is becoming more and more timeless and is now, posthumously, considered art. The work that has for decades been considered legendary and to the human eye and non-professional looks easy because it is so globally accessible. Each one of these ambassadors has played a part in moving this show forward, adding to the study of each vocal lick, every step, every precise flick of the finger or throw of the hat.

His work will never truly be recreated, never perfected but can always be celebrated and we are part of a very chosen few who get to do that on a global platform. What an honour.

It is a delicate and dangerous responsibility and a duty of not only an admirer of Michael Jackson, but a devotee of theatre, of magic, of musical genius and a life dedicated to creating and performing.

This book is for the fans of our show and of Michael's work. But it is also for anybody that has an interest in the entertainment industry, wanting to gain a deeper understanding of how this weird and wonderful world of theatre and music works. Fans of dance, who have an aspiration to train, create and become an all-round performer.

Vocalists who wish to be more than 'just a singer' should read on and learn about what it takes to approach Michael's work and survive in this show, performing it eight times a week.

This is my story. The story of how Michael has been in my life, my whole life, particularly the last ten plus years.

As the director and choreographer of *Thriller Live!*, the live concert musical of Michael's most successful work, I have the obligation and responsibility of presenting this work around the world and in London's West End. On celebrating the tenth year in the West End with this production, it feels only right I should share some of it's amazing stories.

My Life with Michael is a story about a passion for music and the discipline of theatre. It is also, of course, about Michael Jackson and the love that is held for him in abundance around the world.

Thriller Live! has become the West End's thirteenth longest-running musical. It has now been seen by over five million people in thirty-four countries and played over 7,000 performances worldwide

In this book, you will meet people from all walks of life who have had their lives changed by this show and have changed mine by being involved.

Foreword
by Adrian Grant

I am privileged to have known Michael Jackson for over twenty-one years, and since 1988 have been endorsing his legacy around the world. So every time I'm asked what he was like as a person, I take the time to speak from the heart.

Firstly, he was the nicest and most humble person I have ever met. And I truly mean that. Not because he was Michael Jackson, a pop superstar whom I had idolised from the moment I saw him moonwalk, but because away from the stage and hype he was, deep down, a kind, loving spirit who really cared about others and wanted to make a positive difference. And it didn't matter if you were royalty or from south central LA, Michael made time for everyone, often giving something and not expecting anything in return, but to see people happy.

In March 1990, I was lucky enough to meet Michael for the first time and became the first person to have an article published about life at his home, Neverland Valley Ranch. I've told the story many times, but I'll retell a small part here to give you an insight into who he really was.

I had been invited to Record One Studios where Michael was recording his album *Dangerous*. I was there to present him with an award from the readers of *Off the Wall*. Michael marvelled at the award, a six foot by three foot oil painting depicting his twenty-one year career at the time. I then interviewed Michael for the magazine and took some pictures, before being treated to an exclusive preview of a new song, 'Man in Black' (which never actually made the final album). Towards the end of the day, Michael surprised me by asking me if I would like to visit his ranch for lunch at the weekend. I literally fell off my seat and accepted the invitation with glee.

Saturday came and as I was driven through the striking Neverland gates, I remember being amazed at the beautiful lush 3,000-acre valley. Upon signing in, we walked towards the main house and in the distance I could see two chimpanzees rolling around on the grass, giraffes, llamas, the funfair and a lake full of flamingos as classical music echoed out from speakers in the flowerbeds. I commented to the security guard who was accompanying me that this wasn't reality, but he replied, "Well, it's reality for Michael Jackson. This is what he wakes up to every morning." And that was true. Michael had lived a life that, since the age of eleven, when he had his first number one with The Jackson Five, he was able to have almost anything that he wanted. Fortunately, Michael chose to channel most of his desires towards something positive and after getting to know Michael I saw how much he really did care for children – often opening the Neverland gates to the underprivileged or disabled.

I got to see many more examples of Michael's humanitarian efforts over the years. During a trip to Budapest in August 1994, Michael, along with Lisa-Marie Presley, visited a number of hospitals, handing out toys to the sick children. I was fortunate to be the only 'media person' allowed to accompany them into the hospitals and I was happy to help distribute the gifts to the children. However, the press were sceptical and suggested the trip (part of Michael's 'Heal the World' campaign) was nothing more than a publicity stunt. What they didn't see was the moving moment when Michael brought a smile to the face of a very poorly young girl who had lain motionless and silent for weeks. Her mother, at her side in constant vigil, broke down in tears as her daughter reached out and touched Michael's hand. Moments like that mattered to Michael. He had a real caring affinity for children, and I believe he related to them more than he did to adults. Whether that was because he didn't have a childhood or the fact they didn't judge or want from him, I don't know but it was clear that the connection was genuine. I visited Neverland many more times over the years. Sometimes Michael would be present, and sometimes I was there to accompany fans who had won competitions via my magazine, but each trip was memorable and I was always made to feel welcome being invited to enjoy the amenities be that playing in the arcade, the rides in the funfair or watching movies in the theatre.

And I was also fortunate to see him work in the recording studio, when I got to spend a couple of days at the Hit Factory in New York, whilst Michael was there producing his album *HIStory*. Amongst the luminaries present were Janet Jackson, Jimmy Jam and Terry Lewis. They had been putting the finishing touches to the song 'Scream'. On the second day I remember sitting in the studio (alongside Lisa Marie) and watching Michael master the control desk like it was his second home. He treated us to two stellar songs, 'Stranger in Moscow' and 'Smile'. They sounded out of this world, and with the latter I could visualise Michael singing, laughing and dancing in a video with blended footage of Charlie Chaplin. I shared this vision, and he smiled from ear to ear, saying that's exactly what he intended to do. Unfortunately the video never materialised, but that's how easy Michael was to talk to. He was a legend of his craft but always open to new information and letting others have a platform to express their ideas and talent. That's why his music and videos are as good as they are. He has said in the past that for some of his work he was just the vessel through which creativity flowed from above, but I have also seen that he was the vessel that was able to pull together the world's best musicians, songwriters, choreographers and directors and allow them to do what they are best at without ego, combining to produce a volume of work that will live forever.

Thriller Live! was created out of love and respect for Michael Jackson, and wanting to see him honoured not only as one of the (if not THE) greatest entertainers of all time, but to acknowledge his work as a selfless humanitarian striving to make the world a better place through his music and charitable endeavours.

The show's success is purely down to the artistry and creativity of Michael Jackson. His music catalogue spans over four decades and contains songs that have sold a staggering billion copies worldwide from 'Billie Jean' to 'Bad', 'Off the Wall' and 'Earth Song', not forgetting his work with the Jacksons and The Jackson Five, where his career started with four straight number one records, 'I Want You Back', 'I'll Be There', 'ABC' and 'The Love You Save'.

I will forever be grateful to Michael Jackson for opening the doors of his world to me and the chances that has given me. He showed me anything is possible if you work hard enough. And from that *Thriller Live!* has been able to give opportunities to hundreds of people over the years of which I am very proud. From performers who grew up singing his songs and learning his routines to a team of creatives who have been able to use this platform to share not only Michael's genius but build upon that with their own artistic flair.

We have a hardworking and talented team that have kept *Thriller Live!* touring around the world from Hull to Sydney for over twelve years, and in the West End for the past ten. These include, of course, the cast of singers, dancers and musicians. And the crew from wardrobe, lighting, sound and video to stage, and company managers who coordinate on a daily basis. Then at the top of it all are the producers, Flying Music; our brilliant musical supervisor, John Maher; and director and choreographer Gary Lloyd.

It has been a privilege to work with Gary over these past ten years. Not only because of his creativity, but more so because he, like Michael, is kind, loving and humble, and I couldn't think of anyone better to have taken *Thriller Live!* forward as he did back in 2008.

When you buy a ticket to see a stage show you are witnessing the results of years of dedication, auditions and rehearsals. I hope this book gives you a better insight into the world of theatre and the life of a director and choreographer who pulls all that talent and magic together.

Adrian Grant
Creator & Associate Producer, *Thriller Live!*

"I feel very fortunate to have been blessed with recognition for my efforts. This recognition also brings with it a responsibility to one's admirers throughout the world. Performers should always serve as role models who set an example for young people."

– Michael Jackson

Part One
Music and Me

Chapter One

Forever, Michael

As I sat down in the back of the black cab, I dared to look at the front page of the paper I had picked up.

My heart stopped as the image and headline hit me like a blow to the stomach, '*THE KING IS DEAD – days before London comeback Jackson dies of heart attack*'.

It was true, Michael Jackson really had died.

My first thoughts went immediately to the cast: *How will they perform the show that night? They will all be devastated. Would there even be a show?*

At that moment, my phone rang and the seemingly blurred voice on the end of the line asked me to make my way to the theatre (I was on my way there anyway, where else would I go?) as the building was surrounded by press.

Not only that, the fans were starting to appear, swarming in fact, with flowers, candles and pictures as a first tribute to their idol.

The front of the theatre became a vigil for Michael for the next few weeks.

As my cab turned the corner into Great Windmill Street, a small crowd were slumped on the steps of the Windmill Theatre, which is just outside our stage door. It was some of the dancers who had made their way to the theatre not knowing what else to do. All huge fans of Michael, they all looked in complete shock and some were crying.

We had seen each other only hours earlier. Most of the dancers had been supportive enough to come and see my work and their peers perform in a burlesque after hours show I had put together. The show was running for a week at the Arts Theatre in Leicester Square in aid of the TheatreMAD trust for people in the arts living with HIV and AIDS.

It was a fun and very tongue-in-cheek performance, designed to raise money and awareness, and bring people into a late-night environment to have a good time.

The mood was high and all of the 'Thriller lot' brought their usual infectious and overwhelming energy after having a few drinks beforehand.

The cabaret started at midnight so they, of course, had already performed that evening and were buzzing from that.

The show got off to a good start and the crowd was great.

I was in the dress circle operating the sound.

About three songs in, I looked over to the lighting operator who beckoned me over.

Mid cue, I stepped over to see what was so urgent.

He turned his laptop round to show me a news report of Michael being rushed to hospital, potentially dead.

I couldn't quite get my head round this as I had several cues ahead of me and a show in full swing, although I have to admit my first thought was that it was yet another publicity news story around the upcoming tour. It couldn't possibly be true...

At that point I looked down over onto the stalls and saw a sea of mobile phones flickering on, one by one.

How rude! *I thought, but then realised – these phones belonged to one group, the dancers from Thriller, who were clearly getting the news flash I had just been shown.*

Following the show (which went really well, the onstage cast oblivious to the tragedy happening in real time during the show), we walked through Soho and found that MJ songs were blaring from every bar. It was all rather bizarre, yet we still refused to believe it. We made our way to Freedom bar and sat down, where they also had Michael Jackson on loop. The mood had seriously turned to something more apprehensive and dark, and one by one we all made our excuses and left for home, not wanting to admit that this unbelievable piece of media could actually be the truth.

After greeting them solemnly at the stage door, I decided to walk all the way through the dark and suddenly eerie-feeling theatre to the foyer to see what press had arrived.

Through the glass, I could see the press and fans battling each other to gain the best position at the doors of the theatre, the press to get a front row seat, and the fans to ensure their tribute was pride of place.

My attention was taken by the Nimax theatre employee sitting at the box office, head in hands.

I was quite moved by how emotional he seemed, perhaps it won't only be the cast who would struggle to get through tonight?

As I approached him, he looked up and saw me, and gestured towards the computer screen.

"Look at that," he said, "all bookings, I can't keep up."

All I could see was a string of emails ticking upward like a time bomb about to explode.

Ticket sales had gone mad – overnight!

This was hard to take in, incredibly surreal – I couldn't get my head round what was happening.

This wasn't meant to go like this. All we had seen for the past weeks was Michael, 'This Is It', the O2. Fifty shows. The build up was like nothing else… of course, it was Michael Jackson.

We all had our tickets ready to go and witness the master at work. Most of the cast were too young to have ever seen him live.

I was lucky enough to have seen the 'BAD' tour. Leeds Roundhay Park stadium 1988, August 29th, Michael's thirtieth birthday. Barely a teenager, I spent the whole concert standing spellbound, right down the front with my younger sister on my shoulders. The whole thing was so extraordinary, and Michael's performance so hypnotic, I didn't feel a thing, other than complete teenage euphoria.

One of the things I remember most was the crowd, over 60,000 people, spontaneously bursting into a deafening version of 'Happy Birthday'.

Michael stood and cried and the crowd cheered for what seemed like an eternity.

We truly were in the presence of something historic.

The Billie Jean hat was famously thrown into the crowd, and this particular time, it landed right smack in the middle of a crowd of girls next to us. We watched in wonderment at these so called human beings almost ripping each other to shreds to attain this piece of superstar fabric.

Moreover, so was the performance. As time has gone by and I have made the journey from choreographer to director and writer, I realise what I somehow knew then, that this show, although compared to today's productions may seem modest, was a work of art, a genius piece of construction that flowed like nothing else. Michael had the audience in the palm of his hand and it was like we were part of a masterplan that started way back when he was writing and producing this material.

There was nothing manufactured; this was done the old-school way and performed by a master.

This experience just fuelled my obsession with Jackson further and I remain to this day so thankful I got the chance to see him live. I remember the whole thing like it was yesterday.

I looked again at the computer screen, the ticking of the booking emails unrelenting, charging upward. Until this moment (six months into our already extended run), we were poised, ready for our sales to dip, dwindle, even facing the possibility that we might even close in the West End.

It suddenly dawned on me that we were now very clearly in the spotlight. The only place in the UK with any kind of connection the fans could come and grieve and the press could gain an instant quote. It was also clear: the show would benefit from this untimely and horrific tragedy.

I hastily made my way to the auditorium and saw the stage had been set up for a press conference.

As well as myself, Paul Walden, the producer and Adrian Grant, the creator of the show had been called in as well as four of the performers: Ricko Baird (previously one of Michael's dancers) and Mitchell Zhangazha, both of whom were playing Michael in our show; as well as Roger Wright and Ben Forster, two of our leading men. Mitchell, who played young Michael, was only twelve and had been pulled out of school for this and looked terrified.

The remainder of that day was understandably sombre, and as the rest of the company waited for a sign from myself, we entered into the conference with the UK press.

The five of us sat side by side, unusually silent and clearly in shock.

So many thoughts running through our head: the immediate future – should we allow the show to go ahead this evening; what about our 'This Is It' tickets? – to the long term future – how would this affect our show and our life here at the Lyric?

The line-up of journalists asked banal questions about the show, quizzed Ricko and Adrian what it was like to work with Michael, and asked Mitchell how he felt about playing Michael and how much pressure was it to fill the shoes of the King of Pop.

Mitchell, always wise beyond his years (not unlike Michael) answered simply, "I am just singing, which is what I love to do, I am not Michael and I am not trying to recreate his brilliance, I am just singing."

The rest of the day continued in the same heavy, serious, almost numb way as the cast drifted in for a rehearsal for that evening's performance.

We decided, against the producers initial respectful feeling, that we should go ahead with the show.

It's what Michael would have wanted and what he would have done in this instance, to pay tribute the only way he, and we, knew how.

Many ex-cast members showed up to the theatre and I decided it would be an appropriate gesture to allow anyone that wanted to pay their respects to appear on the stage.

This would be in what we call 'The White Section'.

A section that involves some of the more political material Michael recorded named 'The White Section' or 'Whites' due to the all-white costumes the company wear at this stage in the show.

Back in 2009, the songs we performed in this section were 'Man in the Mirror', 'Earth Song' and 'Heal the World'.

During 'Heal the World' was when all the children and ex-cast members would join the existing company in a mass, all-white remembrance of Michael's memory.

We had to rehearse so we could place the extra bodies on stage but as we did so, the tears started to flow, particularly from the men.

The male dancers could barely get through the song as they remembered their hero through the lyrics of this poignant song, so often ridiculed by the media.

It was a moment I will never forget.

This was only the rehearsal, yet so, so difficult to get through, and to see these tough, so often full of machismo dancers, broken by what had happened was truly touching.

The moment came for curtain up on this extraordinarily sad, yet momentous evening. An evening that would change the future of this show forever.

Many fans had been let into the building, and alongside the

nation's press, were standing all the way round the auditorium as we all stepped out onto the stage prior to the show beginning.

Adrian and I spoke as the cameras flashed and the people watched on silently.

Adrian talked of his time with Michael, and about what a gentle and beautiful human being he was. I stepped up and told the audience how devastated we all were and how we had come to the decision to perform that evening. We all felt Michael would have gone on and wanted the show to take place. The stage was the place he was most at home and so we should honour that.

We held a minute's silence for Michael which, at the end of it, the building erupted into deafening applause and cheers.

It was time to start the show.

At the same time, our touring company performing in Manchester, led by principal singer, Ian Pitter, delivered the same speech and they, in sync with us, held their minute's silence.

The show began and you could cut through the sadness and it's accompanying silence with a knife.

At that time, the show opened with our young MJ, Mitchell singing 'Music and Me'. He came out on stage with real determination and strength, the whole evening resting on his shoulders.

As he sang, '*We've been together, for such a long time now, music*', the silence was invaded by intermittent sniffles and then the very clear sound of sobs filling the auditorium.

These were tears that continued for the next two and a half hours…

Thankfully, those tears turned into ones of joy at certain points in the evening as the show became a raucous celebration, with fans displaying that joy and their sadness in alternate intervals and at every possible moment, singing along loudly to all of the songs. Many of the seated ticket holders could not quite believe their fate choosing this date to come and see a show about Michael Jackson. It was the perfect love-in and the only place for this common group of people to alleviate their shock.

Taken from My Notes on That Day

After much deliberation, the director and producers have decided with the cast and crew to perform tonight in memory of Michael. We are deeply shocked by the news but think it is a fitting tribute to share our celebration of Michael's music with you, the fans.

Please join us for a minute's silence in memory of this legendary man.

[Minute's silence – we are cuing this by dimming the house light to half for the minute's silence and bringing them back up.]

"Let's hear it for Michael Jackson."
[Round of applause.]

Cast exit – straight into house lights down, 'footsteps' VT, NO phone announcement.

Here are two emails sent to both companies the following day:

Dear cast and crew,

I just want to say how proud I am of all of you for getting through last night's show and the whole of yesterday.

It truly was the most intense and emotional day I have experienced with a company and I will remember this day and all of you forever because of it.

The show really did reach new heights last night and proved that with a little thought and a lot of teamwork we can keep perfecting and improving this great gift we have in Thriller Live!

It really is now our duty and responsibility as 'children' of this man's legacy to deliver his message and perform his work with more precision and attention to detail than ever before.

I feel that yesterday really unified the Thriller Live! company and although I am still very empty and sad for the great loss we have all suffered, I am filled with anticipation and excitement for the growth of our celebration of Michael Jackson.

It is an honour to work with you all on this very special project and to have shared this moment in HIStory.

With love and much respect,

Gary Lloyd

and from producer Paul Walden:

Hi Sharon/Phil/Gary,

Please send my sincere thanks to all cast, crew, creatives, staff and musicians, in the Thriller Live! family, both on stage and off and in the venue(s) in making what was a very difficult day yesterday go off so well and with sincerity and respect to the memory of Michael. I understand how difficult it must have been for everyone concerned.

The next few days will no doubt also be difficult but judging by the reaction of the audience in London last night (and from the sounds of it in Manchester) what they want more than anything is to celebrate his life and music, and that's certainly what you are all doing so superbly and respectfully.

A special thanks also goes to Kevin for handling the media events so well yesterday.

Regards,

Paul

This was the *Thriller Live!* press release on the day:

After much deliberation and taking into consideration the views of Michael's legion of fans, we can think of no greater tribute to the memory of the man and his incredible music than for this weekend's performances at the Lyric theatre in the West End and Manchester Opera House go ahead as planned. All of the Thriller Live! *cast, crew and production team send out their love to Michael's family and children.* Thriller Live! *was conceived and created by Adrian Grant, a long-time associate of Michael Jackson, and author of* Michael Jackson: The Visual Documentary. *He said: "Words cannot express my deep sense of loss and sadness; I am shocked beyond belief that Michael has died. My full condolences go out to his family – his children, parents, brothers and sisters. The Jackson family have lost a son and a father, and the world has lost one of the greatest entertainers of all time, a true legend. Michael Jackson has been a massive influence in my life – inspiring me to get into the entertainment industry and to produce the best work that I can. I have supported Michael for the past twenty-one years through my magazines, books and now* Thriller Live!*, and I will continue to support and promote his legacy via this musical celebration. But my main focus right now is very much on Michael Jackson the person. He was warm, genuine, funny and smart, as well as the musical genius we all admired. I have lost a friend, and I will be there for his family, friends and fans. Rest in peace, Michael, I love you.*

In Conversation with Ricko Baird
Our first 'MJ' – dancer and associate choreographer
on Michael's 'You Rock My World' video.

GL: You were the first to play the adult 'Michael' in the show – I learned a lot from you in those early days. How much did you learn from Michael, working with him?

RB: *I learned a great deal from Michael as well as prior to working with him. I was able to study him and see how he was able to masterfully incorporate all of his inspirations. I learned how to be inspired by other great performers and make my own unique style. Michael was great at that.*

I also learned that less is more. Sometimes performers feel that they need to do many intricate movements to be interesting and keep the audience entertained and it can work in some cases but Michael's movement taught me the power of simplicity and also to put your entire heart and soul into the work at hand. It was such an honour and learning experience to have worked side by side with him on a few different occasions, including his last music video 'You Rock my World'; I loved it and soaked in every moment.

GL: Did you bring that into your on-stage performance?

RB: *I definitely brought what I learned from MJ to my stage performance; I approached it almost like a method actor diving deep into what I learned from working with him prior. I would keep my laptop computer in my dressing room and before every show I would watch his performances in recordings such as 'Smooth Criminal' or the 'Dangerous' live performance. I would also watch footage of The Jackson Five performing live just to gear myself into the spirit and energy of Michael's legacy and art; it was very helpful and was my mantra before every show.*

GL: What was your favourite song to perform?

RB: *My favourite song to perform was 'Smooth Criminal' as it's always been one of my favorite pieces of his. It's a very powerful song and classic visual. I'm a huge fan of period pieces and I love the natural structure of how the choreography flows in the 'Smooth Criminal' piece. It is sexy, classy and jazzy all in one, it was a ground-breaking video and the fact that we did the famous epic lean live was very magical. I was a bit nervous at first performing the lean live as it takes some getting used to, but, yes, 'Smooth Criminal' was my favorite number to perform.*

GL: You spent over three years in *Thriller Live!* performing as Michael eight times a week. Did the pressure of recreating this icon ever get to you?

RB: *It wasn't so much the pressure of recreating Michael but more of me being able to give my all every time I stepped on stage. Just to make sure I'm giving one of my personal teachers and someone I've worked with professionally, and, of course, the icon 'King of Pop', visual justice. As I said, I approached it as a method actor, so once I step out on that stage it's not about me, it's about the character. The true emotion, feeling and energy I need to bring to the audience. I consider myself very disciplined and focused when it comes to work so I had the movement pretty much down. I'm also a perfectionist so my pressure was more about being honest in my performance every night. But I must admit that theatre has a beast of a schedule performing seven days a week including four shows on the weekends – no need for the gym when you're starring in a theatre show!*

GL: We spent the day and the passing weeks together after Michael died and I know how much it affected you. Did that pressure increase after he passed away?

RB: *I can honestly say that the first time I really felt pressure about my performance was after his death, not to mention crying and bawling my eyes out after hearing the news on that dreadful night. Then knowing we had a show the next day was very nerve-wracking and there came the extreme pressure. There was so much tension and energy right before the show and everyone's emotions were super high. I felt like the world was on my shoulders. This performance was so important to myself and everyone in the cast and especially the audience. I pulled myself together right before going on stage as I wanted to deliver the greatest performance ever seen. I accomplished that to the best of my ability that night but I have to say I was hiding tears through that entire performance. But I did rock and represent for the King that night; it was very difficult but we made it through. Was a great show that night, for sure.*

GL: We collectively chose to perform on the night that Michael passed. The whole evening was very surreal. What do you remember about the show we performed on the night that he died?

RB: *I just remember the disbelief in everyone's faces. I remember it was definitely such a surreal moment that will never be forgotten. And I was playing Michael Jackson, so probably for the first time since I was a kid, I was nervous to go on stage for this particular show. It was beyond overwhelming. I also remembered in that moment how much I had learned from him and how big of a teacher and inspiration he was for me.*

GL: You did a lot of touring with the show. What is the most memorable city you performed in and why? Also what can you tell me about the different audiences?

RB: *I enjoyed all the cities that the show went to and had been to a few of them prior to the show but I have to say that I really enjoyed South Africa. It was my first time there and was an amazing experience. It is so modern and beautiful and yet maintains its very natural tribal element that I was glad to experience. It was a really insightful time on many levels. The audiences would vary in response to the show, meaning some audiences were a bit conservative and it took them a few songs to get into the groove, and then other audiences were up for it straightaway, by the end of every show wherever we performed we had the audience on their feet dancing and celebrating, it was always amazing.*

GL: Do any of the *Thriller* fans still follow you?

RB: *Yes, some of them do follow me still and support my original music and constantly ask if I will ever return to* Thriller Live! *It's a great feeling to be supported and appreciated for your work.*

GL: You have been recording your own music. As an artist, and someone that worked with Michael, how has he influenced you?

RB: *Yes, I'm currently working on my original music projects and they are almost complete and ready to share with the world. Of course, MJ has inspired me a great deal in every aspect of my art but when it comes to my original music, as I've learned from him, you must take your inspirations and create your own unique style. So that's what I'm doing.*

GL: When you worked on the 'You Rock My World' music video, how much of the choreography would you say had your influence? Did Michael have a very clear vision and did you collaborate well together?

RB: Michael always had a clear vision but for 'You Rock my World' I think he was open-minded to try new ideas and bring a different flavor to the visual and choreography. [He wanted] Something a bit different than his previous video work. He would always ask me, "How does that step go?"

I felt very honoured whenever he asked me questions. I wasn't the main choreographer of 'You Rock My World' but Mike enjoyed me being next to him so we could feed off of each other's energy. It was an amazing experience and time that I always keep dear in my heart moving forward with my own career and projects. Much love and light to one of my greatest teachers, mentors and the King of Pop. I love you, MJ.

In Conversation with Mitchell Zhangazha
Our eleven-year-old MJ who performed the night Michael died.

GL: You were eleven years old when you started with *Thriller*. I know it wasn't the first professional production you had taken part in. Before coming to us, you had already been in *Caroline, or Change* at the National [Theatre], *The Lion King* and *Chitty Chitty Bang Bang*. [Mitchell went on to appear in *Oliver!*, *Peter Pan*, *Porgy and Bess*, playing leads in *Five Guys Named Moe* and *Motown the Musical*.] What felt different about coming to *Thriller Live!* after doing all of those massive productions?

MZ: I think what felt different about Thriller, *is obviously I'd grown up with my parents playing Michael Jackson throughout my life. My oldest brothers, both of them just loved Michael Jackson, so, I've grown up with Michael Jackson, whereas I guess with the other shows I was just coming in learning a part. I was having to play an icon so I think that's what was different. Not that it put any more pressure on me, because I was so young. When I came to this audition I just sang like I was just singing at home. But I think, especially as we got into the rehearsal process, it was more, rather than trying to play a character, I was trying to replicate him rather than act like him, which is what other jobs entail. I was just acting a character. This was a real person, all the moves, all the singing, all the [vocal] runs, y'know you had to make it authentic. I think that was maybe the biggest difference.*

GL: What's your biggest memory of starting with the show?

MZ: That's a good question. I just remember walking into the rehearsal room and I don't know why, I'd done shows before but maybe (again) it was the pressure of being young Michael Jackson. I don't know what it was, but I was so shy, do you remember? I didn't even wanna sing – I was like, "I can't do this."

GL: Yeah [smiling] – I do remember. You were always like an adult in a child's body with this gift of a voice but painfully shy in the beginning and for a long time.

MZ: I don't know what it was! That is my biggest memory, just 'cause I look back at the journey I went on performing in arenas, at West End Live, all of that. So starting to look at that comparison from there, I really don't know why but I was just really shy. But apart from that I have to say, I think all the arenas that we did, in Germany and Holland where we had the superfans and there was one place where there was like five thousand in the audience. I think those, especially at such a young age, coming out and having that 'roar' – audiences just going nuts. I think probably the arenas – the arena tours.

GL: And that was first, wasn't it for you?

MZ: Yeah, yeah. I can't really compare anything to that because of the scale of it all, the fans and the buzz.

GL: I have written about the day Michael passed, which was a very big day for us all, especially yourself. What do you remember about that day?

MZ: So it was announced in the morning, wasn't it?

GL: Yeah.

MZ: I remember I was at school, around thirteen, fourteen at the time. And I was in school, it was a normal day and it must have got to break time when we were actually allowed to turn our phones on. I turned on my phone, and I had a mass of phone calls from my mum and then all of a sudden someone from reception ran over and said, "Mitchell, you need to go, we need to get you out of school. Your mum is calling and you've been called into the theatre." I didn't understand why and as I was leaving, somebody, a random kid, shouted, "Mitchell, Michael Jackson has died." I thought he was joking at first and I thought it was a bad taste of a joke. Then, while I was waiting for my mum I was on my phone checking, and it all came up on BBC News, and I just remember the shock and disbelief. With 'This Is It' coming up, I hoped he would maybe gonna come and watch our show while he was in London. All of this came up, and going back to growing up with his music to see that he'd died, the most memorable thing was the shock. I wasn't really one to show tears at the time, but even then I had a tear in my eye that day. I couldn't believe it, he was preparing for these fifty shows and then all of a sudden, he's passed away. Then I remember my mum coming to get me and she was very upset and quiet. It was a really, really silent car journey to the theatre.

I remember asking her, "Mum, are you okay?" and she just nodded and I think that's probably when it set in. My mum had gone to see him live and so to see even her so upset really all brought it all home. Getting to the theatre, the vibe was just, it's crazy to describe – it was just so quiet, everyone just kind of looking at each other, hugging. I remember sitting at the press table and there's actually a photo and I'm just looking depressed. That day was so, so hard – for everyone. And I guess because [Michael] was my biggest role model, in terms of music and inspiration; to know that he'd passed, it was a really, sad day. I remember that day really vividly, all the cameras, the way we were sat, there were mics here (he gestures out in front of him) and so many questions! To be honest I didn't want to be asked questions, just wanted to be... I don't know, it's hard to put into words as it was so soon after it was announced.

Another thing, when you [GL] put 'Gone Too Soon' into the show, and we did that to open, that was just another level, just because all of us on stage together and the feeling, it was really fitting what had happened and how we all felt.

GL: A journalist asked you how you felt about being the first person to perform as Michael after he died and how that made you feel. I remember looking at him in disbelief and we all sat up in our seats protectively towards you. You came back with an incredibly mature and succinct answer – do you remember that moment?

MZ: I do remember that question was asked. I remember feeling that some of them should have had more respect, considering he had just gone.

GL: I have quoted you and we were all so impressed that without any warning you came back with something that felt so media trained and perfect. That's the only thing I remember about the questioning, to be honest. I remember it being really sombre and us all feeling really, naturally, really sad. Ricko was crying – a lot. It was hard.

GL: Do you remember much about the show we performed that night?

MZ: I remember doing 'Music and Me' and when I did the little hat flick, I just remember the audience going nuts, just because of that little movement. I have to say I think I wasn't as [emotional] 'cos in my head I was thinking, Come on, Mitchell, get it together and put on a really good show, *so I got rid of the emotion and just focused on trying to put on the best show and give them 110%. So I think for that show, especially after 'Music and Me' and I heard that roar...*

Oh my God, yeah! [remembering the reaction] That kind of triggered it for me and for the rest of the show. And then obviously 'Heal the World' came and it got a bit more emotional. But I remember that show becoming more of a celebration of Michael as a legend and all of us just rallying together to put on the best show possible. The audience were really amazing that night.

GL: Yeah, it started off really emotional out front and then just became, exactly that, just remembering [Michael] for all the right reasons.

GL: What do you remember about the audiences at *Thriller*?

MZ: The audiences, especially in Europe, there are more superfans in Europe, though the reaction was still great in the UK. In Europe it was a different level. Here it was audiences who loved the songs and came to the show to party, whereas over there, you had the die-hard fans singing along, people waiting out on the street when we all came out just to get photos. Even then, I was so young but I used to get loads of Facebook adds just from superfans. I don't know what it was but we just seemed to attract more die-hard fans out there. Crazy, it was crazy.

GL: You have also great experience in television and radio, reaching the final of *Britain's Got Talent* with your group, New Bounce. Did you write the songs and if so, how did MJ influence that writing?

MZ: We wrote our own stuff and travelled to producers in Leeds, travelled all around. Yeah, wrote our own songs, covers. I don't think MJ really influenced the writing, because we were writing with producers, if anything came out like that, they were like, "No, no, no, that's not the style we want to go for."

GL: Would you say you guys were pushing it in that direction and they were pulling it back?

MZ: Not so much in the songwriting, I would say in the performance, we had a lot of MJ-isms, even on Britain's Got Talent, *we were called the 'four young MJs' so we could definitely have the style in our singing and performing, not so much in the songwriting. I still get it to this day, when I was doing Motown [the musical], when I was singing Berry Gordy and different things in that show, people can hear the MJ influence.*

GL: So that's stayed with you.

MZ: A hundred per cent.

GL: What has been the highlight of your career so far?

MZ: The highlight is a recent one, Motown. Playing Berry Gordy – the lead part. Career-wise, that is definitely the highlight. Because I played a West End leading man at such a young age. He doesn't leave the stage, so getting to do that, after doing music and hitting such a low point, I thought there was no way in hell I would be able to do this again. So to go on and do that feels like my biggest achievement.

GL: That's really nice – your two West End leads, from Michael Jackson to Berry Gordy.

GL: What is your most memorable moment in your *Thriller* career?

MZ: When we met Tito, Marlon and Jackie. For some reason, I never used to feel pressure when I was young, but when I knew they were watching, I was, "Oh my God, oh my God," because you know, I was playing their brother! They worked tirelessly and went through all that with their dad and everything, so just that pressure of going on and doing that to then when we met them and they were so nice and complimentary. Even to this day – in fact that is one of the highlights of my career, meeting the Jacksons. I've got that photo hung up in my room, just to say I've met the Jacksons, who I listen to, to this day. I met them, shook their hands, took photos, we laughed, we joked. Yeah, it was just amazing.

Chapter Two

Dancing Machine

October 11, 1971. John Lennon's 'Imagine' was released.

Rod Stewart's 'Maggie May' was number one in the UK. Our Prime Minister was Edward Heath and the US president was Richard Nixon. *Fiddler on the Roof*, directed by Norman Jewison, was one of the most viewed movies released in 1971 while *The Day of the Jackal* by Frederick Forsyth was one of the bestselling books. Sean Connery appeared in his final Bond film, *Diamonds Are Forever*. In the UK – divorce rates were at their highest ever and terrorism was rife and even closer to home than it is now. The Immigration Act 1971 was brought into UK law and decimal currency was introduced.

In the USA, with civil movements happening up and down the country, the Soviets gained mileage and won the race to space. The Jackson Five were *Goin' Back to Indiana* and already had seven top ten singles to their name, the first four reaching number one on the Billboard chart.

And this was the day I was born.

Every child has a thing. A passion. Something they are good at and should follow with all their heart. Mine was reading and writing stories. And music. I was definitely musical. Not surprising as my mum, Judy had been a DJ and earlier, a singer in a choir and Dad, Geoff spent most of the '60s travelling the world playing bass in many bands touring with the likes of The Beatles (in fact all the '60s rock bands – you name them), Matt Monroe, Vera Lynn – who was still playing the air bases – and Shirley Bassey. He spent a long time in Hamburg hanging out with The Beatles at the 'Top Ten' and 'Star' clubs and has many great stories of that time. If you want to hear him play, that's him playing that iconic bassline in The Walker Brothers number one hit, 'The Sun Ain't Gonna Shine Anymore', probably his most infamous moment, captured forever on vinyl.

Not every child gets the opportunity to chase their dreams or pursue their talents, especially back then in 1970s working-class Britain. Thankfully, I had parents that recognised my gifts and put themselves last, helped me nurture them throughout my childhood and supported my ambition all the way to London at a way too tender age of sixteen (causing my mother's heart to break) and into adulthood.

As a child, it was easy for them to support the wild imagination I had – the reading and in private, writing multitudes of stories, plays and musicals. Scripts for our childhood gangs, 'The Blue Dolphin Gang' and later, 'The Texas Rangers'. Innocent kids in harmless gangs, a meaning very different to that of nowadays. Our gangs were based on the excitement created by books such as *The Famous Five* and *The Secret Seven* or American TV shows such as *The Red Hand Gang*, roaming the streets and falling unexpectedly into adventure, only we had to create our own. I spent hours writing ideas and creating maps to inspire an 'episode' that existed only in my head.

Just leave me alone to get on with it and I'll produce the work, bossing the neighbourhood kids around and producing regular shows in the garden and front room of the house for anyone who would sit and watch. This was a director in training at a very early age.

The music and then the dance, however, was more of a discovery. There was clearly music in me and to begin with, Mum and Dad thought about putting me into piano lessons. An obvious choice but a solid starting block for a musical youngster. This suggestion was aired for a number of weeks. Alongside it came the usual teasing from Dad, this time about how scary piano teachers can be and, "If you don't play the right notes, they'll rap your knuckles with a ruler! Mine did."

Not surprisingly, this eventually put me off that idea…

I remember Mum and Dad sitting me and my sister on the kitchen counter when I was around six years old. The options had always been to play the piano or to take ballroom dancing lessons. Without giving it much thought but following the incessant teasing, the choice became a last minute switch to the dancing lessons and this is how it all began.

The first lesson went well and felt very natural despite never having danced before. It was a 'disco' class and the song we danced to was 'Heart of Glass' by Blondie.

We were both remarkably good at it and these lessons very soon became our lifeblood, happening more and more regularly.

Before we knew it, my sister and I were passing exams and winning regional competitions, dancing to Blondie, Chic, Donna Summer, Queen, all still favourites of mine, as well as dancing the samba to Barry Manilow's 'Copacabana'!

The feeling of dance was the most natural thing I had felt to that point in my life, and still is. Until I discovered cooking (nowadays, the only thing that can really switch my mind off from work), it is the only thing that has ever made me feel free. It is like watching my son playing football – he cannot help it, indoors or out, football is in his blood and he will always love it, want to play it and learn from it.

My blissful ignorance carried me through school with barely a hitch. I was not aware that I, or what I did on a Thursday evening and Saturday morning, was 'different'. Unlike my son, I had no interest in football, so missing out on this at the weekends did not bother me at all. I had my dancing lessons, the exams to focus on and the thrill of the upcoming competitions to create for. And then, the sanctuary of my bedroom and the tiny space at the top of the stairs – my studio, my dancefloor where I created my world, occasionally with a guitar (with the help of Dad and a Beatles guitar chord book), playing out my inner pop star fantasy, or, switching most often to the terpsichorean side of my imagination, showing all the signs of a future choreographer.

I first heard 'Don't Stop 'Til You Get Enough' when I was probably around nine years old.

It made me prick up my ears and pick up my feet all at the same time. It opened my eyes and my mind – despite dancing to all those great tunes, this was different and my whole body felt it.

The intro, beginning with that bass, teasing the listener in, followed by the juxtapositon of Michael's tone against it, not singing but almost moaning about 'the power' and what effect it has on him. Then a dragged out 'whoo!', three hits on the snare and we're off... Strings, swelling horns, bass, groove, guitar. Oh my God, THIS was disco!

The velvet sound of Michael's voice in that first verse, gently licking over two bar phrases with 'lovely', 'fever', 'power' – such a unique sound, then talking about 'the feeling', 'the force', 'my body'; Michael, within the song, describing what each listener was feeling listening to it!

I felt the sonic and kinetic energy coming out of the speakers from this record, instructing my body to do nothing but dance.

Michael and Quincy guide you through three verses and two choruses, coaxing you to 'come closer' and confiding in you that Michael is 'melting like hot candlewax', more of that verse and then BAM! – the instrumental break. Eight solid bars of an incredible, yet understated, solo where you can feel – and hear – a crowded dancefloor (Studio 54, perhaps?).

The break is snatched from you, almost as abruptly as if you were slammed in the face with it. And we are back in the pocket of that groove again, which ticks along to the fade, as the vocals, bass, strings all disappear, leaving that guitar lick and homemade percussion taking you home. Pure genius.

It is still my favourite MJ song and probably has something to do with that visceral feeling I felt when I first heard it.

From this moment on, Michael was the greatest and I needed to know everything about him.

I remember seeing the *Off the Wall* album every time we went shopping – back in the day, ASDA had a significant record department – yet something stopped me from asking for it or saving up to buy it (and I bought every record going!).

There was something untouchable about it and although I bought every single from that album, I didn't feel worthy of owning the album itself.

Then something happened. Christmas morning, 1983.

There were two LPs wrapped and next to each other. Both bearing tags with Mum's handwriting, one with my name and one with my little sister's.

When it came to the two of us simultaneously opening them, I was mortified to see the *Thriller* album – being pulled out of my sister's wrapping!

What? Did we both get it? I ripped the paper off my waiting record…

Paul McCartney – *Pipes of Peace*. I couldn't believe it nor hide my disappointment. Actually, being a lifelong Beatles fan, I wanted both LPs, but the fact I didn't get *Thriller* was beyond disappointing.

I did listen to *Pipes of Peace*, but for the majority of 1984, that *Thriller* LP was in my bedroom and on my Amstrad record player. I already owned the 'Billie Jean' and 'Beat It' singles, but owning the album (or borrowing it, in my case) meant you had that gatefold sleeve in your hands. I never quite understood the inside cover image. The relaxed glamour shot of Michael with the tiger cub? But I loved the animations and obsessed over the lyrics in the sleeve, learning every song meticulously and balancing this between learning those lyrics and imagining being Michael and dancing with him in each of the videos. Anything that didn't already have a video I could copy, I would choreograph my own thing to each of these songs.

Back in 1983, the only way I would have seen a Michael Jackson video or performance would have been on *Top of the Pops*, the famous BBC chart show that aired every Thursday evening at 7.30pm.

The only way to copy any of that choreography or imagery would be to memorise it, hoping it would still be rising the charts next week to see it again, as in 1983 we didn't yet have a video recorder.

Despite being able to put a record on since the age of eighteen months, it was around this time I really started taking music in on a deeper level. Following the musical awakening upon hearing 'Don't Stop 'Til You Get Enough', my thirst for music kept growing. A four-track EP cassette was played on loop in the car, containing the Jacksons' first hits with Epic Records: 'Show You the Way to Go', 'Blame It on the Boogie', 'Shake Your Body (Down to the Ground)' and 'Can You Feel It'.

Hearing 'Beat It' for the first time was momentous, a very similar experience to the discovery of 'Don't Stop'.

The 'gongs' (as we call them in the show) at the beginning of the track evoked an almost hypnotic response, especially as it continued into the whistle kicking in over the beat at the top of the track.

Each element of these early bars of the song were so well thought out. This was MJ doing *West Side Story*, and not the last time the world would see this. The scene was set, only to be hijacked by a two-beat drum fill and Eddie Van Halen's first solo of the song.

The verse vocal was like nothing ever heard before. Michael's high voice spitting out a staccato rhythm, urgently warning, '*They told him don't you ever come around here*'; like 'Billie Jean' before it, this was another story. A three-and-a-half-minute narrative told through song that could be accompanied by a mini-movie. Written by Michael, it was a rock track through and through that wouldn't have sounded out of place performed by Def Leppard. But the purity and emotion in that almost impossibly high soulful vocal married together with the *West Side*-inspired theme made it Michael's rock fantasy and unmistakenly so.

At dance class, it was this song that made us move differently. I took the record in and we set to work coming up with a routine but this one inspired something quite different to the usual. Our movements became more angular, more angry and certainly more informed by the rhythm in the track, following the vocal one minute and the syncopated attacking beat the next. Watching Michael perform the chorus around the pool table in the video was an inspiration. The moves are simple yet delivered so perfectly, so sharp and with such conviction. This visual message buried deep in my memory and was used in every class and performance going forward.

I remember this routine taking my self-confidence to another level. I think the beat and the bravado in the track, as well as the one featured in 'Wanna Be Startin' Something', really made me want to achieve. Something in these songs empowered me to go out and get whatever I desired and not let anyone or anything hold me back. It was these songs, at the tender age of twelve, that ignited my ambition.

The room was smaller than usual. Hotter. I was used to winning these comps both as a soloist and as a partner with my sister, Joanne. We were also used to dancing in the same space, the huge dancefloor at the Scunthorpe Baths Hall (now a major seated concert venue). This time, I had moved up an age group and it would be two years until my little sis would catch up and we could dance together again. Also, this floor was a quarter of the size and it bothered me. The space I had to dance was almost right on top of the tables and I looked around to see where I could place myself without hitting anyone. Every other dancer had the same problem. The song, however, was 'Can You Feel It' and as soon as the throb of that intro kicked in, I forgot everything. I had spent months on the landing at the top of the stairs outside my bedroom perfecting this routine and nothing was going to stop me. Michael and his brothers were carrying me on this journey to glory and for the next three minutes, I was theirs. As the bassline and it's accompanying march took me (and my imaginary army of brothers) to those trumpets, I was away. Then it flowed into the smooth vocal of the verse as the pace came down slightly to allow us to hear its lyrical message.

I spun and threw my arms around in perfect sync to the peaks and troughs of the song, knowing each twist and turn, and every build and cadence, allowing the content of my routine to shine. I was sure that my knowledge of the music would go in my favour, as well as my brilliant routine, the first I had perfected completely on my own. The routine had a journey and I had given it groove with the assistance of Michael and Jackie's composition. As I changed direction I saw other dancers flinging their bodies around aimlessly and without flair. They turned and turned, the fringe on their costumes upstaging their own choreography. I've got this, I thought to myself and turned up the heat.

When the song came to an end and the crowd (parents and generally younger siblings) roared, we waited.

Third? I came in third. Tara Fox (first) and Sharon McIlvenny (second), my nemeses, stood there, both grinning as I stepped up to receive my medal. Smiling to the crowd, inside I was confused and angry. I saw their work and was not impressed, but they had done something to beat me. Something that put them ahead of me. Yes, they were both three years older, but neither the room nor the competition had phased them. They performed like pros and danced out of their head and in the faces of the judges. They did this to win, and win they did. I needed to look inside at myself and see what I did wrong, not look at others and blame. This was my first lesson in self-improvement, my first feeling of real competition and learning how to better myself and my work. I still won bronze and Mum reminded me I was the youngest in this new category. Still, I had to compete with myself to get that gold. A competition with myself that continued my whole life.

The following year was when Dad bought us our first video recorder, so it was months later than the rest of the world before I got to see the 'Thriller' video. It had been recorded onto a blank cassette (or most probably recorded over something) and I remember the anticipation, as we knew the song so well and had heard so much about this video. It was originally aired at 1am on Channel 4 and had the most media attention for any artist at that point since The Beatles. My sister and I, of course, fell in love with and watched it incessantly. Although obsessed with it as a movie, for some reason I didn't get into the dance routine of this one until much later on. Needless to say, my sister and I wore that video tape out. It was *An American Werewolf in London* for a younger generation, which must have been part of Michael's intention and the novelty of being allowed to witness it was genuinely 'thrilling' at that time.

Seeing this and the 'Beat It' video, it felt as though MTV was invented for Michael Jackson. Or was it just a serendipitous continuation of his productive journey, allowing him to creatively capitalise on this opportunity to air his vision to the world? Interestingly though, videos were made for 'Billie Jean', 'Beat It', 'Human Nature' and 'Thriller' but not 'P.Y.T.' or 'Wanna Be Startin' Something'. We were living in the early stages of these mega music movies where it was not always the norm to create a video to accompany a single release, but out of those that did, Michael was the pioneer.

The summer of 1984, when 'Michael Mania' was sweeping the world and certainly the whole of the UK, the *Thriller* album remained in the charts and was still dominating record players belonging to all generations. As well as the new *Victory* album riding high in the charts, with Jermaine rejoining his brothers after nine years as a solo artist, *Off the Wall* made a reappearance in the Top 40, while Motown were releasing their own hits compilations and a 'lost recordings' Michael album. *Farewell My Summer Love* contained archive recordings of Michael songs from January to September 1973. These songs were remixed, remastered and given new musical overdubs.

My memory of this album is a romantic one, particularly the songs that were released as singles: 'Farewell My Summer Love' and 'Girl You're So Together'. Both huge radio songs in the summer of 1984 and welcomed as what felt like new material for those of us who had exhausted the nine tracks on *Thriller*.

My family went on holiday to Margate in Kent that year and this was the first year I was given some independence. I remember hanging out with the son of the owner of the hotel we were staying in, Marcus, who was the same age as me and we would get up early to go fishing and hang around the town, beach and the fairground. Both into music, I bought records by The Jackson Five, Prince and Madonna that summer, but most memorably *Farewell My Summer Love*. I feel like this song was on rotation in every cafe, radio station and fairground ride we went on, and as a teenager starting to feel the beginnings of love towards the opposite sex, I loved singing it and imagining who my summer love would be. I remember as a thirteen-year-old really relating to these lyrics and the feeling behind them. The Motown sound was also fresh in the midst of the sounds of the British supergroups of that time and hearing Michael's voice so pure just added to his appeal and stardom.

The holiday drove towards it's inevitable end; it was July 30th, 1984 and the day before we were due to return home, the Radio 1 roadshow was playing in Margate at the Old Putting Green. Marcus and I went along. The DJ was a lively but not so young and hip Tony

Blackburn (who I've always loved), and who retired from Radio 1 only two months later. Nevertheless, the crowd that turned out to see him went back as far as the eye could see. The charts were jam-packed with the Jacksons, with 'State of Shock', 'Farewell My Summer Love' and 'Ease on Down the Road' all in the Top 100 and the *Thriller* album still in the ether – Tony played a lot of Michael that day.

Chapter Three

BAD – The Teenage Years

In 1986, the family business prevailed and we moved town. Gone was the ballroom and all the competitions. I had reached as far as I could with the exams two years prior, and had to wait until age sixteen to continue with the Associate teaching exams, so it didn't feel like such a blow. This place was full of stage schools and although that world was slightly alien to me, I was eager and impatient to break into that community. Little did I know that this new town, Grimsby and Cleethorpes, was the place Rod Temperton, the man who wrote *Thriller*, hailed from.

My new school was very inclusive of the arts, so in a flash I went from keeping my artistic self under wraps to starring in the school plays and holding my own dance workshops every Wednesday afternoon, putting on regular productions – naturally directed by me! This was all thanks to Richard Dring, my form tutor and drama teacher, a very hip kind of guy who always managed the relationship balance between inspirational authoritarian and mate brilliantly with every student. He gave me the biggest sense of self-worth and access to facilities within the school that may have remained undiscovered without his help. Mr Dring encouraged me to work towards my ambition at every possible opportunity. I remain a big believer in destiny to this day. If my family hadn't have moved here and I had not met 'Dringy', my life and career would be very different.

I still have very close friends from this period and this was the two years of my life I felt most at home, really able to be myself, feeling accepted by others.

The MJ connection continued and when I finally discovered my new dance school, I was plunged headlong into more competitions, only this time, in this world, they were known as 'festivals'.

I remember one particular category, which was choreography, and me and my new partner, Angela Mumby, entered. The song we chose was 'P.Y.T. (Pretty Young Thing)' and the choreography reflected that. Angela was the pretty young thing and I was Michael. We put together a vision of what that music video might have looked like, had there been one. It resembled 'The Way You Make Me Feel', with Angela strutting around the space and me chasing, spinning and using the floor. Once we went into choreography, there was a distinct mix of modern, jazz and latin (a fusion I have used ever since), moves in hold, as well as side-by-side synchronicity. We attempted lifts and I threw Angela in the air and over my back, once again allowing Michael's groove and voice to carry both of us.

To our delight, we went home winners that day.

At the last festival I took part in, following the performance of a classical 'Gypsy Tarantella' duet (for which we came third), I found myself in the wings, catching my breath and sitting next to Janice Sutton, the owner of the school that took home most of the awards. Her dancers were mature, her choreography and work sophisticated – a cut above everything else. There was something different, more professional about this place and I knew I had to go there. I hounded Janice, following her everywhere, asking if I could join her school and although she said she would love to have me as one of her students, she was nervous about poaching students and said 'no'.

The school was located in Skegness in Lincolnshire, at least an hour drive from where we lived but my dad, always wanting the best for us, drove me to the school, uninvited.

Rocking up on the doorstep, boldly asking if I could join in, amused Janice and her staff; my persistent teenage determination, refusal to take 'no' for an answer and the long journey we had made left them no choice but to throw me into their current rehearsal. They were working towards a summer season of *The Wiz* and they were rehearsing 'Ease on Down the Road'. I was instantly cast as 'the Wizard' and spent the next few weeks learning and performing this amazing score, learning more about Michael and his first endeavour into the world of film and musical theatre.

The 'Wiz' season and the rest of that year was a wild ride and a period I always consider my first year of training; I learned so much about the business. At just fifteen, I got digs and stayed away from home in Skegness, working as a waiter by day, allowing me to stay in the town, train at the studio and perform the show at night.

As well as travelling to this new dance school, in the same year I joined a youth theatre group in Grimsby. A cool community of kids from age ten through to twenty-one and beyond. It was a new age amateur dramatic society, a non-operatic group for young people who wanted to be involved in titles created by someone other than Rodgers and Hammerstein. The theatre group was the brainchild of Chris Pearson, a highly energised, motivated drama teacher for the area. At the time she had incredible foresight, not only putting on shows with these kids but travelling the area scouting for and recruiting talent. She had choirs and cabaret groups singing and gigging all over town, as well as the show casts making personal appearances in churches and shopping centres to promote the productions. The company was called 'Stage One' and they had launched a couple of years prior, putting on shows like *Grease* and *Bugsy Malone* – which at that time were the most exciting titles you could get your hands on, not quite as common to put on as they are now (they were also the shows that I appeared in at school as they followed Chris's lead). Chris came to see both my school shows and asked me to join them at Stage One. I went along and never looked back. Here, I learned how to act, sing and create deeper work, and I made lifelong friends. Chris had an immense talent to inspire boys and there were loads of us. Like a theatrical Fagin's gang, we went along every Tuesday evening and Saturday morning to hang out, work hard and see what Chris had in store for us all.

The choreographer at Stage One was Susan Miles. Sue, as she was known to us all, became a great friend and ally of mine, and as dancers, we connected instantly.

I soon attended her classes as well as the general rehearsals.

Sue's style was really unique and like nothing I had been taught before. It was more like the choreography you would see in music videos and she was very inspired by Michael. Always dressed in black, she wore tight leggings with flowing tops and was always in the highest heels. Her hair was platinum blonde and worn in a style not dissimilar to Jennifer Batten on the 'BAD' tour!

I learned that she had trained at Laine Theatre Arts, one of the biggest and most prestigious theatre colleges in London and was great friends with Stedman Pearson of Five Star.

As a big fan of Five Star, this made perfect sense as her choreography possessed the sharp, angular approach and style they were famous for, as well as the groove inspired by Michael and more recently, Janet in her videos, hot on the heels of her big brother.

Sue had worked closely with Stedman, and it showed. I felt blessed that fate had brought me to this town and into this company, as I was once again learning, collecting all the components I needed to progress and succeed as a choreographer and director in this business. It was all starting to fall into place.

The BAD album was released in August 1987, giving us all a week to consume it completely before having to go back to school. The album artwork dominated record shops for weeks before and the anticipation over the whole summer was excruciating. The record was the first to be released on three formats, although myself, not yet owning a CD player, the vinyl and cassette had to suffice.

It was played on loop in the house, especially the cassette, as machines in those days had a reverse mechanism that just switched the tape over and started again!

This album, when I listen to it now, reminds me how cohesive it felt to me at the time. The tracks are all really individual but to me it could all be one song. It is not a concept album, yet so united in it's production and intention. Statistics state that this was a disappointment compared to the *Thriller* album. I'd say (and we comment on this in the show) fans would disagree. Each track is a blockbuster, with it's own identity which *Moonwalker* really helped to visually demonstrate. I love it.

As much as I was immersed in the *BAD* album, it was Sue that brought it into the dance studio.

We did choreography to them all: 'BAD', 'The Way You Make Me Feel', 'Liberian Girl', 'Smooth Criminal', 'Just Good Friends'.

Every week she would pick a different track and had a routine ready to go. The choreography was fresh and born out of inspiration hearing these amazing songs and this new sound. This album was my life soundtrack; I was in heaven and never wanted to leave.

When Michael performed at the Grammy Awards in 1988, I was ready. We had that VCR and I wasn't going to miss this exclusive performance. I can't actually remember how it was aired in the UK – I would hazard a guess that it was an MTV special, maybe even showing just Michael's performance. Nevertheless, I had two fingers poised to push those heavy buttons down, ready to record and own forever.

Michael appeared in silhouette behind a sepia-looking screen. The music was jazzy, held together by slow clicks to which Michael hit varying shapes to. When the screen flew out, Michael was seen at the top of a small staircase, deep in a Fosse-esque pose. And then he hit his trademark freeze.

He flawlessly brought the music back in with a physical hit, and what has become the classic 'chest pop', proceeding to swagger down the stairs.

As Michael started to sing, I realised this was the first verse of 'The Way You Make Me Feel'. (*Oh God, this is going to be good!*)

He stepped forward in an almost gliding motion, seeming to address individuals out in the audience, the most confident I had ever seen him, so in control of his performance and all around him.

He hit moves never seen before and it was clear that the rehearsal process for this show was as intense and aspiring towards perfection as the album session with Quincy in the studio.

This wasn't just a pop artist doing 'his thing'. This was a balletic masterpiece, showing a deep study of Fosse and Jerome Robbins and displaying moments that felt like Gene Kelly in the modern world.

The chosen song showed more of that *West Side Story* inspiration but was all clearly led by Michael's vivid concept for his own song.

This is my favourite performance of Michael's. I think it is pure performance utopia and what gained him the title of not only the biggest artist in the world at this point, but the greatest dancer.

Michael's status following the release of this album is something I think young people will now never comprehend. The internet and the wake of social media has destroyed 'stardom' and what that used to mean. Everything now is so accessible and seemingly easy to reach. In two clicks, you can watch the latest Beyonce video or even book a flight – that Grammy Awards performance is now easily streamed to your phone. Back in '88, these sounds came out of little speakers and their creators were like gods. America felt like another planet and what was coming out of it was truly spiritual and unreachable; it was unthinkable to try and get there... well, not yet anyway.

What is astonishing to me is to see really young people today ne
entranced by Michael and view him as some kind of superhero-type
character, thirty years after this album was released.

Thankfully, then, Michael announced he was going to tour.

The 'BAD' tour was to take sixteen months, including 123 concerts,
playing to 4.4 million fans across fifteen countries.

The UK was in the middle of the tour, as Michael and his team
made their way back round the world to LA, where he would finish.

Sue called to book as soon as the dates were announced and got
tickets to Leeds Roundhay Park Stadium, unknowingly at the time, on
Michael's birthday. There was a gang of us from the Stage One dance
class all going together. We spent the weeks building up to it listening
to all things Michael, especially a tape called *The Michael Jackson Mix
40*, which had all The Jackson Five stuff and early Michael songs in
one long mega-mix. This and the *BAD* album were the soundtrack to
that summer.

Luckily I had been on a coach trip to a pop tour the year before,
to see Alexander O'Neal at the Birmingham NEC Arena with this
same group, so Mum and Dad were quite willing to let me go, even
allowing my thirteen-year-old younger sister to come. It was a day I'll
never forget and another experience that has subliminally formed the
foundations for all aspects of my creative vision and expectations.

I learned later that after this very performance, his birthday concert,
Michael donated $130,000 to the charity, 'Give For Life'.

I still feel lucky finding these like-minded people and thankful to my
parents for moving town when we did. I would not be doing what I do
without this move and it was a pivotal moment of my life.

Before being able to share my inner creative flair and interests, I
lived in a lonely world in a post-punk Northern town, very much in
my head where dance was my only escape.

As a male dancer in the '80s, Michael was my only salvation. He was the technicolour antidote to this monochrome world and allowed me to understand that my fantasy was indeed a reachable reality. I loved Gene Kelly and Fred Astaire, but I couldn't tell that to the football-mad boys in my class. I admired several of the ballroom champions that ruled that part of my world, but stayed silent about that, otherwise you'd seriously get your head kicked in! I remember being shown the whole of *West Side Story* in a music class. I was distraught at being unable to hear a word of it as the whole class thought it was 'boring' and talked all the way through.

Non-dancers, however, somehow got Michael. I could eventually show the moves that he taught me without fear of judgement of my 'credibility' or making assumptions about my sexual orientation.

I became the guy the school bullies would approach, not to dunk my head in the toilet but to push cheap blank cassettes in my hand, ordering me to make them a copy of the latest Jackson album.

Busting out my Michael moves at the school disco got me the most female attention, resulting suddenly in about ten more male 'friends'.

I left school with Michael and the *BAD* album firmly in my head and singing me out of school and out of that town. I wanted to attend the Laine Theatre Arts college that Sue, Stedman and so many of our older dancing friends had auditioned for.

Having seen a show there, the work was mind-blowing, like nothing I had ever seen before and I realised this was the next stage for my career plan. I applied only to Laine, whereas most of my peers were writing to four or five different colleges.

The audition required a self-choreographed jazz routine and there was no question I needed Michael's help. The song I chose was my favourite on the *BAD* album, 'Another Part of Me'.

I set to work getting lost in that intro. The song had to be cut to a minute long so I literally had a verse and chorus to show what I'd got. The routine combined all that I'd learned from Michael. Short, sharp rib movements, peppered with – POW! – an arm shooting out into a strong and focused point, followed by a perfectly executed double pencil spin. I used his *West Side* influence to feature fluid jazz and technical elements, making sure I didn't come across as a disco dancer or one-trick pony.

Nowadays, and particularly over the last eight years or so, dance has developed at such an alarming and beautiful rate, anything different is welcomed in these auditions. Back then, you had to show star quality but still be able to fit in within the curriculum. In 1988, these schools were still developing from being classical ballet schools and although 'Laine' led the way to becoming the most modern at that time, the auditions still strictly required a strong sense of technical training.

Despite bending the truth about my ballet experience on the audition form (to me, 'elementary' meant 'easy', so I ticked the box, not realising it was a rather proficient grade) and making a complete show of myself when brought to the front as the most experienced in the room (lesson learned there!), the audition was a success thanks to my jazz routine and to Michael's inspiration.

My time at this institution was the kickstarter for learning about life. I never imagined that this audition moment and my love for Michael would prove to be the starting point for something that would turn into a lifelong dream.

Part Two

Destiny

Chapter Four

Greatest Show on Earth

The career plan worked, and after auditioning for and attaining a dream role in *CATS* the musical, I left college early at age eighteen. I moved on from that to playing various leading roles, internationally and in the West End, swinging thirteen parts in *Starlight Express* (including the three 'Rockys' and the leading role, 'Rusty'), extensively teaching dance and theatre, while continually finessing my choreography. The last musical I performed in was as 'Sal' in a '70s disco musical called *Oh! What A Night* directed by Take That's creative director, Kim Gavin, and starring Kid Creole. I stayed with this show for over five years, becoming the associate director while simultaneously working alongside Kim as his assistant on other commercial projects.

Let's jump then to August 2006. After a twelve year career on the theatrical stage, I am now a full-time director and choreographer. Having worked around the world, working alongside the likes of Robbie Williams, Pink and the Spice Girls; teaching Jennifer Hudson how to dance; and creating much work for Simon Fuller around the birth of the *Idol* TV phenomenon and all its offspring, both across the Atlantic and on home turf; I was, at this point, making a conscious choice to get back to theatre. My debut outing in this transition to theatre director became my first ever West End show, *The Genius of Ray Charles*. It ran over the summer in 2005 at the Theatre Royal Haymarket (where *Heathers the Musical* would run twelve years later). It was during this period that I was invited to attend a one-off performance of a show completely dedicated to Michael Jackson, being performed at the Dominion Theatre in London on August 16th. The Dominion is by far the largest theatrical house in the West End, so I thought it incredibly courageous of the producers of this show to put it on there; in fact I think any producer is courageous to put something on there, as it is a barn of a theatre with a capacity of 2,163 seats when all on sale. (*We Will Rock You* took seats out to make way for their design.)

That brave producer turned out to be Adrian Grant, creator of *Thriller Live!* and my now collaborator of over twelve years.

In 1988, Adrian launched the world's first Michael Jackson fanzine, *Off the Wall*, approved by Sony and MJJ Productions. Within two years it had a circulation of 25,000 followers and was being read in over forty-seven countries around the world.

In March 1990, Michael invited Adrian to Neverland Valley, and he became the first ever person to write a feature story about his wonderful retreat. Published in the British publication *Smash Hits*, it was surprisingly Jackson's first cover story for the popular magazine.

Adrian has had privileged access to Jackson's world over the years, including during the recording of the *Dangerous* album, *HIStory* album, world tours, photo and video shoots, exclusive interviews, lunches, dinners, and more. In 1994, Adrian wrote the bestselling Michael Jackson chronology – *The Visual Documentary*, published by Omnibus Press.

Jackson has personally acknowledged Adrian's work many times, and in 1998 granted Adrian an exclusive interview for his third book, *Making History*. From 1991, Adrian also produced an annual Michael Jackson show, which in 2006 became *Thriller Live!*

I already knew of this show, as their company of singers and dancers had been rehearsing in the studio right next to me way earlier in the year. This was at Dance Attic Studios in Fulham Broadway, London, one of the oldest and most famous dance hire places in town. They were rehearsing *Thriller* and I was working on *Ray*, and we were about to embark on a long tour of the United States on the Broadway series along with the first national tour of *Wicked*, the hugely successful revival of *Pippin*, and Monty Python's *Spamalot*. We were rehearsing in the large dance studio and the smaller studio next door, while the *Thriller* cast were in the studio adjacent to us.

There were lots of common peers and friends between the two companies (including Lewis Davies and Yasmin Yazdi, who continued with *Thriller* for many years) and we all caught up, sharing stories over lunch and cigarette breaks.

They seemed to be rehearsing for weeks and although I knew it was a Michael Jackson show they were working on, upon returning from the States, I didn't connect that it was the show I had been invited to.

The show featured a music producer I had been working with, Asha Elfenbein, singer Kym Mazelle (whom I had just worked with when she recently starred in the UK tour of *The Genius of Ray Charles)* a young Marvin Humes and what seemed like a cast of thousands. There were several children, including Shaheen Jafargholi, and a very talented young singer named Dominic Smith, both of whom continued into our first tour.

The show was long and rough around the edges but packed full of great performances, MJ hits from across the ages and was overall a very enjoyable evening. I remember saying to Judith Rogers (my associate choreographer at the time) and Aaron Renfree (from S Club 8 – whom I had been choreographer for throughout their career), who had accompanied me, "This could be amazing, I would love to get my hands on it."

I didn't give it another thought until around six months later when I received a call from Tony Rex at Flying Music Productions. I had just worked with them on a touring compilation show called 'What A Feeling!' – starring Sinitta, Zoe Birkett, Noel Sullivan and Jon Boydon.

The call was to check out my availability and interest to work on a Michael Jackson show, *Thriller Live!* – "I saw it, Tony, loved it," I said to him over the phone, "…could do so much with this show. When are you thinking?"

As always, the time frame was too tight and I was not available to work on this initial tryout production. The short UK tour happened anyway and was a regional success, showing the producers Paul Walden and Derek Nicol it 'had legs'.

Here is an account of when another previous cast member of *Thriller Live!* got to meet Michael when performing 'Thriller' with Chris Brown at the World Music Awards during this period:

I met the original creator of Thriller Live!, *Adrian Grant and then-director Kerys Nathan in Reading at my performing arts school Shooting Stars. They enrolled their daughter for the Saturday classes. They were in the audience for one of the children's shows where I had to jump in and unexpectedly cover a part for one of my missing students. We were singing the song 'Respect' by Aretha Franklin and thankfully, I sang it well! It caught Kerys' attention and from that point I was on her radar. Despite not being cast in the first preview show at the Dominion, I became involved in the world of* Thriller Live!

In 2006 I got a call from Adrian asking me if I could teach at an audition. Chris Brown was doing a tribute to Michael at the 2006 World Music Awards and he needed to get dancers together. I got off the phone, watched the 'Thriller' video non-stop, told all my professional dancer mates to come along and then went off to Dance Works to teach. Adrian cast a selection of us, thankfully this time I made the cut and we began rehearsing.

The rehearsals were tough. Kerys made us re-audition. It was all about the face for her. We had to give more... be more intimidating, be more zombie-like! We were getting fully made up, prosthetic makeup sculpted to our faces. It was going to take hours to do but our expressions would be clear on camera. We ran through it over and over again. By the time we got to the day of the event we had it down and we were a really tight group of dancing zombies!

We met Chris Brown on the day of the performance but to be honest I was just desperate to see Michael. We had heard he was singing 'We Are the World' straight after the tribute and would be accompanied by a children's choir.

It felt like we were waiting for hours in our starting positions. The crowd was buzzing with excitement waiting for something to happen. All us zombies were hidden around the catwalk and on cue we would climb out from underneath it, crawl onto the stage and reveal ourselves as the walking dead, taking formation to start what is famously known as the 'Thriller' routine. No pressure!

I might sound mad to most but there are a few people who will completely resonate with this... there is a special energy connected to Thriller Live! that I felt for the first time that day. It's a driving force that has connected hundreds of us on the shows journey. I didn't know it then, while I was waiting in my zombie rags and prosthetic makeup, but now I recognise what it feels like and I can remember it taking hold of me the minute the 'Thriller' track started. I had been fretting about the choreography and making a mistake on TV. I was bursting for the toilet and was petrified I couldn't hold it through the routine. My nerves were almost convincing me to run through the crowd and out the door but all of a sudden I had no choice but to do this performance. Hannah, one of the dancers, was strutting the stage in sky-high heels as she reenacted the part of Ola Ray with Chris Brown. I remember seeing her and growling, physically and aggressively vocalising the sounds of a creature. It was the desire to recreate the video and to do it justice on stage. My body took the form of someone waking from their grave. I felt this uncontrollable twitch moving through, taking hold of my limbs, like they were being woken up, and on the sound of the dance break I pounced onto the platform. I don't remember seeing a single face in the audience. All I remember is how hard I danced with every part of my body. I didn't think about the moves or what came next. I didn't need to. Each dancer was pulled into place by this desirable force to do this tribute justice. We were like parts of a puzzle and the closer we came together, at the point where the catwalk narrowed, it was the most sensational feeling in the world. One rather gigantic male zombie clonked me so hard on the top of my head, but I just kept going. After all, Michael was watching.

We fell to the ground at the end of the number and I just remember the incredible release I got. I didn't want to move. I hugged the floor for as long as I could until the blackout came – our cue to exit. Watching it back is really interesting. I never really heard Chris Brown sing it. It's always Michaels voice that I heard.

Straight after, I wanted to know if Michael was there. In my memory, I watched him live from the crowd but I'm pretty sure that wouldn't have been possible, it must have been on a monitor screen. I got the impression that the childrens choirs weren't doing what they were supposed to do and who could blame them? They were on stage with Michael Jackson. They were actually a teenage *choir and once MJ invited them onto the catwalk they just got so excited. To be honest, Michael seemed comfortable, but for some reason watching him at the time I felt unsure as to whether they were suppose to be touching him and crowding him. After performing 'We Are the World' he got straight into his car. It was a black SUV but I don't remember the make or model. To me, it just looked like a famous person's car. It was parked really close to where he came off and it started to drive away immediately.*

The car stopped and a few dancers whispered we were going to meet him but I couldn't imagine how that was possible. Until Kerys and Adrian gathered us altogether and told us that he was stopping to say hello very quickly.

At this point my inner zombie had left the arena and I was feeling more like myself again, despite my appearance. It was hard to believe what was happening until we saw him in real life. We lined up, single file by the back door of his car. I recited over and over what I was going to say: "It was an honor to have been a part of this performance, it was an honor to be a part of this performance."

When it was my turn, I poked my head into the car and leant into it slightly. There was a man sat on Michael's right, a bodyguard, I'm presuming, but I couldn't be sure. I couldn't take my eyes off Michael. His appearance has always been a hot topic in the press but what amazed me is that despite what changes he experienced in his physical appearance, his eyes were what stood out to me. They were warm, mischievous and intelligent beyond what I could have imagined. I felt so calm in his presence and as I reached out to shake his hand I delivered my line in a high-pitched excited tone of voice and he said back, "The honor is all mine," and he thanked us all for doing the tribute. His voice was gentle and genuine. I didn't want to leave but I had a line of raging zombies behind me all wanting to shake the musical genius's hand. It was a moment I will never forget and one I truly cherish. I believe he would have come to see Thriller Live! *at some point had he lived longer. I count myself incredibly lucky to have had that opportunity. What I loved the most about meeting Michael was that despite how high of a pedestal I had him on he made me feel truly valued for being a part of the tribute. He took the time to stop and meet us all individually and for a split second I saw the real man, the untouchable, the unstoppable, the invincible, Michael Jackson.*

Yasmin Yazdi
my original West End associate choreographer

Later that year, I got another call from Tony, this time more insistent that we make something happen. "It's a long tour. UK and Holland. This one could run, Gary, I need to make sure you are on board. And we need to start casting ASAP."

I jumped on board, delighted to discover that my old mate, John Maher, was the MD for the show. John and I had worked together on the Australian production of *Oh! What A Night* back in 2001 and also collaborated on a European tour of *Jesus Christ Superstar* in 2004. John is an incredible musician and MD, a wonderful communicator and very detailed technician, something that is absolutely vital when working on any Jackson material.

Taking on *Thriller Live!* for me was monumental and meant I had some serious work to do. Being a Michael fan my whole life wasn't enough if I was going to put my name to something representing him.

Research was key so I dived into my record and CD collection and dug out all the old DVDs and video tapes. I had to be more than meticulous with this one.

Undoubtedly, I had to start with Michael. The science of the movement. Embarking on this task became a real revelation to me as, until that time and as inspired as I was by him, I thought Michael's catalogue of moves was a limited one. Aside from the infamous blocks of choreography I needed to learn (or refresh), surely there was only the hip thrusts, spins, varying leg kicks and power arms to study and perfect?

It was not until I really waded through and paid close attention to the various performances from across the years, that my head started to spin.

Studying the evolution of Michael's movement was a key factor in my development of the show. Not only did I need to get this right for this first production but anyone that played the role had to understand each of the elements collected together to create our illusion.

This came into play much more when we brought the show into the West End. This was when we had to think more seriously about understudies and performers coming to the end of their contracts, going on holiday, or getting sick or injured.

It was a long process getting it right but having the foundation in place was vital.

There is a systematic body of knowledge behind all good choreographers' work and Michael was no exception. He analysed work by Fred Astaire, Gene Kelly, Bob Fosse and Jerome Robbins and fused his own inbuilt knowledge of rhythm and groove with their grace and deftness.

His obsession with film came out in all his visual work. Even as a child, I always imagined this came as a result of him never able to go out like a normal person. I saw him in his room, watching movies on rotation and repeat, engrossed in the detail and gleaning anything he liked as his own (pretty much like myself, only I had the ability and freedom to run outside and interact with the world around me). The truly innovative thing about Michael is how he would take this on-screen and classic motivation, magically turning it into something unique only to him. This was his talent when it came to what you see choreographically. You knew where it came from but nothing was the same and it was always sharpened, improved and brought bang up to date, making it feel fresh and brand new.

Ask anyone who invented the moonwalk and more often than not, you will hear 'Michael Jackson'. He has been globally credited with the creation of this infamous move and is most certainly top of the list in the ownership of it.

The fact is, there were many artists who had used a version of the moonwalk in their acts prior to Michael putting his stamp on it at the Motown 25th anniversary on May 16th 1983. Cab Calloway was recorded doing something similar as early as 1932. James Brown used it, as did Bob Fosse, but I would say the closest moonwalk to what Michael presented to the world was seen around the time of 1955 performed by Bill Bailey, an African American tap dancer. Bill called it 'the backslide' and it was a much looser version, with the legs placed further apart than how Michael did it.

The illusion is the appearance of the performer gliding backwards, using the ball on one foot to push the other foot backwards, switching effortlessly between the two with the audience unable to see that switch. This is where Michael has taken something and harnessed it beyond its original form. Despite not being the creator of the moonwalk, he is undoubtedly its perfecter, and therefore rightly claiming the title of the moonwalk king. Michael could flawlessly perform this step, in profile, from one side of the stage to another but also used its variants, moving round in a circle and facing the audience while moving sideways. Each of these versions is choreographed carefully into the show.

As legend would have it, the moonwalk was apparently taught to Michael by Jeffery Daniel of Shalamar, whom Michael sought out after watching him on American dance show *Soul Train*. He also worked alongside The *Electric Boogaloos,* who rank among the pioneers of popping and electric boogaloo, other styles that Michael adopted as his own. Daniel also appears in the 'BAD' video and was co-choreographer on 'Smooth Criminal'.

Bob Fosse and Fred Astaire have both been cited as choreographers Michael has plagiarised. Fosse as 'The Snake' in *The Little Prince* performs a routine so remarkably similar to 'Billie Jean'; it is clear this is where Michael got the inspiration for his live performance from, even down to the black suit revealing white spats. The fit and length of Michael's jacket and trousers in any performance of 'Billie Jean' are key factors in how the choreography looks, highlighting all the right areas. The trousers purposely worn too short to show the crystallised socks and almost oversized penny loafers are all conscious and essential components of the design and to make the movement work to maximum effect.

I ask all our MJs to not only study Michael but to check out *The Little Prince* to deepen their research and see where it all came from.

Michael made no secret of the fact he took inspiration from both of these Hollywood masters, the other blatant mirroring being that of Fred Astaire's final routine 'Girl Hunt Ballet' in Vincente Minnelli's 1953 movie *The Band Wagon*. This was the creative substance that stimulated the birth of 'Smooth Criminal', their similarities uncanny, yet their differences many. Michael once again taking the imagery of this masterpiece and turning it into something more relevant, more exciting and, as we now know, more timeless. The perfection in this work, however, really shows Michael's determination to better himself as an artist. As he did from 'Off the Wall' to 'Thriller', 'BAD' shows a surge in the desire to enrich his movie-making even further. This translates through to the camera work, the choreography and the casting of everything that came out of 'BAD', including the *Moonwalker* film itself. You can see by watching Astaire in *The Band Wagon* how Michael's work with a hat was developed and this features in much of his and the show's choreography.

I couldn't talk about the science of MJ's movement without mentioning James Brown.

James Brown is credited as Michael's first influence and the visceral and highly athletic way he performed informed the Jacksons as a family and Michael's physical language throughout his onstage career. The frenetic and raw quality of a James Brown show was captured beautifully in the 'BAD' tour before Michael moved ahead of the times, streamlining the work and making everything more distinct whilst keeping hold of the 'James Brown shuffle' in his physical vocabulary.

"Study the Greats and Become Greater."
– Michael Jackson

The above are all unequivocally the staple shopping list of Michael's catalogue of moves and idols and this was certainly my focus in those early days putting the show together. The thread that sews those moves together are the steps of the time.

Michael was a trailblazer of the '80s and so much of his movement came from the attack within the music of that era. Michael composed and produced from the dance for the dance, the marriage between them so tight, no-one has since achieved such sublimity.

When working with a new cast, I ask all our performers to listen to the percussion, really study the heartbeat of every song as Michael is each of those instruments. Those sounds came from his soul and without understanding the music we cannot successfully deliver the choreography or the rhythm and phrasing of his vocal.

His lines and shapes so magnificent, you rarely see a bad photo of him. The relationship between what he did with his body, knowing what was in the music, resulted in an exquisite physical version of musical notation. It remains a beautiful secret only to be studied again and again, much as I have.

His attack and linear precision are yet to be matched, especially in the late '80s and have been imitated and developed by sister Janet, Paul Abdul, Justin Timberlake, Usher, Ne-Yo, Chris Brown, not to mention hundreds of modern day dance crews, making Michael, in my eyes, the modern day Fosse or Astaire. The genius was how Michael collected each of these styles from those masters and dared to fuse them. A mash-up of movement, mixing popping with jazz, the moonwalk with the strut. This belonged only to him and became his legend.

My vision for the show was to ensure the audience felt Michael radiating from every pore of the bodies on stage. That every member of the cast and band held a piece of the puzzle, that when put together presented a complete and perfect picture.

For this to work, the show had to contain all the wow-factor moments and it surprised me to learn that the previous version had some serious songs missing. 'Smooth Criminal', 'Man in the Mirror', 'BAD', 'Black or White' and 'Remember the Time' were all omitted from the Dominion show and that original tour. It became a mission for me to ensure these essentials made it into my version.

I started with 'Smooth Criminal'. There were many ways to approach this, as Michael performed it very differently each time he did it live.

His choreography was modified and it was generally a lot less theatrical, highlighting the song but of course always featuring 'the lean' and a machine gun with a thrilling pyro effect. For our show, I wanted this number to be the pièce de résistance amidst all the other massive hits. I told the rest of the creative team, I wanted to recreate the full nine-minute *Moonwalker* version and stage this as a mini musical mid-way through the second act.

The allure of this first step to putting this in the show was a dream come true. I had performed to 'Smooth Criminal' before, again with my sister as the opening act for a summer season in 1989. That performance (also choreographed by me) wouldn't win any awards but it did win me my Equity card, a now obsolete distant memory of a once vital step towards making it in this business. Without that card, you couldn't work and it showed future employers what you had already put into your career before they took a chance on you.

Nowadays, the challenge for young graduates in this increasingly competitive climate in the UK isn't a slip of paper, it is getting the right agent to get you through those doors or impress one of the top creatives who guest at the many colleges across the country.

Now, with the chance to show my authentic love for the 'Smooth Criminal' visual as well as the song, I studied every dancers' track within the video to re-tell this story and make it work for the stage. I wove our 'Michael' through the narrative that would be told by three of the singers acting as reporters at the scene. I recreated and worked up sections, building towards the momentary freeze and deafening window smash. This always gets a massive round of applause when the audience think it is the end of the number.

With barely time to breathe, the song moves on into the 'exorcism of Annie' – the whining, stamping and groaning of the whole group, another example of Michael's extraordinary imagination, taking the lyric '*Annie, are you okay?*' to another level.

We burst into the second MJ and boys' dance break which gives the audience a double-hitter, the moonwalk followed by 'the lean'.

In the beginning, there was much discussion about how to achieve this trick.

The producers loved the idea but thought I was mad trying to put it into the show.

My approach was, "If Michael can do it live, then we have to do it; it's what the audience will expect if we do this number."

When performing 'the lean', Michael has literally done it at the opposite side of the stage, where he and the male dancers have charged across, and with a slight distraction, they're into it. Now I can't go into too much of the process we had to go through without giving it away, but our main concern was achieving the trick eight times a week, nearly 500 times a year! After a lot of research and gaining the patent for the trick itself, I decided we should do it on the bridge. It was the best way to create a distraction while setting up the trick and giving the boys time to 'prepare'.

With the help of our set designer, Jonathan Park, clever lighting by Nigel Catmur, and me putting my counterpoise and gastrocnemius soleus muscles and achilles strength to the test, this was built into the set and has been a huge success ever since.

I am so proud of this as a piece of theatre and it has been an audience and cast highlight since the beginning.

'Man in the Mirror' was the starting point to create what has become known as the 'White section'. The company are all dressed mainly in white to represent the humanitarian and political messages within Michael's music, a vital component for me when first putting together this vision and narrative of Michael's work. In my first outing with this production, the three songs were 'Man in the Mirror', 'Earth Song' and 'Heal the World'.

We now also do 'They Don't Really Care About Us' and for me, this is the conclusion of a three part message that we deliver as what I call, the 'Thriller Army'. The first is the (new) opening, 'Don't Stop 'Til You Get Enough / Billie Jean Remix' where we come out onto the stage, united as Jackson emissaries. The second moment is 'Can You Feel It' at the end of the first half, celebrating, yet urgently sending out the brothers' optimistic message of global unification. The White section goes a step further, especially with the insertion of 'They Don't Really Care About Us' becoming more political and asking the listener to search inside themselves and take a moment to think about what they can do to change some of the wrongs in the world, big or small.

It is the most powerful fifteen minutes of the show and often has the audience on their feet or in tears, or both.

'BAD' into 'Black or White' became part of a three-pronged climax to the show. It was almost impossible to compare or separate the importance of 'Billie Jean' or 'Thriller', and 'BAD' had to be in there even though it didn't quite fit anywhere else.

Following the White section, there is the feeling of a natural and theatrical end, particularly after the power of those three songs. The audience then get what they are really waiting for. Act Three, if you will: 'Billie Jean' and 'Thriller', followed by 'BAD' and 'Black or White' perfectly forming our finale and curtain calls.

Again, this was designed instinctively back in 2008 and has barely changed since.

We have recently added the opportunity in the West End for the audience to use their phones at this point to capture all the excitement and post to social media, showing a real change in the times since we started.

'Remember the Time' did not make the final cut for this initial tour. It was added to the original West End production almost a year later.

Thriller Live! is a show presented and divided by three entities. One is a straight up concert. Michael live – bringing that energy and raw quality to the stage, really showing the relationship between him and his fans. On top of that, there is the recreation of his screen work – the videos, particularly 'Smooth Criminal', 'Beat It' and 'Thriller'. Lastly, there is the representation of the earlier work for where is little reference material and the choreography and visuals had to be re-imagined.

This part of the creation was thoroughly enjoyable as I have been able to use my own originality, together with the inimitable Jackson family style to come up with something new and relevant for a theatre crowd.

Adrian Grant's original concept for the casting of this show was to have six singers representing each strand of Michael's musical psyche. 'Man 1' is the more mature, soulful character, leading the ballads and material such as 'Rock with You', also getting to connect with the audience more through the spoken parts, linking the songs and sections together. 'Man 2' and the 'Female Lead' both have the most dance and video based work with songs like 'Remember the Time' and 'The Way You Make Me Feel'. 'Man 3' is our rock singer and has the task of singing 'Beat It', 'Dirty Diana' and a lot of the high impassioned, screamed stuff throughout the show. Each of these tracks are a tough sing for anyone that plays them and having to do it eight times a week, an added pressure. The fifth and sixth principals play MJ himself, the young Michael and an older singer/dancer. These are the two roles that pay a visual tribute to Michael. This enables us to separate between an impersonation and something more theatrical. Leading with this strong concept, I was able to then create what I call mini-musicals.

Songs like 'Thriller' and 'Smooth Criminal' already come packaged as a mini-musical. I then looked at grouping other songs to take the audience on a more of a journey than just slamming through the catalogue song by song.

The Jackson Five medley comes really early on and has the feel of an Ed Sullivan TV performance, the most famous of J5 performances. Each of our Young MJs makes their way through 'I'll Be There', 'I Want You Back', 'ABC' and 'Rockin' Robin', a back-to-back vocal and stamina test that presents a real challenge when casting this role.

The running order, especially for Act One, has changed quite dramatically over the years, purely through myself and the team all feeling we hadn't quite got it right.

For instance, we originally opened with the Jackson Five medley, 'I Want You Back / ABC / The Love You Save', followed by 'Ben', 'I'll Be There', 'Show You the Way to Go', 'Blame It on the Boogie' and 'Shake Your Body (Down to the Ground)'.

We performed the majority length of these songs, even when in medley form making it difficult to add more content to an already lengthy show.

The end of the first half now pays homage to the *Off the Wall* album which is made up of 'She's Out of My Life', 'Off the Wall', 'Get on the Floor', 'Rock with You' and 'Don't Stop 'Til You Get Enough'.

The concept behind this section is a bustling New York by day, seeing different characters in their mundane nine-to-five jobs. Man 2 lures them to 'live life off the wall' and they shake off their day attire and boogie down to the club. We intimate that this may have been Michael in his days at Studio 54 and the whole section is a dancefloor frenzy building towards the end of Act One.

A more recent addition was putting 'This Place Hotel' together with 'Dangerous', a section that was put in for our Brazil tour. The 'Hotel' is the setting for both songs showing the danger and intimidation in the lyrics from each song. The styling and choreography inspired by the latin vibe of the 'You Rock My World' video.

'Dirty Diana' follows 'Smooth Criminal' at the peak of the second act and we switch eras and characters in a heartbeat. Man 3 sings this one and enters the gunshot world of 'Smooth Criminal', an old rock and roll venue he used to play, reminiscing about his relationship with a crazed and dangerous fan.

Artistic licence ensues and two 'Dianas' appear in a highly choreographed and highly sexualised persual of Man 3, revealing our first 'PG-rated' moment of the night (the other being the zombies in 'Thriller').

When you have so much material to choose from, it is tricky to please everyone.

I personally long for the day when we are performing 'Scream', 'Blood on the Dance Floor', 'In the Closet', 'Ghosts', 'Liberian Girl', 'Give In to Me', 'Will You Be There', 'Is It Scary', 'Stranger in Moscow' and 'Love Never Felt So Good'. All personal preferences, but when you only have around two hours to tell the whole 'story', sacrifices and wise commerical choices have to be made.

All the actors that have played 'MJ' often ask me, "What is my motivation for each performance?"

The truth is that each of these experts bring a different 'Michael' to the stage, depending on their age and physical ability. David Jordan, for instance, is able to capture Michael at the height of his performing career, slightly more mature and with a confident glint in his eye, emulating the 'HIStory' era. In a David Jordan version, the choreography contains more robotics and popping and is a slick and knowing presentation, whereas the more youthful Kieran Alleyne flies around the stage at speed like Michael on the 'BAD' tour with the same fierce agility. This was another eye-opener. I hold each of our MJs talent in very high regard, each one of them a master of movement, but it would take putting all of them together to get anywhere close to Michael himself.

We show a variety of Michael's guises from each era, which can be a demanding ask for our boys.

The opening number which includes our 'drop-in' of 'Billie Jean', is Michael at his best – the ultimate performance. We only show a glimpse as a device to let the audience know that someone who looks and performs like Michael will be gracing the stage throughout the show.

'Dangerous' is directed as the 'American Bandstand' TV special. I discovered this performance and think it is his best. 'Wanna Be Startin' Something' is the live opening of the 'Dangerous' tour, slipping into 'Dancing Machine' as a nod to The Jackson Five's various performances of this song where Michael showed a youthful and experimental attempt at the Robot. 'Smooth Criminal' is a recreation of the music video, combined with some of the live elements of choreography. 'Thriller', again, is the music video combining Michael's playful side as much as possible in the storytelling of the first verses and choruses to help set up the dramatic change as we enter the graveyard for the iconic zombie dance break.

'Billie Jean' is the only number we discuss as an option for each of the MJs to take ownership of.

There are so many wonderful versions of Michael doing this and I feel it is important that each actor finds his most comfortable.

From the beauty and innocence of that first Motown 25 reveal to the amazing Victory Tour performance and then of course, 'Dangerous' in Bucharest and 'HIStory' in Brunei '96. So many options – all different and all phenomenal in their own right.

Each of our MJs find their own identity with this song and is often the basis for their whole journey.

Chapter Five

Triumph

The announcement from the producers that we were taking the show into the Lyric Theatre in London's West End gave us very little time to prepare or get too excited. That first tour under my direction had successsfully toured the UK and was now out in Rotterdam. After another stint back in Manchester and then Belfast they would all be done. The creative team back in London got right down to working out what this West End production would look like.

Rehearsals would happen through December and over the Christmas period. We were to tech the show over new year with the first preview taking place on January 2nd.

We had to audition for an all-new cast, including the young boys and I had a lot of new material to construct. We decided to hold open auditions as well as go through the usual channels via agents, organised by Debbie O'Brien, our casting director.

We ran a televised search for both dancers and the boys. The dancers open auditions were held at the Urdang Academy, a top London college recently relocated to the old Finsbury Town Hall. The listed and very ornate Great Hall was our home for the day, a beautiful backdrop for the cameras.

Thousands of dancers arrived in their droves, having to queue around the block and down Rosebery Avenue. Various news stations turned up to interview myself, Adrian and some of the auditionees and once the room was set up with our banners and posters, we were ready.

These clips were aired on Sky, ITV, even shown across the pond on CNN news!

The day was long and a little crazy. We had two rooms running; one was the Great Hall where we would bring in a hundred dancers at a time. To get through it all in time, they stood in lines of ten and came forward to show their freestyle. I went through every up-tempo MJ song that day!

There was some incredible talent and of course there were also the die-hard MJ fans and those that just wanted to be seen on TV. They came in their costumes, lined up with everybody else, each with a desire to show their two minutes of 'Michael'. This was great for the cameras and the TV crews lapped this up as part of their item.

Anyone that showed a glimmer of talent appropriate for the show, was asked to stay.

The other studio was used as a recall room with my assistants, Jo Dyce and Yasmin Yazdi, teaching those candidates a short routine. At the end of the day, those groups were brought in to perform for myself and the panel. That routine was 'Thriller'.

The open auditions for the 'Young MJ' boys were held at the Lyric Theatre on the stage we would eventually perform on. Again, there were hundreds of boys who this time were seen in groups of four to sing their own choice of Jackson song to the panel sitting in the auditorium.

The boys with promise were kept and taught a short routine from The Jackson Five medley and then asked to sing again. The stand-out from that day was Kieran Alleyne, a totally untrained boy from Leicester. Layton Williams was cast through private auditions as he was performing as *Billy Elliot* at the time. The two completing the final line up from the opens were Sterling Williams and Ashton Russell.

While working on all these open auditions, we were seeing singers privately through agents calls.

Ricko Baird, John Moabi and Roger Wright, who were all lead performers on the tour, had agreed to return to the show, so we were only looking for a Man 3 and our diva.

We were gifted with a young Ben Forster and Five Star lead singer, Denise Pearson.

Ben did a wonderful few auditions and although the deliberations within the panel involved discussions about his aesthetic being 'right' for the rock track in the show, he soon proved his worth, showing the versatility and invincible range of his vocal. Ben went on to set the bar for what we now look for in the role.

Denise was another level altogether. I was a huge Five Star fan back in the day, so having not seen or heard of her since, was quite starstruck on the day of her first audition.

She was clearly not used to auditioning, as she turned up with hardly anything prepared and in a very cosy-looking woolly jumper and jeans – very *America's Next Top Model*! However, when she sang, there was no question we had to have her in the show. I recall her singing a Whitney Houston song but even then, there was a distinct Jackson quality to the vocal.

We asked Denise back for a recall and producer Paul Walden requested a more 'show appropriate' look to help him envisage her in the role.

She did not disappoint. Denise came back, dressed all in black leather, with killer heels, a hair piece in and a full face of make-up. We had given her material from the show to learn and she came back with it packed tightly in her arsenal, blitzing us all with each song, beautifully navigating her way through each Michael riff and nuance, assaulting all four of us on the panel with her brilliance.

This was an audition masterclass from Denise's day one as a theatrical novice jumping to day two showing all her experience as a global star of the '80s.

There was no question we had found our leading lady.

Denise came into the show and has remained an enigma. Truth be told, her performance is the benchmark for all the singers in this show as not only is she one of the best female vocalists this country possesses, she is so steeped in the Jackson feel, it pours out of her naturally. In a Jackson show where four of the principals are NOT dressed as him, it is essential each of them possess or develop an essence of Michael. We still look to Denise as an example of just that.

Nevertheless, even though Denise came into rehearsals wowing us with her virtuosity, she was terrified. I recall teaching her the staging for 'The Way You Make Me Feel'. Denise asked me to clear the room, not because she was being a diva, she was so scared her whole body was shaking!

Of course, when the company were finally allowed back in the room, she knocked everybody out with her performance (and Denise never did anything less than full out!) and has done so ever since.

It felt like no time at all between finalising our casting and starting rehearsals. With so much being added to the show (the whole *Off the Wall* section, new J5 Medley, 'Remember the Time' and new choreography for 'Blame It on the Boogie'), I had to create while we rehearsed. This meant early starts and very late nights. When you are so creatively invested in something, adrenaline prevents feeling any kind of fatigue and this was an opportunity that needed an unstoppable sense of adventure.

Also equally invested, the producers brought in a costumier and spent a fortune on all new costumes. When we got to the theatre, the cast got to fit and try these on. Sadly, after weeks of meetings and a great deal of prep in this time, the costumes were just not right. The cast spent most of that fitting pulling me outside to complain and show me the dreadfully unsuitable and ill-fitting garments that were being presented. It felt like hell with only days to go and the cast ended up wearing their own clothes for not only things like 'Beat It' but also the white section. It was a little soul-destroying after all the work put in, but there was little we could do during the Christmas and New Year period, while frantically putting this monster of a show together to present to the public only a few days later.

In the end the producers lost that fortune and we brought in my partner and his team to style, redesign and make the costumes for all future productions.

These designs, like the show itself, have developed over the years. The show leaves no time backstage for any member of the cast to relax. They are all either onstage or backstage changing. So many songs featured in the show means many iconic looks and you cannot do one dressed as another.

In total there are now over 250 costumes in the *Thriller Live!* wardrobe department for one show alone.

The longest process within a technical rehearsal of any show is usually the lighting. This is what the tech is for, adding anything 'technical' or 'technological' to the already rehearsed content and can take anything from three days to three weeks depending on the production. The lights take the longest to set up, to focus and then to program to fulfil the designer's and eventually the director's vision. But the tech is made up of many other elements including sound, sometimes video (which is also very time-consuming) and running the show cue to cue for the stage management team.

The band, or orchestra, led by the musical director, simultaneously rehearse in a separate location.

This is where the musicians, design team and the backstage crew – the people you rarely see – come together and become as important as the performers on stage, bringing the whole team together as a 'company'.

The critics have given much attention and praise for our lighting over the years and rightly so, Nigel Catmur is one of the best. He is yet another creative who works constantly to keep the show looking fresh and will always attend with his team to make any design updates himself.

The sound department, led by Chris Whybrow, are less likely to receive praise. I find sound to be one of the most thankless jobs in entertainment as people only seem to notice it when there is a problem. It is expected that sound should be perfect and when it's not, these guys certainly hear about it.

(On the American tour of *The Genius of Ray Charles*, a fist fight broke out between a guy in the back row and our sound operator, all because the audience member wasn't happy with how the show sounded!)

We now use in-ear monitors for the singers and the band. This technology is more common in music than it is in theatre but with *Thriller Live!* being a sung-through concert with the make up and volume of a pop band, we have found that this monitoring system is vital. It also assists in us getting the precision we need from the singers. The singers each have their own 'mix' that they can individually control and request what they need to hear to ensure they give the best performance. They rely solely, however, on the sound number two, who is situated in the wings and controls each of their mixes.

When the equipment fails, which does happen sometimes, it can be very distressing for both performer and technician, especially if you imagine having a room full of sound going horribly wrong, total silence or screaming white noise plugged into your ears. Our sound team are as dedicated as the rest of the company and take these issues to heart.

Back in 2009, however, we were still using traditional monitors in the wings and at the front of the stage.

As our opening preview fell upon us, I remember standing on stage and telling the cast, band and crew, "Thank you all for your commitment and hard work over these past few weeks. I know how much we all believe in this show but it's not the kind of product always welcome in the West End. We are about to go on quite a ride with this, so please all enjoy every moment, as it may only last a couple of weeks."

The reviews were mixed but not terrible. Paul Vale of *The Stage* stated, "Those looking for history of Jackson's personal life should look elsewhere as this theatrical extravaganza is a breathtaking celebration of a musician whose work spans over three decades... Jonathan Park's set design and Nigel Catmur's lighting are complimented by LED screens creating some wonderful theatrical set pieces that are simple and yet remarkably effective." Benedict Nightingale of *The Times* said of one performer, "What [he] lacks in physical similarity to Jackson he also lacks vocally. The coarse, sandy qualities of his voice are as suited to 'Rock With You' as custard is on a steak." Karen Fricker of *Variety* wrote that the musical had 'remarkably high production value' but was too long. Fricker continued, "Jackson's hits sung by four strong-voiced, charismatic leads, backed by a crackerjack team of singer-dancers—is effective and entertaining." Sanjoy Roy of *The Guardian* noted, "It's cute, kicking and retro, but also highlights a danger that looms large in this show: that even as a tot, Jackson was supremely gifted performer—both as a singer and a dancer—and this tribute, however well intended, inevitably pales by comparison."

And Charles Spencer of *The Daily Telegraph* commented, "Gary Lloyd, who doubles as director and choreographer, keeps the energy level at fever pitch almost throughout, and his dance routines, featuring daring leaps from an on-stage bridge, break-dancing, and, yes, the moonwalk, are spectacular."

Ten years later, after 7,000 performances and five million people around the world having watched the show, I look back at my comments when addressing that original West End company. I have realised since then, that with every show we work on, you just never know which one will capture the public's love and imagination.

Chapter Six

One Day in Your Life

"It's a mess," I exclaimed as I slumped in the tatty, yet strangely comfortable, armchair in the company office. "I really need to come in and do a session with these kids. Halfway through their contract and they seem to have forgotten who we are representing."

Sharon, the company manager, sat there silently, waiting for me to suggest a time and a date so she could start scheduling.

"It's embarrassing how lazy some of them are being out there!"

At that moment, the phone rang.

"Company office," Sharon said perkily as she picked it up. "Uh-huh," she said, looking at me, her expression changing. "Right, okay," she continued, starting to look concerned.

The conversation continued for another minute or so and Sharon finally put the phone down.

"Okay," she said, "brace yourself." I took a breath.

"The Jackson family want to come and see the show tomorrow."

"What?!" I cried. "You have got be joking!"

"I'm not," she answered gravely. "Three of them are coming and that's not it." I looked up, waiting for the punchline. "They're filming a documentary."

"Okay," I replied hesitantly.

Sharon continued, "They're filming and they want to come, be filmed entering the theatre, watch the opening and then they want to leave."

"You have got to be joking!"

How was that going to look to a theatre full of people?

The most famous family in the world come to watch a show about their brother, the most famous man in the world, and leave after five minutes!

It that doesn't kill ticket sales, I don't know what will!

I started to panic.

The show looked a mess. It needed at least a week to go through and sort it all out. The team needed a boost but maybe it was more a rocket underneath them that was required.

And how would they feel, watching the Jackson brothers getting up and leaving, not ten minutes into Act One!

We planned to call the company in the morning and left it there for the night. The next day, the rehearsal went well and we worked on the worst bits.

The cast were excited and understandably nervous about that evening's guests. I didn't tell them about the fact they would only be watching the opening. That would certainly have been counter-productive.

Showtime arrived quicker than you could imagine and I began pacing.

The show would go up late as the brothers were arriving with our marketing team after the general public were seated.

I went out to greet them.

What struck me initially was how wonderfully ordinary they looked.

Aside from Tito's signature bowler hat, the three of them just looked like regular guys out for a night at the theatre.

Until you really looked at them.

They each radiated a warmth, a positive glow that just said – superstar.

We entered the auditorium together.

It had already gone beyond seven-thirty so the audience were all in and waiting. As we walked into the stalls, I felt the entire theatre look and the buzz started.

It was like a whispering spirit that ricocheted from right to left.

The Lyric Theatre is quite intimate so it's easy to feel exposed in these moments.

I walked the brothers to their row (G) and watched as they shuffled down the aisle passing people in astonishment and amazement.

As they sat down, a gentleman behind Tito dared to ask if he would remove his bowler hat.

Tito simply said, "No."

I took a deep breath; now the show could begin.

I watched the opening sequence and then ran up to the company office as I couldn't bear to watch them leave and hear the reaction of the audience.

I viewed the show on the TV monitor and was happy that our surprise guests had helped pull this team together. It looked great and the audience were really responding, the atmosphere helped no doubt by the presence of, not only Michael's family but pop royalty in their own right.

The brothers leaving didn't seem to upset the flow of the performance AT ALL and the cast remained energised, giving that night's crowd an unforgettable time.

I made my way down to the auditorium towards the end of act one and to my absolute delight, discovered Jackie, Tito and Marlon standing in their seats, joining in with 'Can You Feel It' and seemingly having a ball.

No wonder the show maintained its energy level.

I found out later that the brothers were enjoying the show so much, they cancelled their dinner plans, sent their film crew home and stayed to take in the whole thing. Wow.

Once the auditorium had cleared, the cast, band and crew were called back on stage after this momentous performance. A performance so high, even higher than an opening night, followed such haunting memories of Michael's passing, which seemed like only yesterday.

Adrian and myself escorted the brothers to the stage after hearing briefly how much they enjoyed the show. The relief was huge and the smiles all round could have lit up the theatre.

As Jackie, Tito and Marlon walked onto the stage, you could feel the anticipation and almost smell the hero worship.

As expected, they spoke gently and, talking over one another, congratulated us in small groups, looking around.

At that point, Jackie spoke loudly and clearly and the whole stage quietened.

It was almost as if we were witnessing the older brother pulling rank and calling for silence as he spoke.

"I want to thank all of you. The show was really great, you really, really touched my heart and both my brothers."

There was a unanimous smile of triumph from us all, but it was at this point that he began to cry.

Through his tears he proceeded to thank us all for putting on the show, and sobbing, he continued, "We have become so used to other people, the media... talking about Michael in a negative way. He was our younger brother, y'know, and that was always painful." Tito and Marlon moved closer to him, nodding in agreement. "This was the most positive celebration of his life and we are not used to seeing that." Tears appeared in many eyes of the crowd surrounding them.

Tito looked at him. "I told you" he said, smiling. "You could do with some more of our songs, though..." he almost joked.

By now, there was yet another feeling of surrealism and euphoria, a surge of warmth and positive electricity buzzing through the company.

This moment was a proud one, but also very sad as we saw three older brothers grieving for their younger brother, not only for his recent death but for the life he had to lead.

The brothers kept us on that stage for an hour and a half, connecting with each and everyone of us, Marlon and Tito talking to John and the band, Jackie to the singers and performers, and all of them addressing the crew and theatre staff. We took pictures and swapped stories. They showed real interest in us all, our backgrounds, and our roles in the show and it's development. We really were in the presence of old-school showbiz royalty and I relished watching the younger generation drink all of this in.

To this day, I always tell this story on the first day of rehearsals with a new cast.

In Conversation with Haydon Eshun

Haydon Eshun was the lead singer of '90s boy band
Ultimate Kaos and starred on ITV's *Reborn in the USA*.
He also holds the record for the longest-running male lead
in the West End for his time on *Thriller Live!*

GL: You have had links with the Jacksons thoughout your
whole career; tell me how it all started.

*HE: Going back to when I fell in love with Michael, I'd say I was
about eight years old and my mum won tickets for the 'BAD'
concert on the radio. I hadn't heard much about Michael as I
was really young at the time, so my older brother got to go and
see the concert with her.*

*I think it was at Wembley and my brother came back raving
about it so then I wanted to research everything about Michael.
My mum bought us the records and – it goes to show, being in
this [show] for over ten years, you see how kids fall in love with
Michael and his music – instantly, and I feel that was something
that happened to me when I was really young.*

*So that led to me wanting to get into music, and loving music
but then randomly I got into a band – Ultimate Kaos. My school
teacher had told me that I could sing and I ended up going to an
audition for Simon Cowell. It was actually Simon Cowell that
put the group together because two of the guys from my band,
they were backing dancers for Sinitta. This is how it all started.
At the time I wasn't good at spelling or reading and I was really
shy when it came to being around people. Somehow, I ended up
doing this audition at Dance Works on Bond Street in London.
I walked out and my mum grabbed me and pulled me back in,
saying, "You can do it, you can do it," and it was all because,
y'know, I did have this love for Michael.*

I loved dancing; back then it wasn't so much the singing, it was more the entertainment side and I loved that. I did the audition, got into the band, but at the time they were looking for two bands. Rahsaan from Damage was cousins with a guy from my group and they were all putting together these two groups: one was Damage, one was [Ultimate] Kaos.

After that, we left Simon Cowell – I think it was 1992 – and then we signed a big deal with Polydor in '94. We had a good amount of success and being the first black boy group of the time, they wanted to make us out as the English 'Jackson Five' – there were five of us, we were young, it made sense.

But we had that pressure to be this big group and we were so young, it was really difficult to live up to that expectation. So then in '95, Motown jumped on the deal with Polydor and we were planning to release through Motown. We had meetings, did a photo shoot and planning to go over to the US and meet the execs and stuff. And then every interview we had it was, "Oh, so you guys are the new Jackson Five?" We felt like we were but then after six months, the deal fell through, the labels clashed and it all kind of fizzled out. But all through my career with Ultimate Kaos, we were compared to the Jacksons.

And I just found I've always been inspired by (Michael) – he put everything into his music, into his craft, and that's something you can't teach someone, someone has to have that ability and that passion. He didn't think about himself, he thought about everyone else and I feel like that's what he did for most of his life.

So, when I left the group I ended up doing a TV programme with some '80s and '90s artists – it was called Reborn in the USA *[I smile remembering this show – Haydon laughs], which was a great experience. We got to go to America, and each town we did a different genre of songs. In Detroit, I sang 'Rock with You' – we went to the Motown studios, saw how they recorded. I remember*

*it was so small but there was like fifty people in the one studio,
'cos they used to play everything live and it would be done in
one take/two takes. It was a great experience to see how back in
those days, how they made that magic happen.*

GL: You have been awarded the honour of being the longest-
running male lead ever in a West End show. How does that
make you feel and what is your secret for such endurance?
Eight shows a week is really hard for most people ,but you just
seem to keep getting better.

HE: *I think we are all blessed to do something in life and I feel
that when you get given opportunities, it's important to grab
them and appreciate them. Being in a band, leaving that band,
not having so much success and being all over the place – being
part of a show gives you stability, it gives you focus, it gives you
discipline. And one thing I needed was discipline and this is why
I am able to be consistent, because one: I love Michael Jackson,
I love Michael Jackson's music; two: I love the team, I feel that
is so important to have a good team around you, good people.
I sacrifice a lot of things to be able to do eight shows a week. I
don't party. I don't drink. I don't smoke. Because I know, when I
step on stage, I want to be one hundred per cent. I don't want no
distractions, no, "Oh, but I went out last night and I was tired,"
stuff like that, because this audience are paying twenty to a
hundred pounds for a ticket, so the trick is to look after yourself.
Be focused, whatever you do, whether it's musical theatre, music,
acting. It's just having that focus and desire and passion, and
that has what has got me through ten years of doing this show.*

*It's hard, I admit. I do have vocal problems and I do want to
go out and have a great time and to be fair, I have in my past.
But if you live for the weekend, go for a nine to five. If you don't
have the discipline and focus, this is not the business for you – it's
just not. Mind, body and soul you have to be healthy and love*

*what you do. I get to sing Michael Jackson's songs every day –
there's no better place to be. That's what kept me here. I love my
job.*

GL: I talk about your audition in the book. It is one of the most
exposing and high pressure auditions we have ever done. Tell
me about it.

HE: *My manager, Gary Wilson, called me one day and said,
"Haydon, I've been contacted about this* Thriller Live! *show, a
Michael Jackson show, are you interested?" Straightaway, my
reponse was, "I'm not really interested in musical theatre yet."*

*I said that because as an artist, you look at that later on
in your career, especially not coming from a musical theatre
background. This is people's passion. Sometimes you don't want
to venture into those areas where you're not one hundred per
cent in it, y'know? Because these people, the musical theatre lot,
they go to the schools, they study, they know every line and every
word, so I wanted to respect that and at the time it wasn't for me
but then he said, "The show is more like a concert."*

*Then I thought, That is interesting, so I said, "Let me get
back to you."*

*He kept calling me. I didn't pick up my phone but I was
talking to friends and my family, asking them, "Shall I go for the
audition?"*

*Auditions are nerve-wracking, especially when you don't do
it a lot, it's very nerve-wracking. So I built up the courage and
the advice was, "Go on, do it, you've got nothing to lose, it's in
the West End."*

*So I went for the audition, and I walked in there [we both
laugh, remembering] – who was in my audition? You were there,
Adrian, Paul—*

GL: And John.

HE: *Yeah, and John, of course, and that was in Husky studios [in Elephant and Castle, South London].*

So I walked in; I can't remember what I sang. But I felt a connection with you and Adrian, as soon as I walked in there, I felt like I knew you guys. So when I walked out, like with every audition you think, Ahh, I didn't get it, or, Did I do well? So then I got a callback and my second audition, I had to come to Three Mills Studios, where you were rehearsing the tour cast. You made me sing in front of the tour cast, but not only that, with full sound, and in front of the whole production team.

I remember walking in, and the lights were shining, the stage was set. I got given the mic and you said, "Can you sing 'Man in the Mirror'?" I remember I was so nervous as I walked on that stage. I had already done it; I'd performed in front of a hundred thousand people, done tours all over the world, but when you've got twenty-five people you don't know sitting there... But the thing with me is when I get on stage, like with Michael Jackson, y'know, he is very shy, very pleasant, just very low-key. Behind closed doors, he didn't like to do interviews, but when he got on that stage, he was just, y'know, he was just someone else. I feel like that's something that I have, which is unique and you can't rehearse it.

Going back to the audition, as soon as the music started, I feel like it's hard with his songs, the amount of emotion and passion and feeling he has in his songs, I remember feeling it was a blessing to be on that stage – when that song started and I started singing 'Man in the Mirror', I just closed my eyes, the song started and I just sang away – I was in my element, that was a great feeling for me and whether I got the job or not, I felt I was meant to be on that stage. I feel that's very important for anything you do is to love what you do and really embrace it. That audition was crazy but it was an amazing audition because I got to perform on the stage that ten years later I am still performing on. I remember afterwards, I came outside and I saw you and Jo [Dyce] both with smiles on your faces and I kind of knew, without you guys saying anything, 'cause you couldn't just say straightaway; I could tell that I did a good job. And I think you kind of hinted to me that I did well.

GL: You have been shipped off to certain countries to help out with the tour. What are your memories of these trips?

HE: *The worst tour experience was the first tour to Japan 2012. I think it was Tokyo. During the interval, we were getting ready for Act Two and out of nowhere an earthquake erupted and shocked the building for over a minute. All our costumes, wigs, make-up were thrown everywhere. When we got back out there to start Act Two, the audience were on thier feet cheering like nothing had happened! My best memory has to be the arena tour in 2009. Thousands of like-minded people coming out to show their love for MJ and screaming for what we were doing. Such a great feeling.*

GL: You were in the charts with MJ during Ultimate Kaos – did you meet him or the brothers then?

HE: *No, we didn't, but in 1999 we were the opening act for Janet on her tour at the Docklands Arena. She was amazing and very encouraging when we met her.*

GL: You recently toured with Tito and his band – what was that like?

HE: *It was an amazing experience. They came to see the show in 2009 but I didn't get to meet them then as I was rehearsing to come into the show. Meeting a Jackson is surreal. You see them on TV, you know their history and their background. You know the discipline they had to go through and the trials and tribulations, and for me, to meet someone who had to go through all that, coming from a hard background with their father being so strict, there was so much I wanted to talk to him about.*

The thing about Tito, he is so cool, so down to earth, we just connected straightaway. And I think the reason we connected is he knew I had a passion for what I do and I have a passion for Michael. So, he actually just let me do whatever I wanted to do! He would say, "Can you sing this song?" and I would say "Yep!" The first rehearsal was in London. He was famously two hours late, he came in and I was starstruck but I played it cool, but as soon as we started playing it was magical. The first show we did was in Chelsea – Under the Bridge. It felt like we knew each other and we just knew what to do on stage. This show has helped me so much – we fit in and we just smashed it. I felt like we'd known each other forever. And we'd performed hundreds of time, because of that connection. Him, playing this music for so many years and me singing and performing Jackson material every day. As soon as we'd done that show, he was onto his agent the next day, saying, "We need to do more shows."

GL: And now working with the Jacksons – what a payoff!

HE: *Randomly, my manager has in the last six months become The Jacksons' manager. So I recently got a call: "Jermaine's been ill and we need a singer and a backing singer. It's tomorrow and it's in Brazil, can you fly over?" and I was like, "Gary, this is too much pressure, man! I need to know what I'm doing." 'Cause as amazing as it is to jump on that stage, it's really important to know what you're doing, especially on that level. So, I turned it down. But I've been offered to do some gigs in the summer, doing backing vocals for The Jacksons. That's going to be unbelievable. This is all because of this show. It has helped me grow so much in my career. I've met so many amazing people. I love you guys. It's the people you work with that makes the experience better and that's the reason why I'm still loving it.*

Chapter Seven

Who's Loving You?

On July 7th 2009, the world got to witness a very public memorial for Michael. Held at the Staples Center in Los Angeles and televised globally, thousands of fans, still in shock, gathered alongside the Jackson family and Michael's star-studded line-up of friends to mourn and celebrate their idol.

One of our original 'Young MJs', Shaheen Jafargholi, sang 'Who's Lovin' You' at the memorial, right after Smokey Robinson read a eulogy for Michael. Shaheen had been invited to perform at the 'This Is It' shows after Michael saw his performance on *Britain's Got Talent*. Still only twelve years old, Shaheen stood alone, in front of a room filled with the most famous faces you could imagine, to remind us all what a unique talent Michael was at his age.

The image of Shaheen singing his little heart out as the camera pulls back to show Michael's casket beneath him, then sweeping around revealing the picture of Michael aged twelve on the screen above him, still gives me chills and rocks me to the core. To this day, I don't know how Shaheen got through that. He was always a fiercely tenacious young talent. We were, and still are all so proud of him.

By September of that year, the hype around Michaels passing had subsided somewhat, yet the spotlight still shined glaringly upon us. We were still the only live non-tribute show that represented Michael anywhere in the world and we felt the pressure to keep pushing towards perfection. At the Lyric and on tour, we were still performing 'Gone Too Soon' as our opening and although it felt like the time to move on from that was upon us, we didn't quite want to let go of our own modest memorial.

The demand for our little show had gone crazy and we now had companies performing two productions, one in London and one out on tour in Germany, soon to be travelling the whole of Europe. We were also casting for what we called Tour 2 (the World Tour), starting with arenas in the UK, then to follow in territories in Sweden, Finland, Denmark and then onto South Africa, possibly China and beyond. *(We are still on that world tour, by the way, performing on rotation to different territories in regular bite-sized chunks.)*

So much was going on with *Thriller* we could barely keep up and then we were hit with yet another curveball. I received a call from the Flying Music general manager, Mark Strange.

"So, dear. [Mark's term of endearment for everyone he speaks to] BB [our German co-promoters] need us to do this TV promotion. It's in a month and the tour is in Denmark but the TV is filmed as live and will be in Munich."

"Right?" I slid up to the note, knowing there was more.

"They want us to do 'Smooth Criminal', 'Thriller' and the Jackson Five medley all in one number, and with a Michael and a young Michael."

"Well, that's impossible to do that properly with the same person playing Michael," I said, and after thinking for a beat, "and who's going to do it? All our performers are either out on the tour or on stage in the West End."

We put our heads together and decided an all-new company would be the best idea and we would need two Michaels. For such a big TV opportunity (and to please our new German partners) we had to use the best, which meant Ricko Baird coming out of the West End and Michael Duke leaving the tour for a couple of days. Luckily we had great understudies in Sean Williams and Simeon Henry.

The show was called *Menschen 2009*, a famous German live music and chat show that had been running since 1996. The host was Thomas Gottschalk, also the host of one of Germany's biggest TV shows, *Wetten Dass*, and he was to present what would be a Michael Jackson special, featuring Michael's sister La Toya.

I had met La Toya at our premiere party, opening night in the West End, 21st January 2009.

She didn't make it to the show as she was attending the final of *Celebrity Big Brother* that she had appeared in and where she came seventh, being evicted on Day 20 with politician Tommy Sheridan.

As far as I remember, she came across really well and the other housemates warmed to her, as did the British public.

She did come to the party to join her brother Tito, who had been present at the show. The two of them were very relaxed and fun to be around. There is a great photo that was taken for the press with myself standing with La Toya, Tito and Adrian Grant. You can see a cheeky smile on both mine and La Toya's faces as she was squeezing my bum as the photo was taken! She giggled just like Michael after it was taken and found my more than slight embarrassment really funny.

So, I looked forward to seeing her when we made it to Germany for the filming of this TV show.

Much was to be done before then, though, and we got stuck into making rehearsal plans, costume arrangements, casting and how we would record the music. It's astounding how much goes into making five minutes of TV.

John and I went to work working out how we would present this musically. At the time, I was working on the film premiere for the Will Smith movie *Hancock* with a lot of the dancers from the show. I remember constantly checking edits of the music for the promo in all my breaks and because this was live television, the medley had to be exactly five minutes long.

We had to recruit two teams that would perform on two stages. One team would perform 'ABC' and then change into zombie costumes to perform 'Thriller', the other team were the 'Smooth Criminal' dancers. Of course, our dancers were all performing in both shows, on tour and in the West End so we couldn't use any of them. I drew on a lot of commercial dancers that my agency represented at the time. They had to learn all the choreography from scratch, which is not unusual for TV and for commercial dancers. The teams were made up of a variety of dancers, including Jessica Powell, who became the resident director on both the Australian and Brazilian productions of the show.

We then had to discuss how we would do the 'Smooth Criminal' 'lean' trick. What actually happened is that the TV company built a set similar to ours with steps coming down and a bridge that enabled us to do the 'lean' safely and effectively.

After rehearsing the medley over two days at Pineapple Studios in London, we flew to Munich.

We were on the first flight out at about 5am so we could go straight to the TV studio and rehearse.

Many of the dancers turned up in pyjamas, hoodies and leather jackets, as well as the mandatory pair of sunglasses, most still looking half-asleep. As commercial dancers, they were used to this drill, the early-morning flights and journeys to far off places, long days and late nights.

Michael Duke was there on time, bright and breezy as always but on my arrival to the terminal, my attention went immediately to Ricko. "Has Ricko arrived?" I asked the few standing there.

"Haven't seen him," was the general muttered response.

As brilliant as he was, Ricko needed a chaperone and was renowned for not turning up either on time or sometimes at all.

As we didn't have a company manager assigned to the group at this end, I paced up and down, as the only 'grown-up' until Ricko arrived.

I smiled as he finally appeared, trademark Russian 'cossack'-style black fur hat, black leather jacket and shades, tapping his head as though he had Michael's fedora on instead of the fur. This was a nervous tick of his which he did constantly, hat or no hat! I got this new gang through security and onto the plane. All was good.

On our arrival in Munich, we got through the airport pretty quickly until we reached passport control. There were two lines and seemingly some issues and discussion along the way with some of the performers. I scanned the group behind me to find Ricko, who was at the back on one of the lines, and shuffled down to join him. When we eventually reached the desk, I gestured for Ricko to go first. He passed his US passport through the window.

"*Nehmen Sie hut und brille ab,*" said the officer firmly.

Ricko simply replied, "What?", lazily and barely looked up.

The officer repeated in German, "Take off your hat and glasses." Ricko understood and slowly took off his glasses. "*Und der hut.*" I could see the officer starting to lose his patience.

"Ricko, take your hat off," I whispered loudly.

"Ah, it's okay, he can see it's me," Ricko retorted nonchalantly. At this point, the passport control officer had called two other officers over and they were talking very seriously in German, passing Ricko's passport around from one to the other.

"Ricko," I said urgently. "Just take your hat off, dude, otherwise they're gonna put you back on a plane!"

"I don't wanna take my hat off." I could not believe how indignant and stupid he was acting.

This childish act could ruin the whole performance and we had no back up!

The whole company were waiting for us and could see what was going on.

Heart in my mouth, I pulled Ricko out of the way and stepped up to the window.

"*Entschuldigung*," I said. Thankfully I knew a bit of German, having lived in Hamburg when performing in *CATS* the musical there, aged eighteen. "I am the director of a show called *Thriller Live!* and we are all here to perform on your TV show, *Menschen*."

The officers nodded. They knew *Menschen*. Good, this was a start.

"Ricko, here, is from America and he plays Michael Jackson in our show."

They nodded again and this time a couple of them smiled. "Ahh, Michael Jackson, *ja!*"

The others looked confused, looking back and forth from Ricko to each other as if to say, "*How can this be Michael Jackson, didn't he just die earlier this year?*"

"Erm, may I show you something on your computer?" A stab in the dark as this was potentially going so well…

Officer number one reluctantly turned the laptop that was in front of him round to me.

I typed in the show's website as I knew there were lots of images of Ricko on there.

After what felt like an eternity, the site came up. The homepage shot was a production photo of Ricko performing 'Dangerous' – as Michael, of course.

I turned the computer back round.

All three officers responded together, "*Ja!*" and they laughed and pointed at Ricko.

"Hey, Michael Jackson!" They came out of the control box to shake his hand and pat him on the back. I was not quite sure whether they understood we were a show and Ricko was portraying Michael or they actually thought this was him.

As we walked away to collect our bags, relieved, we could still hear them: "Michael Jackson, Michael Jackson!"

They didn't even check my passport.

The rest of the trip went without a hitch.

We were taken straight to the studio, fed and shown the set and bridge that had been purpose built for 'Smooth Criminal'.

It was way lower than ours but fine for TV and the 'lean' mechanics had been organised perfectly. That's one thing you can count on when working in Germany, the details are always triple-checked and will always be precise and on time.

We hung out in the studio until it was time to rehearse.

I exhausted both teams with dress rehearsals in London so we were all feeling well prepared and quite relaxed.

There were two very large spaces to hang out in so we spread out and took over one of them. Interestingly, although we all had mobile phones, this was in the days before the extent of social media so we all actually sat around and TALKED!

There was a lot of storytelling and general banter, as well as starting to play some group games. These games were developed around the bar later that night and consisted of concentration games, replacing words and rhythms with dance moves. After a few drinks, this became quite fun and went on into the early hours.

The camera rehearsals went well and when it came to showtime I found myself wandering to check the entrance for the zombies. Stage 1 was where we would be set to start the medley and the floor managers would take care of little Mitchell and the rest of the cast, but I wanted to double-check the last entrance, as the zombies came from different areas of the studio. I turned a corner to discover I was right behind the main entrance of the TV studio and the show was already live and in full flight.

I turned to see La Toya standing alone, waiting to make her entrance.

We were practically on the stage, merely a wooden screen between us and the audience, and ten million viewers. We silently greeted one another and grabbed a quick double air kiss.

A loud audience applause interrupted us. She squeezed my hand and whispered, "Catch you later," as she prepared to make her entrance. At that moment, Thomas, the host, started to talk about Michael, the lights went down and a video montage began to play.

The montage started with 'I'll Be There', sang by Michael as an adult, with images of him as a child and the hype of The Jackson Five era, moving into 'Blame It on the Boogie' with a voiceover talking about Joe Jackson and his hand on making the band a success. It moved into 'Billie Jean' and was spliced with fan hysteria and then in quick succession, the MJ rise to fame through 'Thriller', 'BAD' and 'HIStory'. An exciting but pretty standard montage of the success of the King of Pop. Suddenly there were images of Neverland, the tone of the voiceover changed and there were images of children, Michael looking drawn and then clips of him being frisked as he entered court. I suddenly went cold. This jumped out at me at being really odd, almost cruel, when Michael's sister was about to walk out there and be interviewed just after losing him so tragically. I looked over at La Toya and she too, was watching the same backstage monitor I was. Her face was expressionless and she just stared. I found it hard to believe she was there on her own with no PA or friend. She seemed so alone, especially with the horrific images being shown before her. I remember thinking it was so trusting to turn up and expect everything to be positive about Michael. The video then showed Michael with Lisa Marie Presley and then Debbie Rowe with baby Prince. The last few shots were of Michael announcing 'This Is It' and then global bulletins announcing his death. The music went back to 'I'll Be There', only this time, hearing a combination of Michael's adult voice duetting with himself as an eleven year old. The clips that followed were of Paris, Michael's daughter, speaking at his memorial, and Janet and the family comforting her, then closing on slow motion images of Michael performing at his peak.

I looked back at La Toya and she looked in so much pain, a solitary tear rolling down her cheek.

What are the producers of this show thinking? I asked myself.

Before I knew it, her name was being called to the stage by Gottschalk and in a flash she was gone.

I didn't even get to see her wipe that tear away. I just remember thinking how normal she looked and it dawning on me no matter how famous Michael was, or how much we, his fans around the world grieved for losing him, he was just a human from an ordinary family who were all devastated at losing him.

La Toya stepped out there like a true Jackson, no sign of the tear that fell only moments before.

She descended the few stairs with grace, only to have her microphone pack fall out of the back of her dress. Thomas Gottschalk bent over and picked it up, and La Toya apologised, seeming a little flustered. I felt so sorry for her. I stood and watched the interview on the monitor and my little knowledge of German helped my understanding of what was being asked. A translator spoke over La Toya but I got most of what was being said. La Toya looked bewildered but answered each question professionally. I could see she was shook up by what she had just seen and was still reeling at the fact Michael had gone. She talked about how the family still couldn't believe what had happened and so much had to be done following Michael's burial. She told Thomas how they all made a vow not to watch TV for months after his passing, so they were blissfully ignorant as to what was being said. La Toya talked about how Michael was not a difficult man to understand and was a very sweet, kind, loving and generous person. The public should have known this about him, how he was very playful. He loved to joke, he loved to have fun and loved children and animals. "You guys never saw that, you always saw the serious side."

La Toya was asked if Michael felt alone. She answered that Michael was never happier than when with his friends and around people, but sometimes felt secluded due to the level of fame and it could get very lonely and he often felt sad as a result.

The questioning moved on to the 'This Is It' shows at the O2. La Toya made it clear that Michael had agreed to ten shows only. The fifty that were announced later were pushed on him by the promoters and he did not agree to them or feel he could physically get through them. She had not, at that time seen the *This Is It* movie, as she could not bring herself to watch it. She did, however, comment that from the clips they had seen, the family did not feel that this was Michael at his best and he would not want the fans and the public to see him in this light. At this point in the interview I was horrified to see that they started to play the montage again out on the screens in the studio. La Toya had relaxed by this point and I really did not want her to see those images again, especially out there in public. I turned my attention to hyping up the cast about to go out there and perform.

Thankfully, the interview came to a close and Thomas got to thanking La Toya and introducing us: "…here is Michael Jackson's *Thriller Live!*"

As the lights hit the cast, the music started and Mitchell began to sing 'ABC'.

I looked over to see La Toya smile for the first time.

Chapter Eight

Working Day and Night

October 2009.

We spent the first part of rehearsals for the World tour broken, disconnected and hanging onto each other by a thread. We had just completed a cast change in the West End, only a few months into its run, followed by a full rehearsal period putting on the European tour.

By this point, swine flu had swept the nation and had seemingly found us.

The virus reached the United Kingdom in April 2009 and was announced as a pandemic of a new strain of influenza, colloquially named 'swine flu'. The first cases were confirmed on 27 April 2009 in passengers returning from Mexico. The first case of person-to-person transmission within the UK was announced on 1 May 2009 and of course the media went to town reporting many cases of people contracting this disease and dying from it. The actual number of deaths reportedly rose to over 360 (by January 2010) so we had reason to be concerned.

It hit John Maher first, so we started without an MD, then Yasmin Yazdi, my associate, went down with it and eventually me. I think

Hayley Evetts, our lead female, had it too at one point, but to be honest, this whole period is a bit vague!

We took the Tamiflu drugs and all came back way too soon, as most showbiz people do when there's a show to put on.

We were juggling two companies, the arena tour company and the European tour, which we were re-casting and adding new material into the show.

I had created an opening that involved many different MJ looks, iconic imagery and a mash-up of choreography – 'MJ through the ages'.

The song was 'Remember the Time'. We had to make some changes to the show as it was a little long. 'Remember the Time' came out of the second act where it had been since our opening at the Lyric, and was placed as our new opening.

It started with the boys styled like the dancers in the 'You Rock My World' video and the number then travelled through different eras, with singers and dancers coming on as Egyptians, mixing in a bit of Janet style for the girls. The idea was to set up to show the audience that this was an ensemble piece with four singers as well as a guy that plays MJ. Not my finest moment, when I look back, and certainly not a number I miss. However it did serve a purpose and was a great transition from 'Gone Too Soon', which we had used as an opening for almost four months after Michael died. This new number still had a sense of tribute and nostalgia but was upbeat and seen by many over three productions: the West End, the European tour and the tour we were currently working on, the Arena (World) tour. It had great visuals and the fans loved it. I prefer, however our current 'Remember the Time', a more authentic tribute to the iconic video.

Eight years, and many opening numbers later, I was able to finally succeed in delivering the desired message by putting together a remix of 'Don't Stop 'Til You Get Enough' and a part of 'Billie Jean' which involves the whole company. This is the opening we perform today.

The rehearsals for the arena tour were fraught, not only with illness but with various issues caused by clear signs that the company was being stretched. We had struggled to cast this second tour, particularly the singers, and went into the rehearsal room with barely a full cast.

The production was managed by a new company manager and DSM (deputy stage manager) that hadn't done the show or worked for the company before and this put a strain on the day-to-day running of things.

On a show as complex as *Thriller*, you need a team that knows what they are doing, know what to expect and can communicate between producers and creatives and cast, with one foot always firmly in front. The demand for the show was high and we were already maxed out when it came to staff and crew familiar with the gig.

Thankfully, everyone recovered from the (swine) flu over the weeks of rehearsal and we got the show together, as well as farming out various people to different productions that needed them. We had to send singers into the West End because we were down and Britt Quentin was to fly out to Europe to join that company. (He is still touring with that company and has done irreplaceable work as our resident director on that tour.) This has become a familiar story across the years and cases full of costumes are kept in strategic places for when we need that 'body' to come in and save the day.

The World tour cast had signed up for the UK arenas but were to begin this tour in Finland, a territory we had not yet ventured to. The idea was to bed the show in and gel the company together, however the chaos of company management ensued and despite the show and its company being ready to travel by the dress rehearsal, we had not received our flights.

Mid-way through the dress, I was handed a slip of paper with some hand-scribbled info on it.

It seemed the cast and band were being handed scraps of paper as they performed their dress rehearsal. "Whoa, whoa, whoa," I yelled at the person handing me my scrap. "What is this and why are we doing it now?"

Dress rehearsals can be extremely stressful, especially when there is a clock running against you.

This particular dress (rehearsal), we were in a film studio and a crew were coming to load out the set and the lights in less than an hour. That pressure was real as the truck companies charged by every hour incurred. I could not stop and there was no room for error. This was our only dress run before this cast would perform in two days' time in front of an audience. The show had to be loaded onto a truck and make a ferry to get it all to Finland in time for opening.

"These are your flight details," said a small voice.

"I can see that." (We had been asking for this information for days.) "Why now? Oh, forget it." I turned my attention back to 'Smooth Criminal', which was in full chaotic flow in front of me.

At the completion of the dress rehearsal, we gathered together, only to discover that all our flights were different. We were in small groups all flying via another European city: Paris, Amsterdam, Berlin. WTF? Not only that but we were to wait for the last flight to arrive before we could all travel together to the hotel. I was tired, frustrated and I was not happy.

The fatigue and frustration continued throughout the next day. It is always physically harder when you have a day off or travel day following a very long stint of creative and physical work. I dragged myself to the airport, still very unhappy about a number of things to do with the production and concerned about how we would get through the next day. I was also very worried about the cast all going off on various detours around Europe and hoped they would all make it to the meeting point.

The girls, Yasmin and Jo, still laugh about the time I arrived at the airport and went to check in.

Yasmin and a number of the dancers had been upgraded and were checked into business, which Yaz took great delight in announcing to me as I walked up to the desks.

When I checked in, I was literally given a seat at the back of the plane!

I feigned annoyance and gave the girls a bit of tongue in cheek drama to entertain them and adding to my already annoyed state. Lucky they knew I wasn't serious but found the situation hilarious anyway. I threw my hand luggage over my shoulder and sloped off to departures.

Depsite turning down Yasmin's offer to switch seats with me, I was very happy sitting with Jo at the back of the plane. To add insult to injury, however, we were served 'reindeer' as our meal...

The flight was fine but the trip worsened when at Amsterdam we were forced to wait for all the other cast members arriving at varying times from other airports around Europe.

There followed a very long coach journey. When we finally arrived, we were checked into what felt like a student hostel. Everything was made of wood and all the amenities totally basic. The beds were all smaller than your regular single and the place smelled like a hospital. Well, at least it was clean! Outraged and beyond tired by this whole palava, yet unable to think about sleeping on my child-sized block of wood, I threw my stuff down and searched for the girls. It was most certainly time for a drink.

We headed out and poked our heads into a couple of bars, both playing 'death metal' at thunderous levels. Not searching for quite that much excitement, we thankfully found a small cocktail bar who were playing music to suit our mood and complement the much-needed nightcap.

Early next morning we set off for the venue, again all together on a coach for quite some time.

The venue seemed to be in the middle of nowhere, on top of a hill with nothing at all surrounding it. It turned out to be an old ice rink and once we stepped inside from the penetrating Helsinki air we were subjected to an even colder environment. This was the first of our problems on that day.

Denise Pearson, who was our female lead for this tour, had arrived unwell and unable to sing, so we had to fly Carole Stennet, our understudy, out from London. Now, considering how difficult it was for us to get out here, I didn't hold out much hope for her arrival, so I was already subconsciously planning an emergency show for the first date on a huge high-profile tour with this brand new cast.

Luckily Yasmin, who was only here in the capacity as a temporary resident director, was also an understudy to the female lead so we put that idea 'in the bank'.

The stage wasn't quite ready for us, and although the audience that night would be over two thousand people, the seats only took up a third of the venue meaning the great deal of empty space attracted more cold air. The whole group, wrapped in coats and scarves, got to work. We rehearsed and cleaned choreography, waiting for the stage to be safe and free to work on.

Leo Tierney and Darren Holt, two of our longest-serving stalwart production managers, were doing all they could, as ever to make our set work for this venue and safe for the cast.

Because the space was so open and the stage almost floating in the centre of it, they had a job trying to 'mask' our exits, having to create wings either side of the stage.

In these early days, there was always extra for these boys to do on arrival to a new venue. Ten years later, having played so many of them, we are generally armed and ready.

All hands were on deck and I was immensely proud of the team spirit that emerged from this unforeseen scenario.

On day one of any tour with a new cast and in a strange location, the nerves begin to show. This is natural, having got used to the venue where you have made a home during the technical production period. Suddenly, your quick change is in a different place, the wings are smaller and your internal compass has been completely thrown. Part of my job is to keep everybody's levels down, while reminding them that 'they got this'.

Amazingly, at around 5pm, Carole breezed into the venue! Without giving her a moment to take her coat off (not that she would have wanted to!), she was whisked onto the stage, handed a microphone and we started to run her songs.

As we reached the end of this unorthodox technical rehearsal, it dawned on me that I hadn't smelt any food all day, or noticed any area that served snacks – in fact, I hadn't even had a coffee!

We had been here for hours but as there was so much to get through, not one person had been aware of the lack of catering in the building! I checked with the staff and nothing had been provided. Nothing at all, not even water.

As we went into the break, it was only a matter of time before the cast realised they weren't being fed. This was a potential ticking time bomb, as it would be minutes before hunger would strike each of those cast members, preparing to put their bodies through one of the most strenuous shows around.

I had to do something.

I called each of the team back home but typically it was bank holiday Monday in the UK, where everything shuts down and nobody works. In those days, people were not glued to their phones so most of my calls rang out until I finally reached Andy Sharrocks, the Flying Music production manager. Within minutes, an abundance of pizza had been ordered and water, enough to create another ice rink. The audience poured into the venue as we waited, ravenous.

When I got word of our much-awaited delivery, I sped past the company manager, who gleefully waved a good luck fax (yes, a fax!) at me. "Happy first show, everybody!" she sang.

You have got be kidding me. I shook my head, cursing her under my breath while gathering the cast together as quickly as I could. Surely this was her job?

By the time the food arrived, the whole cast were in costume but because of the nature of this venue's layout, they had to walk across the back of the stage to an area in full view of the paying customers walking in!

The cast were so in need of sustenance, they tore into these pizzas like wild animals, giving the audience a preview to their pre-show ritual, only two hours too late.

The show went up half an hour late, but thankfully the cast, now satisfied, went from being too full to 'full-out', forgetting the carb overload devoured only moments before.

Thankfully, this dreadful start to the tour was a one-off occurence and an unlucky mismatch of new touring management and a first-time promoter. There was no more illness or bad luck, and the company were soon able to enjoy packed arenas in the UK, playing our show and the work they had invested in to hundreds of thousands of screaming fans.

Chapter Nine

This Is It

On October 28th 2009, towards the end of the rehearsal period for the World tour and right before we headed off to Finland, we received an invitation for the whole cast from Kenny Ortega to attend the premiere of the highly anticipated *This Is It* movie.

We had also just been informed that Katherine Jackson had politely declined an invitation to come see the show as she would still find it 'too painful'. It was clear, then, that she wouldn't be part of the *This Is It* circus that was happening around the world and of course we all knew that she was now taking care of Michael's children.

There was a bittersweet feeling around receiving this invitation, as it all, together with the recent opening of the Michael Jackson exhibition at the O2, felt very soon after his passing. The fact the invitation came from Kenny himself made us feel special and we were of course intrigued and excited to see the film.

The invite, when it arrived, was a beautiful personalised A5 card based on the recent *This Is It* album artwork. It has since become a collectors' item and felt very luxurious, yet something about it gave me an odd sense about being part of all this.

Nevertheless we went along, en masse and in solidarity together and as always, for Michael.

"The guest list for the London screening includes Leona Lewis, JLS, Estelle, Peter Andre and the cast of the Jackson tribute show *Thriller Live!*" reported *The Independent*. *The Telegraph* gave a timed breakdown of who arrived: "4.55 pm (LA): 'There are so many stars!' says the female co-host. But she fails to name a single one. Oh, I just saw Jermaine Jackson," and what entertainment took place around the event: "11.55 pm (London): Boy band JLS do an impromptu rendition of 'The Way You Make Me Feel' and spark hysteria among the girls in the crowd. Harry Connick Jr turns up and goes unrecognised by everyone under 30 years old."

The Guardian gave a more interesting and colourful account of the red carpets from around the world. The first screening was at 4am and this was, of course, as with any MJ release, a huge deal.

Sadly for this one, Michael himself was not in control of it or would ever be present again.

Following a scrolling heartfelt explanation of how and why this movie was made 'for the fans', the film began with close-up shots interviewing each of the dancers upon getting the job, speaking emotionally to Michael on camera about their audition. Each of these stories of how Michael inspired could have come from the mouths and hearts of any of my dancers. This was something we all related to and knowing what was about to happen, this sequence was shattering to watch.

The heartbreak of all these dancers was something myself and all my cast sitting around me could connect with. Not only the personal loss and shock they must have felt, but the deep hole left by not performing the show they had been a part of creating. The most anticipated set of shows of any artist living, the dream of all dreams. Dancers work harder than anyone in this business on the way up, auditioning and auditioning to get through the door and make those contacts to fight their way up the ladder. Some of these kids had jumped right to the top only to find the mother of all snakes bring them back down the board with a bang.

Of course, this wasn't the end of their careers, far from it. Tyne Stecklein appeared in the films *Burlesque* and *No Strings Attached*, as well as TV hit shows *True Blood* and *Fuller House*. Misha Gabriel Hamilton performed in *Boogie Town*, *Step Up 4: Miami Heat* and *Step Up: All In* and Charles Klapow has become a choreographer, working on *So You Think You Can Dance* and working with will.i.am, Jennifer Lopez and The Rolling Stones. Mekia Cox has come out of this group most prolifically as an actress, now known for appearing in *90210*, *Grey's Anatomy*, *Gotham*, *Modern Family*, *Once Upon A Time* and *Chicago Med*. Not all of them have been quite as successful as this but the platform created by *This Is It*, provided by Michael, has helped them all move forward as recognised experts in this competitive field, undoubtedly giving each of their careers a boost.

But, devastatingly, they never got to perform with their idol.

This Is It was the ultimate goal and the kind of job most dancers reach for. After all that hype, the excitement of being chosen and working with the man, that bubble burst the night he died. For everyone involved, *This Is It* became and will always remain the dream that turned into a nightmare.

There followed an exhilirating insight into what would have been the opening video sequence for the 'This Is It' show. Narrated by Kenny Ortega, it was a two-minute adrenaline rush building to the stop at the end of 'Wanna Be Startin' Something', only to then hear Michael say, "You know what, I want that more." [*He demonstrates the bass sound he wants*] "It's funki-er, I'm not feeling that part enough."

Michael goes on to 'bass-box' what he wants to hear, a poetic example of Michael being one with the music and leading his band. "It's all for love. We'll get there," he says.

The rest of the movie was inspiring, enlightening and very interesting to see Michael at the heart of the process, directing (and fighting with) the young musical director, teaching these kids who the master was. There was nothing he didn't hear or see and he could still really, really move. He was completely in control when it came to the creative and he knew every nuance, every beat and every frame of video content. However, there was something slightly dark about the way it was filmed and was at times, uncomfortable to watch, leaving me questioning how well Michael was, even at this point. The show would have been out of this world, and knowing how much work goes into this kind of production, I understood why Kenny would want the world to see the film.

I believe Michael would have wanted us to see it too.

Daniel Kreps, for *Rolling Stone*, wrote:

> *What began as a 10-night stand at London's O2 Arena has exploded into a 50-concert affair as Michael Jackson added another 20 shows to his 'This Is It' run. All the tickets allotted during yesterday's presale, roughly 360,000 of them according to MichaelJacksonLive, sold out yesterday, and the tickets that go on sale to the public tomorrow will likely do the same. As it stands, the 2009 concerts will end on September 29th, and then Jackson will return to the O2 on January 7, 2010 for at least 15 more shows, bringing the grand total to 50.*

Many believe it was this pressure that killed him.

Two days after the premiere Kenny Ortega came to see the show.

Alex Buchanan, one of our long standing 'Man 3s' recalls him coming backstage.

Kenny walked onto the stage and congratulated everyone. He was so warm and really enjoyed the show. "You guys were great, really great," he said. "It is such a beautiful show, you all did amazing. You know this is the day Michael was due to come and see this show." The cast all groaned at how sad this was and looked at each other regretfully. "He would have loved it and loved you all. We were discussing what disguise he would wear – he had several!" he joked.

The fact Michael would consider coming to see a show dedicated to him in the midst of the general public on a Saturday afternoon was quite the unbelievable thought.

Alex then remembers how Kenny spoke to him personally. "Adrian has just told me that this was your first-ever show, is that right?"

It has almost become standard practice for anyone (particularly anyone learning Man 3) to get plucked from the end of their rehearsal period and brought into the West End on a four-show weekend, where singers will, from time to time, struggle with their voices.

This very thing happened to Alex after four weeks in the rehearsal space working on the World tour. He was grabbed prior to our final run-through to perform in front of a West End audience and Kenny Ortega.

"That was incredible man, you look like you have been here for ten years."

Praise indeed from the man who directed Michael.

Uber-confident Alex also confessed to me that he always hated learning choreography. Alex can dance and has never shown any fear in front of a crowd but reminded me that I would teach him choreography, in this instance for 'Beat It', in front of the company.

"I was terrified," he said, "but I had to get it together 'cos everyone was watching!" He then went on to say, "I didn't go to college, so I wasn't used to that whole show and tell thing. It's scarym man! But I will say I've taken it with me and it's helped me with everything I have done since *Thriller*. You directed me, Gary. You got me to think about everything I did on stage, making sure I had a reason for every step, every arm gesture so all my solo ventures since then have benefited from that training and direction."

I think this is a major difference between *Thriller* and other shows I work on or theatre productions in general. We attract the untrained. The show needs that raw talent to perform Michael's material with the range, sense of abandon and musical understanding needed.

With that comes an extra level of learning that everyone has to go through.

Once some of these artists have learned the show, they go on an unexpected crash course of the discipline that comes with that eight shows a week contract. Go to a theatre school and you will learn this over your three years. To those that haven't had this experience, it can come as quite a shock as there is a tsunami of rules and social etiquette that take over your world in a heartbeat on day one.

To quote dancer and choreographer Cris Judd: "Michael didn't demand perfection, he expected it."

This is the level we have to work at to keep his legacy alive and true.

Chapter Ten

JAM

As the house lights dimmed and the front of house announcement resounded in the ever-recognisable and maniacal Vincent Price laugh which always gave the cue for the start of the show, the anticipation grew as we sat awaiting and willing the show to start.

This afternoon's dress rehearsal had not gone well and (as usual) we had not really been given enough time to perfect this, so I was naturally apprehensive.

These were the moments, it was very clear we were mimicking the world of Michael Jackson and not actually in it!

The overture started and there was a ripple throughout the audience. It was almost as if they knew they were the first audience about to witness yet another new opening number under a great amount of pressure. That new number was 'Jam'.

The video montage ran through the accolades and achievements of Michael's career with the booming over-dramatic music, synonymous with the start of one of Michael's arena tours.

Then we heard, "1, 2, 3…"; the beat kicked in and we were off.

The lighting looked fantastic and the cast got off to a great start. They looked fierce, controlled and like they were loving every moment.

The costumes were all black and white and looked like suits of futuristic armour, the boys with headphones on, 'jamming' to this opening track, hypnotised by Michael's music.

The number built with each of the principal singers entering the stage and performing their part. The rap went down a storm with the audience, as did the first fake stop that led into the dance break with the whole theatre bursting into applause.

That's when I noticed it.

One of the boys was dancing out of sync with the rest of the group.

Not just out of sync but gradually starting to perform what could only be described as a tribal war dance. It looked as though he was purposely moving in the opposite direction to everyone else.

And because the whole group were dressed identically with sunglasses and headgear, it was almost impossible to work out who it was!

My eyes followed him around the stage, casting my mind back to the rehearsal room to figure out who it was by where he was placed.

It was Lewis.

I glanced over to my assistants, who were both looking at me intently to see if I had noticed.

By now, Lewis was flapping around the stage, running up and down, back to front like he was being stung repeatedly by a furious wasp. The other boys starting to look around, also wondering what had gotten into him. Of course I'd noticed, the whole room was looking at him by now, audience members pointing and laughing.

"What the hell is he doing?" I hissed at the girls.

Jo shrugged and tried to suppress her laughter. Yasmin, who was also Lewis's fiancée at the time, looked down at her notepad, clearly mortified by what was going on.

Why didn't he go off stage?

He was one of the most experienced performers on the stage, what was he doing staying on and turning this new number into a train wreck?

The really weird thing was, every time the choreography demanded the group to freeze, he did so, without moving a muscle. He held each position perfectly and for the right amount of time. Then, when they had to dance again, off he went spinning and flailing like a boxing kangaroo on acid.

The three of us decided we had to run backstage and find out what the problem was. We charged through to the pass door and waited for the cast to come off stage.

As the music changed and our young MJ, Mitchell, changed the mood with 'Music and Me', the dancers all swarmed into the tiny stage wing, sweating and ripping off their costumes ahead of the next big number.

Amidst my congratulations and pats on the back to those that passed me, I waited for Lewis to come off. I could hear a few of them: "What the hell was he doing out there?"; "I nearly stacked it when he ran into me"; "God, what a loser, that was a nightmare!"

Just as I was starting to get a little concerned about where he had gone, a figure, all in black came charging up to me.

"This." Lewis said holding up a plastic jock cup in my face. A hard plastic jock cup that had lots of teardrop-shaped air holes through it. "This – I put the damn thing on the inside of my jock…"

They were meant to be placed on the outside.

The poor boy was cut to shreds.

Another story about Lewis (who, by the way, despite being one of the more larger than life characters ever to hit our stage, is an amazing performer and has been in several of my productions) involves a far more serious accident.

It was a Sunday afternoon (we were one of the first shows in the West End to introduce Sunday matinees and after proving to be a big day for ticket sales, most shows have since followed suit). I arrived at the theatre a little later than intended, missing the start of the first show following a meeting and as I reached the stage door, it flew open, and two ambulance men burst out carrying a stretcher and on it a body that looked very much like Lewis! Sharon, the company manager, was hot on their heels as they flew up Great Windmill Street towards two waiting ambulances.

I ran into the building to discover that during the intro of 'Blame It on the Boogie', Lewis and Scott Maurice had had a collision. The number used to start with two boys running on stage and crossing one another while performing two backflips. The stage at the Lyric is rather shallow in front of the set, so this was always a little risky but with regular rehearsal and with the trained acrobats in the company doing the tricks, there was rarely a problem.

On this occasion, and probably through fatigue, the boys misjudged their take-off, and mid-flip, instead of crossing to land on opposite sides of the stage, hit one another full throttle, head to head, both landing flat on the stage.

Now Scott is a six-foot-three powerhouse, whereas Lewis, although stocky, is a mere five foot five/five foot six. They both got up and carried on, somehow making it to the interval of the show. When they both collapsed in the wings on opposing sides of the stage, there were two ambulances waiting for them.

This was not one of those showbiz moments you could just smile and carry on unbeknownst to the audience. Scott and Lewis were the only two on stage at that time and the collision was audible, even over the band. The audience saw it and heard it and that show took a while to recover as cast and audience alike wondered what had happened to Lewis after Scott helped him off stage.

Lewis was fine. He came out of it with a mild concussion and a bit of lump and a couple of days off.

It is, to this date, one of the most shocking accidents we have had and is still talked with great fondness but always with wincing faces on the people recalling it.

Chapter Eleven

With a Child's Heart

We have made more than the occasional trip to the US on the ever-taxing search for our principal singers.

Thriller Live! is truly the hardest show to cast due to the sheer demand of the vocals and the incessant physicality for the singers, dancers, band and children. As a result, we have to cast the net as wide as possible to get the best.

One of the highlights is always getting to travel to the US in the search for talent.

Two reasons really. One, we get to sit in a room listening to Michael Jackson songs all day sung by incredible vocalists, the other, I get to hang out with my friend and creative sidekick, John Maher. We always have a blast in the air and on the road inspiring each other with talk of improving the *Thriller* show and working on other projects together. We have made many long-haul trips together, for auditions and to visit or mount the show in a new territory. These moments are a big part of what makes a group of touring travellers family, especially after ten years.

It was January 2011 this time around and we hit New York just in time for the blizzards.

Auditions were going well and we did the usual rounds at Schetler Studios, right by the Neil Simon theatre and Studio 54. We saw so much talent, most of whom at that time were performing on Broadway in the likes of *Rock of Ages*, *Hair* and *Memphis* as well as some pop and gospel singers.

I love the audition routine in New York. The morning coffee, a theatrical experience in itself, followed by the long walk through the hustle and bustle of rush hour in NYC. We always stayed at the Hudson Hotel right on Central Park so it was quite a walk. But there is so much energy on the streets, it gets you ready to start the day and experience the well-drilled machine that was run by Benton Whitley of Stewart & Whitley casting.

John and I always take in a couple of shows when in New York. I think on this particular trip we saw *Rock of Ages* where we went to support John's old friend MiG Ayesa. MiG also performed on one of the original tours of *Thriller Live!* and again in the West End, as well as starring in the Australian tour. In *Rock of Ages*, MiG played 'Stacee Jaxx' and was absolutely incredible. I loved the intimate nature of how they staged the show on Broadway; you really felt part of the action and it worked brilliantly. The charm of this inclusive feeling was something they lost when brought to the Shaftesbury Theatre in London, although the production itself was amazing.

The other show we saw was *American Idiot* – the Green Day musical, a one-act punk rock frenetic riot through the album of the same name, following the story of 'Jesus of Suburbia'. We both loved it but naturally launched into the obligatory autopsy, only to be concluded over dinner. It had already started snowing when we came out and was settling really quickly. Not used to the New York snow, we decided to take dinner at Sardi's, the theatre restaurant which is right opposite the St James Theatre. We had a lovely time, happy to carry on dissecting what we thought of the show as well starting conversations about new material for the next incarnation of *Thriller Live!*

Before leaving for the US, we had had a meeting with Paul and Adrian about some new ideas and whether we should look at adding material and moving some songs around.

This has become a regular exercise over the years. The management of the show is quite different to any other I work on. The producers and creative team are very hands-on throughout the whole process. We still audition together, make decisions together and ensure the quality of the show is not only maintained, but constantly improved.

Each year we get to play on the West End, we take on more of a commitment to provide our audience with the best we can find. Over time, I think this has been a combination of testing our luck, seeing how long we would remain the resident show at the Lyric and working as a committee, regularly checking in to air our thoughts on the show and how the material was working.

This duty of care has spanned into looking at the show and its setlist, sparking discussion on how we all feel about it and acting upon those feelings.

Act Two barely gets touched in terms of its songs. It's the *Thriller* and *BAD* catalogue and it works like a dream. Since we added 'Dancing Machine' into the opening medley, we have only really added production to songs such as 'Dirty Diana' and I have made some choreographic changes to 'Beat It' and 'Wanna Be Startin' Something' very recently. The one thing we did change – and this was part of our conversation in Sardi's – was moving 'Dangerous' to the first half. This was part of a big shake-up and additional songs that followed mine and John's meeting.

When John and I left Sardi's, we could barely get out of the door. The snow had settled like nothing I had ever seen and was two-feet thick above ground. We pushed our way through it and looked for a cab. The snow was really coming down and we could barely see through the blizzard. There were no cabs, or people, for that matter; it was like everyone had fled while we were obliviously enjoying our dinner!

We were in ordinary clothes and shoes. And we had to walk back to the hotel…

Our main concern was, this was our last day in New York and we were due to fly to LA the next morning.

This looked highly unlikely and we both went back to our rooms wondering what tomorrow would bring.

Next morning, the snow had stopped and cleared a little. New York was back to its usual bustle and apart from the cold, felt like nothing had happened.

We jumped into our cab to the airport, leaving in plenty of time. We arrived at JFK and it was chaos. Most flights had been cancelled. There were queues of people as far as the eye could see and there was a mixture of travellers going nuts about their cancelled flights and some that seemed used to it. We stayed in line like good English/Aussie visitors and then reached the front to find that the quickest way to get to Los Angeles would be to fly to Fort Lauderdale, stay overnight and fly to LA from there, taking two days out of our trip. We decided, looking at the queue of irate people behind us, that we should take this option. John bought the tickets, and I called Benton to explain and to get him on the case rescheduling all our West Coast auditionees.

We made the trip, did the overnight in the motel that was provided by the airline and got to LA (two days late) as planned.

What did come out of this trip were the creative plans for the new show. John and I sat for hours in one of the JFK terminals, bouncing ideas and editing songs.

I wanted to build 'Dangerous' together in a section with 'Blood on the Dance Floor' which we looked at. (This later became 'This Place Hotel' segueing into 'Dangerous'.) We toyed around with a new opening, moving 'Wanna Be Startin' Something' to the beginning of Act One instead of opening Act Two, and a new Jackson Five medley.

The whole of Act One had a hell of a shake-up, including putting 'Show You the Way to Go' in what we call the disco section, adding 'Rockin' Robin' and putting 'Jam' at the top of Act Two. We also wanted to do more of 'Working Day and Night'. The trouble with being such fans of all this music is we wanted to do it all! A lot of these changes took a while to introduce into the show, some debuted in Brazil two years following this meeting, some a further two years on from that when we made some major changes in the West End. Some ideas didn't make the final cut at all and remain on our wish list.

We arrived in LA very early morning and checked into the wonderful The Standard hotel on Sunset Boulevard. I even got a swim in before we were picked up for our first day in LA.

It was beautifully hot and hard to believe that two days prior we were battling snow in New York.

The smell of the heat beating down and the feel of it on your skin really had an effect on both our moods, our tempo and of course, our attire. The great thing being that we didn't have to worry about the possibility of rain.

We got through over twenty singers on that first day, including Stacy Francis, a whirlwind of a character who was part of girl group Ex-Girlfriend, appeared on the American *X Factor* and even popped up on *Celebrity Big Brother* in the UK. We recalled several of these, including Stacy, being sent away with material to learn to come back in two days' time. The next day we were seeing young performers all auditioning to be Michael.

The following morning, I had arranged to meet a good friend before we started the long day.

I first met Gloria Jones when working on a musical I developed and directed *20th Century Boy*, the story of Marc Bolan, lead singer of T. Rex and the pioneer of glam rock in the UK. It was a fascinating period working with that music and learning about Marc and his rise to fame only to die tragically young in a car crash age twenty-nine. His girlfriend, Gloria Jones, was driving that car and as part of a re-write of the script, I wanted to feature Gloria and their son Rolan leading the storytelling. We, of course, had to gain their blessing and so I spent a wonderful few days in LA meeting Rolan and Gloria and hanging out. We all really hit it off – 'three Librans and a love-in', I called it, as we all have similar birthdays (Marc, too, was a Libra) – and we have stayed in touch ever since. Gloria was also in the original LA company of *Hair the Musical* (I directed a European arena tour a couple of years later). Marc actually met Gloria when she was in this show, so the fortuitousness nature of this relationship and our meeting has never failed to amaze me.

On this trip, I had reached out to Gloria to let her know I was in town. We were still working on the Marc Bolan show at this time. John was musical director on this show too, so I wanted them to meet, as well as bring Gloria up to speed with how the show was developing. We were about to go on a national tour and at the time, it felt like things were really moving with the project.

Time was ticking so I kept an eye on the door and out of the window, hoping Gloria would arrive before we had to leave for our day of casting.

As she entered the diner, I stood up. "Gloria!" I sang, beaming that she had finally made it.

We hugged like crazy and I introduced her to John. We sat down and ordered some breakfast and coffee. "So, boys," she looked us both square in the eye and asked in a sincere and serious tone, "how is it going with the musical?"

We chewed the fat on all things Bolan and then Gloria naturally started to tell us stories.

She told us of the time that David Bowie ("Oh, Marc and David were best friends but so competitive and paranoid of one another.") invited Marc to sit in on the 'Spiders from Mars' tour dress rehearsal. Heartily laughing out loud, she regaled how Marc took great pleasure in taking David backstage to give him pages of notes after the run-through. She also told us a story of how around that time, Marc took his band to Germany to record a new album. Marc's star was already starting to fall.

He was terrified of looming failure and showing signs of insecurity, he used to hide under the desk in the studio. That studio was Music Land Studios owned by songwriter, producer and artist, Giorgio Moroder, who by chance (and at the time of writing this) I am working with as creative director on his live UK and European Hits tour.

According to Giorgio, it was Marc that discovered Music Land and once he got home to the UK and spread the word, Giorgio was inundated with British bands booking their album sessions in. Before he knew it, he was working with The Rolling Stones, Led Zeppelin, The Three Degrees, Sweet, Iron Maiden, Deep Purple, Thin Lizzy, Elton John and Queen, all of this almost stopping the flow of work with his famous partnership with Donna Summer. Well, almost.

As the producer to be seen working with throughout the '80s, Giorgio was also heavily involved with the Jackson family, producing Janet's first album, *Dream Street*, in 1984 and later in 1987 working with Jermaine on 'All Revved Up', a track that featured in the soundtrack to *Beverly Hills Cop 2*. He said to me he was particularly impressed with Jermaine's vocals and that he felt he had, over the years been very underrated as a singer.

Giorgio had also been working with Michael on a film project where Giorgio would create the soundtrack. Michael had just set up his film company with Sony-Columbia and yet to release a project with them. Michael was a musician, writer, producer and dancer, but his big passion was film.

He is quoted as saying, "What I really want to do more than anything is film. Film will last forever." He felt that film, even more than the music would leave a more everlasting stamp on the world. His work on *The Wiz* (1978) showed a natural acting ability and then undoubtedly displayed a flair for producing when it came to *Moonwalker* (1988) and *Ghosts* (1997), not forgetting Michael's collaboration with George Lucas, *Captain EO* (1986), which was brought back by Disneyland in each of their parks in 2009 as a tribute to Michael after his passing. Prior to this, of course, each of the music videos from the *Thriller* album showed a narrative that clearly came from deep within Michael's imagination and desire to pursue this artform.

The project with Giorgio was going to be the *7 Faces of Dr. Lao,* a remake of the 1964 Tony Randall film, directed by George Pal. Dr Lao is a wise and mysterious character, several centuries old, who arrives in a strange place to arrange bringing his travelling circus to town. Giorgio told me, "Michael was so intrigued by the concept of this wise, ancient being using his many faces to impart his wisdom. He couldn't wait to make this film. It was all going so well and then that first scandal hit. His house was raided and then production ground to a halt."

One thing for me that is almost more tragic than not seeing Michael live on stage again, is that he passed so soon, we will never see what more he may have created as a filmmaker.

Gloria Jones, to me, is best known as Marc Bolan's girlfriend and the mother of his child. The singer of 'Tainted Love' – the original Northern Soul version which was actually a B-side to a song called 'My Bad Boy's Coming Home' and the writer of 'I Haven't Stopped Dancing Yet' – a track I knew very well as a child, my disco roots coming through yet again.

In 2013, Gloria went on to star in *20 Feet from Stardom,* the Academy Award-winning documentary about the lives of backing singers, also starring Darlene Love, Martha Wash and among others, Sheryl Crow who started out her career as Michael's backing singer on the 'BAD' tour.

However, Gloria's career and credits go back a bit further and even more impressively.

As a singer and songwriter in the '60s, Gloria became good friends with Pam Sawyer, who asked her to write for Motown Records. Gloria and Pam fast became the second string of writers at Motown, but still wrote for artists such as Gladys Knight & the Pips, Commodores, The Supremes and The Jackson Five. The most memorable song that Jones wrote was Gladys Knight & the Pips' 'If I Were Your Woman', which was nominated for a Grammy in 1971. The song Pam and Gloria penned for The Jackson Five was '2, 4, 6, 8' which featured on the *ABC* album, produced by Hal Davis, someone who Gloria credits for giving Michael and his brothers a lot of inspiration in those early days.

As our breakfast came to an end, we hugged, and not wanting to let her go, I said to Gloria, "We are auditioning for *Thriller* today, why don't you come along?"

"Could I?" she replied, showing excitement and humility in equal measure. John and I looked at each other. To have her in the room would be a thrill, not only for the auditionees, but for us too.

I gave her the details of where we would be and told her when the 'little Michaels' would be arriving.

After a morning of back to back 'little Michaels', we only discovered Gloria had arrived when we took a break to get some air. We stumbled across her as she was sitting politely in the reception area of the audition space. This is Gloria all over – so beautifully unassuming.

It was a modest place, not like the endless studios on multiple floors of the New York audition rooms and she was sitting on a small sofa waiting for someone to come out.

We took her back into the hall, I introduced her to Benton Whitley and we picked up with the rest of the auditions. Throughout the remainder of the afternoon, Gloria pitched in with the feedback (with our encouragement) and gave the boys lots of amazing comments as they belted out the early Motown material. "Oh, that's just how Michael sang that," she would say, or, "Can you do that again, but this time take it nice and easy at the start and work your way up to those notes," when working on 'I'll Be There'.

At the end of the session we held back our few favourites and Gloria stood before them.

"You are all amazing," she said earnestly. "So much talent, you should all be so proud." She meant every word. She went on, "Y'know, when Pam and I recorded with Michael, he was so naughty." She giggled as she remembered. "Always playing tricks in the studio. He worked so hard but he was the naughtiest out of all of 'em. He had those big brown eyes that everybody else around the world saw as their own but he was just a little boy wanting to play outside. We would be teaching him lyrics but he would be watching his brothers and say, *'Why can't I play out there?'* He just couldn't wait to join them. So we were like, *'Okay, Michael, just give us three more lines, and than after that, you can go and run and do whatever you want to do.'*"

Later Gloria went on to tell us how much Katherine and Joseph (she referred to them as 'Mr and Mrs Jackson') embraced her and Pam, as they were both young mothers. "They liked the fact we both had young children and could nurture the boys in a maternal way as well as in the studio."

Gloria talked about how Michael was always very special and so wise for his tender age.

How he would always tease the adults but had such power and presence when working.

She began to tear up. "It's so sad he's gone." She looked at me wistfully as she thought of that little boy and all he had to sacrifice to give the world their star.

Gloria now devotes her life to raising funds for the Marc Bolan School of Film and Music in Sierra Leone, which she founded in 2011.

In Conversation with Kieran Alleyne
Former *X Factor star* as lead singer with 5 After Midnight,
also known as 5AM. The first to ever play both
child and adult MJ roles in the show.

GL: You came to our first ever open audition for Young MJs, which we held at the Lyric. Tell me about that experience, coming down to London from your hometown of Leicester. How did you hear about the audition?

KA: *My sister was living in London, doing a uni course and she saw the auditions in the paper. And she was like [to me], "They're looking for a young Michael Jackson, and you're small, you've got a 'fro and you sing... you kind of look a bit like Michael, why don't you give it a try?" And at this point, I wasn't even into music that much, I was a massive Michael fan and I listened to music but me doing music personally wasn't my goal. I was set on being a basketballer, which I'm glad I didn't pursue 'cause I never grew [laughs – Kieran is five foot eight]. So, I was like, "You know what, why not? I'll just go down to London and see what happens." The whole time I was talking myself out of it: "I can't do this, I shouldn't go down, I can't do this, I'm not a singer like Michael," and it was my mum that said, "Just go down and give it your best shot and whatever happens, happens."*

GL: Yeah, good old Mum.

KA: *Yeah she said, "You just keep playing basketball and you just continue on."*
So you know, I got down there and I could see that everyone else was kind of theatre school trained or had been doing this, that and as a whole, I thought, "I'm a real rookie at all this, compared to all of these people." I was like, "I'm probably not

gonna get it so I'm just gonna go in there and give my all and just come out. And then say yeah, I'm happy with how it's gone."

GL: Right. A great attitude already at such a young age [Kieran was eleven when he auditioned].

KA: Yeah, I remember when we did that very first round and I sang the first line of 'Ben', and you guys stopped me, I literally felt my whole heart sink and thought, "Oh. Okay. There you go, I get it, that was quick, back home!" And then you said, "Kieran, thank you, can you come back?" I was like, "OH. I didn't expect that, okay awesome!" [He laughs.]

GL: You sang one line!

KA: Yeah, that was it, it was like a line and a half?

GL: Wow!

KA: Yeah and you guys were like, "Yeah, that's enough." I think because I picked 'Ben'.

GL: Yeah, a hard song to sing and cuts right to the chase.

KA: I remember when it used to be in the show. So, that was a moment I thought, "Ah, I must have been alright then." Then it came to the dancing round. Now I wasn't a dancer, at the time, that was one thing I couldn't do – dance. At all. I could two-step but I was the guy that would stand at the back and try to copy other people. For some reason, I just seemed to be picking it up and when it came down to performing it, I was like, "Yeah, I'll just give it my all," and I discovered I wasn't actually following people anymore, I was just doing it in time and... [Kieran smiles as he remembers that surprised feeling] "Oh, so I managed to get through that round," and again, an amazing feeling. Looking back at the third round, we had to sing 'Stop (The Love You Save)' and that was one of my favourite Jackson Five songs and I was one of two kids that knew it so when you said, "Can anybody sing it?" I said, "Yes I can!" so stepped up and sang that.

The waiting process afterwards was the hardest, just [constantly] thinking, "Have I done alright? Don't think I'll get it" And I think it was three days went by and I was like, "Ah, okay, I didn't get it. It's fine." And then when we got the phone call [laughs loudly, remembering] and the reaction was, "Oh! I'm gonna be in the West End, I'm gonna be in the West End, alright... okay..."

GL: So, it was a bit of a fateful experience for you then, wasn't it? Because obviously you didn't think you were cut out to do what you're doing now, so it's kind of paved the way for you becoming a performer. Y'know, doing the whole *X Factor* thing and then coming back to 'Thriller'.

KA: It changed my whole life.

GL: Yeah.

KA: The moment I went on the stage for the very first show, I quit playing basketball the same day. I said to myself, "Music is my goal in life. I want to be able to perform and do this. Every day." And if I hadn't have come to that audition, I wouldn't have ever done that. I don't know where I'd be right now without that one audition.

GL: That's answered another question I had. You have such a passion and a loyalty to the show but this has kind of explained why that is. I think because your journey was so different to everybody else's.

KA: Yeah [nodding in agreement].

GL: And when you were chosen to perform on the opening night, our press night. I remember this being a big deal at the time [smiling].

KA: Yeah [nodding], yeah…

GL: How did that feel?

KA: All the Young MJs… [tails off as he remembers] er… it was amazing. I was so nervous, especially when I found out that Tito was watching. I was like, "Oh my God, there's actually a member of the Jackson family, there's a Jackson here. I need to rehearse, go through everything in my head, need to make sure I'm on point. Vocals are warmed up, legs are all ready to go and I just remember practising in a mirror all the way up until the show started. Then I was like, "Okay, let's go." I just remember thinking hopefully I can deliver for the crowd. It sounds crazy, but on a thirteen year old's shoulders, it felt like so much pressure. But when I first heard the cheer after that first number I thought, "Okay – let's go."

GL: Do you still feel that pressure now, now that you are performing [Michael] as an adult? Or is it even more of a responsibility?

KA: I feel like it's kind of worse. Y'know like, as Michael, you are the one person in the show that gets judged… immediately. [the audience] are like, "Oh no, you didn't kick like Michael, you didn't do it, you are bad at MJ." That's the hardest part, and that's why I sit here now and I study Michael so much to try and build new things in so I can give the most, the closest kind of replica to Michael as I can get. Yeah I definitely feel the pressure more now. As older MJ. Just to really go in and deliver, y'know, and show I was inspired enough to study him and do the best job that I can physically do.

GL: And that hasn't faded, the more you've got used to being on tour, it's the same level of pressure for every show?

KA: Yeah. I think, I enjoy it more now, because I've relaxed into it but I still feel the same pressure to deliver and if I do something wrong, I feel like I'm chasing redemption for the whole show.

GL: Right. Can you give me an example?

KA: If I trip on a moonwalk or if I overspin, I need to make it up in the next number, I need to go even harder.

GL: That's interesting. The pressure you put on yourself to perfect and honour Michael's performance is the same pressure he put on himself. Earlier in the book, I have written a whole section on the science behind Michael's movement, because for me, as a young male dancer growing up, Michael was the only thing I had to look at that wasn't old-fashioned or perceived as 'gay'. He was like a spaceman that had landed from another world and was doing something that I really connected with and so I studied... I loved all the music and the wow factor of the videos but it was the movement that fascinated me. Obviously there's a lot of freedom in your track in the show, because I think every 'Michael' that we've cast embraces a different... [thinks] it's not even a different era, it's just that the movement is so vast that you, as a dancer, have to pick up a different element and find a different way of presenting it, based on your body and physical ability. What has been your process when working on all the steps?

KA: For me, I watch the way his body shapes. His moves are quite awkward to do, they're not natural.

GL: Mm, yeah.

KA: I sit and watch how he positions his body and try and copy it as much as I can. I get so fascinated by the fact that it's, he could be doing something simple, like his arm is twisted but his body? It's like, "How is he doing that?" That's the stuff I've been trying to study the most because that's the stuff that made Michael 'Michael' for me. He did things that weren't ordinary and weren't natural so he literally created a different move from the same thing that anyone else might do. He just made it his own way. That was his genius...

GL: So, it's a lot of repetition in rehearsal, mimicking the movement and then trying to master it?

KA: Yeah, y'know I've had to film myself a lot of the time just to see how low the hat should come down so I can adjust that or, okay, the hip wasn't all the way out there, so work on that a little bit more, just continuously trying to improve on it.

GL: What's your favourite song to perform?

KA: Ahhh... [thinks] I'd say probably 'Billie Jean' just because it's so iconic for Michael, for me. That's the first song that comes to mind. Yeah, Michael Jackson, 'Billie Jean'. The white sparkly glove, the outfit, that's just what I picture and I get to go out there and do that. And he's done so many different versions of the routine so I can almost get to play around every time I do the show. I enjoy that. But I also enjoy 'Thriller' for the playful aspect of it. I love trying to get into his... the video, the character that he has, I enjoy that part.

GL: Yes, that's almost the most musical theatre moment in our show, that moment of storytelling before the dance break, you can have a lot of fun with it.

KA: *Yeah, especially with 'Ola Ray', he's playing around and kind of like silly and not serious so I enjoy that. I can do anything and—*

GL: —and it works.

KA: *Yeah, I switch it up every time I do the show and do something different 'cause it's kind of free—*

GL: —and keeps that feeling of spontaneity Michael has in the video.

KA: *Exactly.*

GL: And what's your favourite MJ song, and why? Just in general.

KA: *I'd probably say 'Show You the Way to Go'.*

GL: Is it? Yes, you've said that before.

KA: *I love that song! I was so sad when it got cut from the show. That for me, the Jacksons section, when they all came out in their silver suits, that was my favourite section in the whole show. I was like, "One day..."*
   [GL/KA both laugh] I don't know, I love how he almost doesn't sound like he's trying on the song. He sounds more like he's feeling what he's singing rather than trying to sing it. That's what I love about it, he's not pushing his vocals too much, he's not forcing it, it's just a fun song.

GL: Do you know what's interesting there... The reason why we cut the song is because the boys generally found it really hard to sing, like a lot of them. When you get to the end, those riffs at the end, there was only really Britt that could nail it, eight shows a week. Everybody else struggled and we got to the point where we were like, "*This isn't sounding good, we need to do something about it.*" It's weird isn't it? Michael makes it sound so effortless.

KA: But in reality, like all his work, it's actually really hard!

Part Three

BRAZIL – Another Part of Me

Chapter Twelve

Skywriter

I love to travel. I hate London.

As I write this, I am in a queue at Costa in Waterloo station and reminded how much I hate (central) London and why I love travelling the world and exploring different places around the UK.

The guy behind me barks his order at the expressionless girl behind the till who barks it back to the barista.

The girl in front turns around and her backpack nearly knocks me over.

She glares at me like it is my fault.

I eventually emerge from commuter coffee hell to be met with a stampede of a hundred more commuters all charging in the opposite direction as myself, none of them paying attention to my luggage, my coffee or me.

I make my escape to an area that looks clear where I can breathe, check my train time and platform, and perhaps get a sip of that coffee.

I try to block out the pretentious noise of the city boys and middle-class working women who all seem to insist on shouting loudly into their phones, at their colleagues or just into mid-air, either with just a blatant disregard for the people around them or arrogantly wanting to be heard.

This is London and despite the gift I have been given to create and work here, deep down, I do not fit in.

Lucky then, I have been fortunate enough to travel with my amazing so-called 'job'.

As a director/choreographer, I have lived and worked all over the US, worked in Australia, Scandinavia, Mexico, Germany, France, Switzerland, Italy and Malaysia, among other great countries. I've loved them all but nowhere has touched me like Brazil.

I have so much to say about this place because it really changed my life.

The London life and working in such a high-pressure, frenetic industry can wear on your spiritual being and self-esteem and it is so very easy to lose yourself.

Brazil, its beauty and its people brought me back to me and I will be forever grateful.

The Brazilians truly have an unconditional love affair with Michael, different and seemingly deeper than any other fanbase. (I do not say that lightly as MJ's fans globally are without a doubt the most loyal and loving in the world.) He is like a God to them, a big brother and someone both men and women aspire to be. So it was a rite of passage for our show to go there, and I was more than happy to be the emissary.

The *Thriller Live! Brazil Tour* was our first ever co-production. This meant that the producers in Brazil could have a say and assist financially into making certain things happen. The two producers (that we met initially) were both assertive and charming as well as really hands on.

Our first meeting was late summer 2011 in London at The Ivy restaurant. It amused me that dinner had been scheduled for 6.30 yet we had to be in our seats for the show by 7.15.

Just time for a starter then?!

The (then) Brazilian producers, Paulo and Junior, were both very enthusiastic about the show and the brief meeting was a chatty one.

Paulo, who was short and a little older than Junior, seemed to have the most experience. Junior, who was tall, handsome and the quieter of the two, felt like the new boy. The show that evening was a good one and they both left with great energy and promises of a wonderful partnership together.

From then on, regular meetings were held about how the show would work with Junior returning to London alone this time to discuss the way forward with the show.

It was January 2012 by the time we got to Brazil but we were still a few steps away from having a production.

Each trip was a long one, the longest being the production period where John Maher, Jo Dyce and myself were there for almost three months. The others varied but we got a chance to take in the culture, see the sights on the surface and be cast under the charming spell of our hosts.

When we arrived in Brazil for auditions, Paulo seemed to have disappeared under the radar and Junior was leading the direction on all things regarding the Brazilian side of the production.

We were introduced to his co-partners at a company called Future Group, an incredibly plush yet corporate environment specialising in advertising.

Their energy and style was very American with a top layer of the smooth and hypnotic Brazilian charm we were quickly learning about. There was a real smell of success about the place, and Junior and his partners delighted in filling us in about all their other contracts and clients.

There really was a buzz about us being there and though the building we would meet in felt like money with floors and floors of thriving businesses, there was poverty around every corner.

'A developing third world country', Junior would describe Brazil as, and he was right. In the beginning, we were shielded from the real sights, having a driver provided to take us door to door anywhere we pleased, making it almost impossible to walk around. This was clearly the idea, although that did change much later on.

We were taken to Credicard Hall (now Citibank Hall), in the Santo Amaro district, where the show would be held in São Paulo. São Paulo was the last venue, though, as we were scheduled to open in Rio de Janeiro. Credicard Hall was a gigantic concert hall, holding 7,000 people.

As a result of seeing the vast hall and learning of its capacity, discussions turned to the production.

I turned to John, "We should be looking at doing the arena version of the show."

"There is an arena version?" Junior's ears pricked up. I looked at Adrian and John; I would probably get into trouble for this. "Yes, we have a much bigger production that toured arenas in the UK two years ago. Extra pyro, fire effects, 'toaster' stage lifts to shoot people out onto the stage. We used these for the dancers but also for the guitarists and the zombies in 'Thriller.'"

"We need this version," Junior said emphatically. "Okay…" was my response, loving Junior's no-limits attitude towards this meeting. We went to work planning what eventually became a hybrid of the regular touring show and the arena version.

There were many meetings that followed, all driven by this Brazilian enthusiasm and infectious energy. They wanted to take care of their own costumes, making everything from scratch based on our designs. They really were shooting for the stars and aiming for a first-class production they could be proud of and call their own. Paulo popped up every now and again at the odd lunch meeting, but Junior was most certainly now in the driving seat.

We discussed stage effects; he wanted bigger and better. We talked about wigs and despite explaining that hardly anyone in the show had time to change wigs, they still went on the list... in every section of the show.

The VIP treatment was intoxicating, as was working in such wonderful weather. Every person we met was as vibrant as that weather. We were taken to Credicard Hall as VIPs to see Seu Jorge – a famous Brazilian artist considered 'the renewer of Samba'. Seu Jorge, raised in Rio, became homeless at nineteen and started making music while he was living in the streets becoming known in the favela communities. On August 12th 2012, Seu Jorge performed in the Handover section of the 2012 Summer Olympics closing ceremony in London. This was an eight-minute segment that introduced Rio to the world. Jorge performed alongside Rio artists B Negão and Marisa Monte, and the whole thing ended with a surprise appearance by Pelé.

The concert in São Paulo was like nothing I had ever seen. The music was almost tribal and felt improvised yet really together and the sound almost acoustic yet booming. The atmosphere in the hall was so raw and people were not only up and dancing, it felt like we were outdoors – everybody was so free with their reactions. We were wined and dined by all the 'Future' partners – they were so proud of their culture and their artists, and Seu Jorge was their star of the moment. And us – we were to be their star of the very near future.

Chapter Thirteen

2000 Watts

We arrived back in São Paulo on February 4th 2012 to kick off the casting, this time starting with the dancers. This was going to be exciting. Searching for the vocalists and the children was tough, as it always is, but even more so as Brazil is such a gigantic place, but without as much natural opportunity for performers. Like in London, we discovered later in the year, the really good ones were already taken.

When we discussed how we were going to cast this production, it was a no-brainer for me to want to cast all the dancers in Brazil. This was, of course, a plus for the producers and would add to their sense of pride and patriotism in the production as well as being able to sell it. I had never travelled to Brazil but I had seen lots of footage of Brazilian B Boys and breakdancers, as well as all the real samba dancers, so the thought of having a cast full of this talent was a dream for me and for the show.

I have always been drawn to the Latin culture but Brazil was different. Yes, it is Latin but there are many other influences in this culture, particularly African, that gives the country its own unique identity.

My assistant Jo, Adrian Grant and I arrived in São Paulo, fired up for this first leg of our audition tour. Musical supervisor John Maher followed on and was arriving later as we were to start with a search for singers during this visit as well as John having to audition and work with the suggested Brazilian musicians for the band.

We had two days scheduled to get through hundreds of dancers. The studio provided was a place called Espaço 10 x 21, a perfectly sized, well-lit space with several rooms. It transpired that, because I was so impressed with it, this became our rehearsal home too.

Work started on the morning of the 6th with a room full of very nervous yet hungry dancers.

A film crew, who were to be filming our whole journey from auditions through to our opening night fruition in Rio arrived with all the equipment guaranteed to add more than a sprinkle of extra tense energy in the room.

We started with split calls: first the girls, followed by the boys.

At that time 'Jam' was still our show opener and I used that as the group routine to see overall level and to cut down from. The boys were way stronger than the girls, this was clear from the off but it was too early to be concerned. The energy in the room from both groups was not only electric, but awestruck and almost desperate. This was the biggest thing to come to Brazil and everyone we had met, espcecially these dancers, were acting like it was Michael himself coming to town.

We made an initial cut and then brought mixed groups of boys and girls back together to see the routine one more time, giving them some more choreography to learn and also see their freestyle.

This was when we got to see their individual characters and the real contenders started to show: Gustavo, the youngest male in the room at only eighteen, showing great flair in his tricks, a raw but well accomplished B Boy, doing good work in the routine; Lunna Gomes, a slightly reserved but really interesting redheaded girl; Fernanda Fiuza, a strong vogue dancer who was the hottest girl on the combination.

And not forgetting Eric and Ana, a couple who made the whole proceedings feel a little more like *A Chorus Line* than *This Is It* – unlike Thiago Vianna who could have just walked off an MJ tour, they did not let their relationship stop them from being two of the most memorable powerhouse performances of the day. Renan Tenca, a wiry six-foot-four guy with a million-dollar smile who was just the most incredible dancer. He had the choreography down within beats of learning it. These were the stand-outs and already making it through, but there were others that, as the process unfolded, came to the fore and helped us put our jigsaw together with ease.

The love in the room that day was something that you barely see in a dance audition at home. It does happen, but it is rare and everybody knows that it's been a special day when it happens.

These guys were able to separate their competitiveness, and shout and holler at every flip, flare and 'coin drop', as well as appreciate the different personalities coming from all these dancers who had travelled from all over Brazil. They were creative and fierce, stopping at nothing to show us their determination and to prove how talented Brazilian dancers were.

There was a naivety to some of the movement and a wide variety of technical dancers versus the street talent. These guys got to take masterclasses with some of the best choreographers from LA but only when they visited their city. Otherwise they took to YouTube to learn the latest dance styles and moves, but it was not all natural.

This was exciting for me as it meant we could mould the show onto these dancers and they would learn new stuff when working on my choreography, as well as perfecting the Michael moves their bodies so craved to dance.

Before sitting down to deliberate and go through our notes in detail so we could announce our list of who to return later that week, I was approached by a production assistant who had brought Gustavo, the young dancer over.

"Hi," she said politely, "this is Gustavo."

Deep in casting thoughts.
L to R: Gary Lloyd, Jo Dyce.

The West End opening night party at Cafe de Paris.
L to R: Tito Jackson, Adrian Grant, LaToya Jackson, Gary Lloyd.

Rehearsal for 'Gone Too Soon'.
June 30th 2009.

Reveal of our memorial plaque.
L to R: Diversity's Perri Kiely and Mitchell Zhangazha.

Meeting the Jackson brothers.
L to R: Jackie Jackson, Tito Jackson, Gary Lloyd, Marlon Jackson.

Madame Tussauds reveals new waxworks of Michael.
L to R: Britt Quentin, Eshan Gopal.

Jermaine Jackson
visits the show in Paris.
L to R: Jermaine Johnson
(Dancer), Nathan James
(Man 3), James Anderson
(Young MJ), Jermaine Jackson,
MJ Mytton-Sanneh (Young MJ).

MJ meets the Phantom.
Ben Forster and David Jordan.

With Gloria Jones.
Los Angeles 2012.

The Brazil company.

Visit to the Liga Solidaria.
L to R: Rodrigo, Gary Lloyd, John Maher, names unknown.

Performing 'Heal the World' with
some of the São Paulo children
suffering with cancer.
L to R: Leilah Moreno, Ryene
Chermont, Diego Jimenez, Zoe Birkett,
Renan Tenca, Thiago Vianna,
Eric Santos, Renato Max.

Our Young MJs visit the MJ Shrine
Mosaic, Santa Marta, Rio de Janeiro.
L to R: Diego Jimenez, Isacque Lopes,
Pedro Henrique,
Felipe Adetokunbo.

Brazil final curtain call.
L to R: Gustavo Della Serra, Fabiana
Figueiredo, Eddy Lima, Lunna Gomes,
Samella Nathielle, Ana Zgur, Eric Santos.

Tito Jackson mentoring
the students at the Young
MJ Academy

Rehearsing with Peter Andre for our 4,000th performance.
L to R: Wayne Anthony Cole, David Julien, Peter Andre,
Haydon Eshun, Vivienne Ekwulugo, Gary Lloyd.

Ten-year Anniversary Show.
Front line L to R: David Julien, John Moabi, Layton Williams,
Mitchell Zhangazha, Ben Forster, Eshan Gopal, Vivienne Ekwulugo.

Some of the Thriller Live! alumni backstage at the ten-year anniversary reunion.

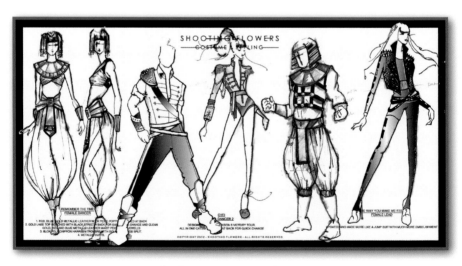

A selection of costume designs.

I smiled and nodded. "Yes, I remember, is everything okay?"

"Er, yes," she answered in her broken English. "We need to tell Gustavo whether he is called back to the final audition on Wednesday. He is leaving now to take part in his national service test."

"Okay," I said hesitantly, "what does that mean?"

I discovered that Gustavo would leave the audition and go straight to the National Service barracks where he would take a physical and mental test. If accepted, he would stay at the barracks and serve for a two-year period. If not, he would be allowed home and he may make it back for the final audition for the show. Or not.

I was horrified and when I looked over at Gustavo, he was in tears.

I put my arm around him. "Hey, it's okay," I said, trying to comfort him. "You have a recall, my friend, you were wonderful today." And then, spelling it out: "Very. Good. Dancer," putting both my thumbs in the air. "I really hope to see you back here Wednesday and will pray for that to happen."

He smiled, thanking me and bowing more like someone from Japan, he left the room.

I looked at Jo. My God – he might walk out of this room and not be seen by his family for two years!

We also learned that day that Lunna Gomes, who was also down on the recall list, had sold her only television to afford the bus fare to come down from Rio, a six-hour journey.

Who knows what other tragic stories there were to enable these kids to get to this audition that was clearly so important to them?

After a gruelling few days, the final dance recall involved the partner work from 'Rock with You' and used to demonstrate a contrasting flavour, something more sensual and controlled than the precision and athleticism required in the slamming 'Jam' routine.

The remaining girls stepped up on this one and showed us a real sophisticated shift in what they could offer, clearly finding this style easier and showing a relief there was something more feminine than what we had done in the previous audition. Some of them were not the best dancers but they did evoke a style that was both compelling and irresistable. A natural performance that sought attention without appearing desperate or exaggerated. It was thrilling and curious to behold.

More faces came out of the crowd on this day – we were in a smaller room and they all began to fight even harder for our fourteen slots. Samella, Fabiana, Edson and Felix brought style on this day and Tiago Dias had more dance technique than anyone we had ever seen. The picture of our Brazilian dance team was becoming clear and despite us all, and the walls dripping with sweat, we were having a ball.

We brought them into the room in smaller and smaller groups, making them dance in pairs, solo and seeing both routines and their freestyle again, and again, and again.

In the height of the final hours, and as time was running out on the studio hire, I requested a break, as the heat and intensity was affecting my judgement and I desperately needed some air.

It was almost as if I sensed it because when I left the studio and turned right to head down to the entrance, a car pulled up. Someone ran round to open the door and in the car, rushing to get out, was Gustavo!

He ran in, panicked that he missed us all but when he saw me and Jo standing there, he jumped on us like he had known us for years. The relief was mutual and emotional for all three of us, as Jo and I had spent the last three days wondering what would happen to this poor boy in this rather alien circumstance.

We were more than thankful for this positive result and so happy to see this familiar-looking stranger who, hell or high water I would find a slot for in the show.

I gave Gustavo the option to warm up (which he declined – adrenaline would get him through this one!) and we got to teaching him the routine he had missed that morning.

We filmed his audition, as we had everyone else, and he joined the final group for one last look at each dance combination.

When it finally came to the end of the day and all our discussions together with Adrian and Junior had reached a resolution, we were asked, "Can we announce to them now?"

This seldom happens at home as often there are other conversations to be had, or the casting professionals would take over and make those calls and give out the offers.

In our world, it was unusual not to have Paul, our producer, sitting in on these final auditions and as he wasn't here, it didn't feel right to announce.

Junior, however, was as persuasive as ever and pushed for this to happen, making an impulsive and unprecedented executive decision.

The film crew were still present and filming every second. Junior set up that we would get the final contenders in and I would announce in Portuguese that they had made the show.

We brought them into the room, the strength, bravado and self-assurance gone from each their faces. They looked on nervously as I stared at the piece of paper handed to me by Junior.

"*Vocês são es Escolidos*," I spoke clearly in my virgin attempt at Portuguese. It translates as '*You are the chosen*'. There was a pause. And then – deafening screams. Then tears. Friends found each other and the couple, Eric and Ana, hugged each other tightly. Edson and a couple of others fell to the floor and many looked up to heaven to thank their God. Then the dancers all jumped on each other and began to chant, "Hey, hey, hey," over and over as they jumped around in a circle for what seemed like an eternity. It was a good feeling and we had an astonshingly good team of dancers.

Fuelled by this injection of energy, they all wanted to perform the dances again. Of course, I obliged by hitting 'play'.

Junior took the opportunity after this to film them all chanting, "Put your hands up," to assist with the advertising campaign. The show was to be sponsored partly by Gillette and this was their current slogan. The dancers took great joy in jumping and shouting this as another celebratory mantra. This was the beginning of many days like this and I could not wait to start working with them all.

Following this trip, the footage was very quickly cut together, creating a very exciting and well-executed series of videos showing our last few days searching for dancers. Along with the footage of the kids auditions, these were posted on YouTube and shown on TV appearing almost immediately on shows like *Bom Dia Brasil* (Good Morning Brazil) and quoting my tweets about what an experience we'd had and how I found the dancers 'phenomenal' and the people 'beautiful'.

This was all true and we got to experience them and their work ethic sooner than we thought.

The Brazil dancers were:

Girls: Fabiana Figueiredo, Fernanda Fiuza, Lunna Gomes, Samella Nathielle, Glaucia Fernanda de Oliveira, Ryene Oliveira, Ana Zgur.

Boys: Gustavo Della Serra, Tiago Dias, Edson Lima, Felix Pimenta, Eric Santos, Renan Tenca, Thiago Vianna.

Chapter Fourteen

Childhood

We returned to São Paulo in October 2012 and we were now searching for our young talent, the nine to thirteen year old boys that require that triple threat, all-round talent to perform as Michael in his early years.

The camera crew were more present than ever, every second being filmed for the *Thriller Live! Brazil* documentary. We saw lots of boys (and even a few girls) over a number of days all auditioning to be little Michael.

We found four incredible young performers each with their own story and I write about all four of them later in this section of the book.

I was asked by Junior on one of the Young MJ audition days if I would consider seeing boys from a local orphanage. *Orphanage?* I thought to myself. *Do those places even exist anymore?* Then I remembered where we were and realised there were probably hundreds of them all over Brazil. Daniela, a girlfiend of his, volunteered at a high level at the Liga Solidaria, a very famous institution in São Paulo that took care of not only children, but adults in desperate need from the risk of homelessness and domestic violence. With a father who spent his early years in an orphanage in the UK and soon to be a father myself, the answer was not one I had to mull over for long.

I, of course, said yes and on the Thursday of that week, we braced ourselves to meet these young men.

Only two of them were brave enough to come into the audition room and sing for us. One of them, a larger boy, had an abundance of confidence and bounded into the room ready to impress. The other, a boy much smaller and slighter, was very shy and only managed to get a few lines out.

Neither were disciplined nor technically trained enough for us to consider them for a recall but I was happy we had spent the time to give them the time of their lives.

We congratulated them on their talent and bravery and said that Michael would be so impressed with them for coming in. They beamed with pride and thanked us several times.

Although these were the only two that made it to the audition room, in the holding room upstairs was a room full of ten year olds who had come down on the bus but didn't want to audition.

I asked if I could go up and meet them.

As I walked into the empty room filled only with crazy ten-year-old energy, the boys stopped what they were doing to stare at me. Halfway through being introduced, they all started to chant, "Michael Jackson, Michael Jackson." They approached me and each of them grabbed my arms, still chanting, "Michael Jackson, Michael Jackson." I felt like Jesus and through my laughter at how ridiculous this was, I tried to tell them, "No, I am not Michael Jackson, I am Gary Lloyd, the director of the *Thriller* show!" all falling on deaf ears.

Daniela, came over and said to me, "They do not know who Michael Jackson is or what he looks like. These boys have only heard of him but have never seen anything of him, that's why they think it is you." Gradually, they each got bored and carried on with their games of tag and play fighting. Apart from one boy, Rodrigo.

He kept hold of my hand, still whispering to himself as he looked up at me, "Michael Jackson."

I didn't have the heart to keep trying to tell him that wasn't me as he seemed to find some comfort in my presence. I kept chatting to him, telling him about the show and what we were doing here in Brazil. I made conversation about what we had done here and how beautiful I thought his country was. The other boys kept coming back to intermittently listen to what I was saying and then ran off to rejoin their game, but Rodrigo stayed transfixed on me, hanging onto every word despite not speaking a word of English.

We eventually had to say goodbye as the boys went to get back on their bus. They were not allowed to come into the audition room and see the keyboards, mirrors, cameras and crew. They did not understand what we were doing or why they were there. They didn't even know who or what Michael Jackson was! They had literally walked into the building, walked straight up a narrow staircase and sat in an empty room for two hours but somehow this had made their day. These boys who had come from a world of trauma and neglect and possessed nothing had been given the opportunity to come to the city for one day and meet people from another country. This was a lifelong gift for them and their appreciation was clear, each of them filled with so much joy.

This resonated at the time and has stayed with me since.

How could these boys, abandoned and left alone, radiate so much happiness and gratitude? It was a pure example of how the simple things in life can really matter and how the more we pursue, the more complicated life can be. These boys were living in the moment, grateful for anyone who gave them attention and love in that moment. It was becoming apparent these profound moments would become a regular feature during our stay in Brazil.

On Wednesday 31st October, right before we were due to fly back home, Daniela arranged for myself and John to visit the Liga Solidaria.

The Liga de Solidaria (Solidarity League) is a non-profit organisation, run completely by volunteers, founded on March 10th,

1923, driven by the belief that 'a fairer society with more opportunity is possible if we promote the encounter of love, solidarity and work'.

In this ever-revealing country, while working on *Thriller Live!*, this could not be a more insightful venture into Michael Jackson's humanitarian side and felt so poignant for us both to be there.

More than 10,000 children, young people, adults and elderly people in situations of high social vulnerability attend the Liga Solidaria during the year, in eight education and citizenship programs that work to rescue dignity and foster their autonomy.

There are also many children and women that live there as a result of loss of family, homelessness and domestic abuse.

The programs that are run at the Liga Solidaria include early childhood, children and adolescents, professional qualifications, working on bringing families back together, adult education, looking after the elderly, education through nutrition (cooking), sports, and music. The fundraising events that were (and still are) constantly held to provide these vital services include bazaars, samba parties, feijoada, workshops and talks on domestic violence, and Junior music festivals.

We were already moved and impressed by all of this before we even got out of the car.

I remember this day. Baking hot even though it was the end of summer during São Paulo's rainy season, all the vibrant colours of Brazil's nature being lit by the sun.

On arriving in the astonshingly beautiful grounds of the 'Liga', we were greeted by Maria Louisa, clearly the matriarch of this vast institution. She had been well prepared by Daniela as to who we were and we were welcomed with an authoritive yet maternal warmth. Daniela smiled during this introduction and there was clearly a great love and respect between the two of them.

We made our introductions and she took us into the main building. We looked around the offices and Maria Louisa explained about all the work they do. There were rooms with people working at desks and computers but we also peeked into rooms where young women were sitting, either making things and working at stations or being counselled. These were the young women suffering from domestic abuse and had nowhere safe to go.

Some of them went out to work but came back to the 'Liga' to sleep. Others were training as part of one of the many education programs the 'Liga' had to offer. Some had children there with them and were living there together while waiting to be rehoused.

The Liga Soladaria is a really beautiful old building. We breezed through it and ended up out in the grounds. The place felt desolate but Maria Louisa quickly explained that most of the children were having their lunch. We walked this vast green open space and saw where the children took their sports classes, football and tennis, walking around to a row of huts and where we finally saw signs of life. Some of the children were sitting in the shade, some playing lazily in the heat and others tapping on basic percussion instruments.

Like the boys who came to audition, these children all seemed so content, calm and full of life. *I'm sure this isn't the case all of the time*, I thought to myself, but still it was very noticeable to me.

The love and care coming from Maria Louisa, her staff and the volunteers like Daniela was apparent and clearly doing wonders for these desperate children.

Just when we thought we had seen the majority of these incredible grounds, Maria Louisa started to explain that we were about to visit the children's living quarters – the dorms.

As we turned a corner, looking up to see even more buildings, we followed our hosts to what felt like a simple little village built into this hill.

Maria Louisa chose one house to take us into and we were met by two sweet young girls, one around twelve years old and the other who must have been about fourteen. Like the other children we had seen, they were just hanging out, not really doing much at all. Again, there was no TV and the whole place felt silent.

As we were saying hello to the girls, a young boy came from one of the other rooms.

It was Rodrigo! I couldn't believe my eyes and I could see he felt the same element of surprise.

"Michael Jackson," he yelled and ran towards me. He gave me the biggest hug around my waist and then grabbed my hand, darting off and pulling me with him.

We shot down a corridor and I heard a voice behind me. "He wants to show you his room," yelled Daniela, laughing.

We walked into a decent-sized room, clean and immaculately tidy, that had eight single beds in it with a stack of what looked like square, wooden school-like lockers covering the wall at the end of the room.

Rodrigo let go of my hand and ran into the room. He stopped at the bed nearest the wall and pointed at it. "That's his bed," Daniela said. He then opened one of the lockers on the wall and pulled out a few items: a book, a handful of clothes and a pair of sandals. He came towards me with them all in his hands. "These are his things," said Maria Louisa. I looked up at her and then back at Rodrigo. "What – all of his belongings?" I asked in disbelief. Maria Louisa simply smiled. "Yes, all of them," she said.

My heart broke. This boy hadn't stopped smiling since we arrived, yet had nothing in the world. Well, nothing apart from the love and security this place was giving him. The Liga Solidaria had saved his life – was his life, in fact – and he and all the other children were clearly grateful.

We left the room with all three children in tow and moved back into the lounge. We chatted a bit further, then went outside. We carried on asking the children what they liked to do, telling them a little more about what we were doing in Brazil (via Daniela and Maria Louisa as our interpreters, of course!) with Rodrigo grinning the whole time. We got a photo together with the children and then went on our way. My heart sank when we had to say goodbye and I couldn't stop thinking about Rodrigo. I asked Maria Louisa how many of these children were successfully adopted and she told us, as we made our way back down the hill, that it was mainly international adoptions that were successful, particularly with couples from Italy, but they would always go for babies and the younger children, and that Rodrigo was unlikely to ever be adopted. I thought momentarily about pursuing adopting him, but the reality of this very genuine notion was way too complex. My work involved too much travel and time, he was a ten-year-old from a polar culture to ours and we spoke different languages. Not impossible, but too difficult to consider. My heart felt it needed to do something but for once, my head took over. I had a show to put on, a way too busy life and a partner at home to consider!

By this point in the day, the sun's heat was beating down more than it had done this whole trip and we enjoyed the walk back down to the main building. Maria Louisa showed us round a new annexe that was being used as music rooms for therapy and teaching. There were desks and some basic musical equipment, mainly percussion. These rooms had large windows so were filled with light.

I suggested to John that he and I come back to do some music and dance workshops with the kids and left that open to discuss with Maria Louisa at a later date.

As we came to the end of our visit, we had to pass through the main building again.

We were met and gently 'shushed' by one of the office volunteers who ushered us into one of the ground floor rooms that had previously been empty.

To my horror, every inch of the floor was filled with over a hundred babies, all fast asleep! I couldn't believe my eyes, firstly at the sea of tiny children, who at first I thought were all orphans, then by the fact they were ALL silent and sleeping. It turned out the majority of them were children of single female parents who had to go out to work and either lived at the 'Liga' or left them there and picked them up at the end of their working day.

"How on earth do you get them all to sleep like that at the same time?" I asked in amazement of the smiling volunteer. "With lots of practise," was the answer, delivered with a wry smile. In the background were more babies being fed or rocked to sleep by more caring staff.

We eventually left the company of all these incredible human beings – superheroes, really – in this country where a lot of people are so in need of compassion and love. Thankfully, the Brazilian people possess these qualities in abundance and they are not afraid to selflessly distribute them.

I felt sad for these children yet my heart was so full – overcome at how this community has come together to do right by one another and by humankind. This genuine, almost holy love radiated by each of the people working and living here was something I felt I would never encounter in this way again.

***

Following the string of auditions for vocalists and children, John and I had to extend our stay in São Paulo. A TV appearance had been arranged to introduce our four Young MJs to Brazil and officially launch the show. The boys would perform a medley of Jackson Five hits and each sing solo, while being interviewed by one of the top TV presenters in Brazil, Rodrigo Faro, on his show *O Melhor Do Brasil* which simply translates as *'The Best of Brazil'*.

To give the boys a little on-stage support and to make the performance feel bigger, representing the broader look of the show, we added four of the chosen dancers to the mix.

Thiago, Eric, Ana and Fabiana were brought in and we spent days putting this medley together, sourcing costumes and wigs. John was as usual, having to edit music and vocal together, this time requiring a master version for TV broadcast. I had decided to make a start on the new choreography I intended to put in the show for this very special production.

It was great fun and gave us all a sneak preview of how this team were going to work together.

It soon became very apparent that we would need interpreters for the duration of our stay in Brazil, as the language was the main problem.

The work ethic, however, was not and each of these performers gave me everything, making the whole process a dream.

Here is an email sent from John Maher to Paul, Derek and Adrian after the promo:

4th December 2012

Hi all,

Just wanted to give you a brief account of the launch yesterday.

As you know, we were doing a medley of 'I'll Be There', 'ABC' and 'I Want You Back', with the vocal workload divided between the four boys. For the purposes of this event, the lines usually sung by adults in these songs were covered by the boys, and they sang all four parts of the breakdown in 'IWYB' (the 'bom bom bom' bit).

I had recorded a backing track for 'IBT' just for this event, and it came out sounding rather good (if I say so myself!). We decided to pre-record the children's vocals and have them lip sync to themselves, as is pretty standard for TV, and a lot safer both in terms of vocal security and controlling the mix. The promoters here organised a recording studio and we put the vocal tracks down on Saturday.

Gary did his usual outstanding job of staging the number with all the boys plus four of the Brazilian dancers. We are fortunate that he has had so much TV experience, as it is very different to putting things on a stage.

We were at the studio all day yesterday. I had thought we were just presenting the number with the boys, but in fact several hours of the show were given over entirely to Thriller Live Brazil. As you know, they have been showing weekly segments about the audition and casting process, so their audience is already familiar with the show.

Unbeknownst to Gary and me, we were to be interviewed as part of the programme, and in fact we spent the entire 'Thriller' segment on set. The host interviewed both of us to start the ball rolling. They then presented each of the boys in turn, showing footage of their auditions and backstage interviews before presenting them to the live audience. After a chat with each boy, the host then interviewed each boy's parents, who were in the studio audience. He then carried on interviewing each child in turn, asking them about their favourite songs, their experience, when they started singing, etc. He asked each of them to sing something a cappella, to rapturous applause from the studio audience.

Once all four boys had been presented, he interviewed one of the dancers. After all of this buildup, they finally had the boys do the medley, and the place went completely mental! The boys did well, with two in particular really performing to the cameras and looking like absolute stars. There were a few little errors, but nothing very serious. There were six cameras, so the coverage should be very good. The impact of the presentation will depend largely on how well the director of the Record TV show edits the various camera shots. If they edit smartly I think the number will be absolutely terrific. If their editing isn't great the impact will be reduced but I suspect it will still be pretty strong.

Still we weren't done. The host then pointed out that with four boys performing together they looked like the original J5, but were one short. So, after a 'magic of television' break, he appeared made up in J5 clobber and joined the boys in dancing through 'ABC' (for which we used the German TV track featuring Mitchell's voice; indeed, this was played repeatedly throughout the broadcast to vibe things up).

Still not quite done, the host's 'comedic' midget sidekick then appeared in a glittering pink suit and afro wig, attempting to join in. He is a much-loved part of their act, and again the place went nuts.

Finally we were finished. During the following break some of the boys were called over by members of the studio audience for photos, etc. This escalated rapidly, and very soon all four boys were in the middle of the crowd, with groups of girls literally screaming for them. Shades of Beatlemania. Even Gary and I got roped into the action.

All in all I think it's safe to say that the event was very successful, and with a peak audience of something like 5/6 million, I imagine the publicity value for the show will be enormous.

What John omitted from his email is that he and I were not informed we were to be on camera, so we both rocked up in shorts and tees, expecting to work and be on set but not in vision. We ended up having to borrow shirts from Junior (who oddly happened to have spares in a suit bag…) and sitting on set, fully in shot. This was quite stressful for both of us, as we had worked so intensely with the boys and the dancers, we wanted to be off camera to gee them up and experience their performance privately without being seen. This was most certainly the shape of things to come in Brazil and surprises like this came a-plenty.

Chapter Fifteen

Mama's Pearl –
The Young MJs

Isacque's Story

Isacque Lopes, at the point of writing this, is the star of Brazilian film *Tudo Por Um Pop Star*.

Not surprising this boy is succeeding in the industry as he was a star from the get-go.

From Rio de Janeiro, Isacque bounced into the audition room with a head full of long afro hair, a winning smile and incredible dance moves.

One of the first boys we saw, I felt we had struck gold and, to top it all, he could sing. Singing was not something he had focused on to this point, but he had some talent and man, could he perform!

The remarkable thing was Isacque came from the favelas of Rio.

The passion of the parents in Brasil is undeniably something I have never witnessed. Isacque's mother Rosa would have done anything to get him to the audition and she did. After hearing about the audition from a friend, Isacque told his mother but as we were only auditioning in São Paulo, she could not afford to get her son on a flight.

Isacque had been a fan of Michael's from age three and started to perform as Michael from the age of five! This was in his blood – he had to be there.

We were floored to discover that the community this family lived in had put everything they had together to pay for a bus fare for Isacque and his mother to make it to São Paulo for this audition period. Everything they had. Even then, they could only raise enough for a bus fare taking over six hours to get to São Paulo rather than the hour flight most people would take for granted.

It meant everything to me to make it into this show. Having the chance and opportunity that I had was incredible. The sensation of being next to Adrian Grant, who had met MJ in person, was the greatest feeling and to be seen as MJ, and feeling like I was him on stage, to represent him in Brazil for Brazilians who love MJ so much, was amazing. I can say now, that everything I have today in my career, started after Thriller Live!

I enjoyed the auditions very much but it made me anxious. I had done auditions for other things, soap operas and such, but this did not compare. Rehearsals were a bit exhausting but I knew it had to be this way to the make the show perfect like Michael did in his shows. Thankfully my mother speaks fluent English so I could communicate with the UK team.

I was primarily a dancer and joined a ballet company because of Michael's influence, then started singing because of him. My whole career is influenced by Michael Jackson.

Now I am starring as an American musician in a movie about a boy band, Tudo Por Um Pop Star – *translates as 'Everything for a pop star'.*

It's the story of three teenagers, the biggest teen stars in Brasil – Maisa Silva, Klara Castanha and Mel Maia – all trying to get closer to their idols, exactly like MJ's life. I had a chance to feel that in the movie. I have also recorded some music and music videos. I have worked a lot after Thriller Live!

The show opened many doors for me and my dream is to perform in London someday.

What I learned from Thriller *is discipline. If you have discipline you can get anything in life.*

I discovered much later that Rosa, Isacque's mother, had to quit her job to get him on that bus.

There was such love and belief in these people, all for this young man and the hopes and possibilities this one audition could potentially bring him.

These extraordinary stories were collecting in my soul like a jigsaw, creating a love for this place like I had never known.

Felipe's Story

Felipe Adetokunbo became a finalist on *The Voice Kids* Brazil.

An unapologetically feminine boy, he was an enigma from his very first audition and throughout the audition process.

This child had the most beautiful gift and could sing this music the closest to Michael out of any other MJ we'd ever had (to that point). But he was a complex teenager and had no experience at all.

He really struggled with the movement side of things and felt very self-conscious around these other boys, who were either already steeped in MJ's world or desperate and so willing to learn.

I could see he saw me as a threat and it was because of this I realised I had to learn Portuguese to help us both communicate.

Rehearsals were really time-consuming and problematic, and Felipe would behave like a much younger child, running out of the room and wanting to eat or drink to try and escape learning choreography.

I know now, being a parent, that this was him crying out for attention and help. The help that he was getting and, thankfully, was eventually able to accept.

Felipe became a wonderful asset to the show and once we opened and he got his audience, he really flourished and started to relax.

It was wonderful to see him become more socially comfortable (once he understood that everyone accepted him) and properly hang out with the other boys.

I already did singing lessons at a gym in my city. Music has always been very present in my life. In family, at parties, in the religious environment. I'm a young black Brazilian. Afro-Brazilian music is very strong and was present in my family. I knew some of [Michael's] songs from my aunt's computer. She had been a fan since the Jackson Five. She had vinyl records and she went to watch the group when she was young and they came to Brazil. She said they were wondeful and she then followed Michael's career. She had a lot of songs on the computer that they did not play on the radio anymore. I went to see her. A lot. Then I started to listen to myself because I liked a lot of songs and the way he sang. I did not know anything about the Thriller *musical. I had no idea this was happening.*

I had had a highlight of the year-end presentation at the music school and the singing teacher told my mother about the application for the audition for Thriller Live! *She suggested that my mother enrol me because she thought it would be a good experience for me. My mother was a bit reluctant because she did not believe it would be an honest assessment and since we are poor and without an agent, she thought it would not be good for me to participate. But the teacher insisted, the principal of the school and my aunt were also insistent so my mother accepted and made my application by email. I was called the next day which surprised my mother. So we then had to face the financial problem of how to get to another city to participate in the audition. But my family collected money for basic accommodation and boarding, so my mother and I could attend, the whole time my mother always telling me not to get too excited, because we did not have the resources and were neither known nor had an agent.*

The audition process was a challenge. We did not have any money for many days. And there were a lot of strange people, a lot of kids, a lot of people with agents, a lot of people who were already doing shows and some had already appeared on TV. I was unknown. But I also had little idea of the importance and weight of an international audition. Nor of the importance of Michael Jackson. I wanted to sing those beautiful songs that my voice allowed me. But it was very dramatic every day and waiting to hear whether you would be asked to stay. On the one hand it was good because I was not eliminated. It was very tense. My mother very distressed, afraid I would be devastated by the elimination. She saw people she knew and thought there would be some favour to those who were already famous. That was the hard part of the audition. Singing and dancing was a pleasure. I went there to do this. And they did not treat me badly.

Rehearsals were important but at times they were very tiring. We were four children and each with their own potential. Some picked things up faster, and others took longer. This is normal but then everyone was forced to pass everything. Then it was dull for me. And I lost the patience to keep repeating what I had already learned. Besides that, I was out of my city, away from home, away from everything I liked, and there were days when I was sad, and there didn't seem to be much understanding about it. I gave them a product, but I was a child, a childish person, with feelings, sensitivity. But I'm not hurt. I think it was good for me to mature a little.

Entering the show was very good. At first I had no idea what it meant. For me, the good thing was that I went and could sing more and dance. I understood that they liked me, and I felt appreciated. That was great. I was very young. My family never put foolish vanities in my head and I was always treated the same way at home. Everyone was happy but without starlets.

They started talking to me about the future and if this was what I wanted to do. That it would be hard to move on and that I would have to make some sacrifices. My family was very nice and they supported me a lot, but not letting me get off my feet. Then I realised it was kind of magical to be on the show. I had never been to a major production. I used to sing in many places but this was so big and new to me. But I was never uncomfortable. I felt being on the stage was my home. It's a place where I always feel very good. Joining Thriller *was an important milestone for me. To realize my own ability. That I could do what I liked that made other people feel good too. I came to understand that I liked people in general, not just my family.*

The talent and charisma of MJ were things that impressed me a lot. I discovered that he was a dedicated guy, committed to doing the best ever without measuring efforts or sacrifices for the art he did. That was one aspect of him that has encouraged me to this day. I keep trying to always improve myself. And I want to do my work, my art, perfectly. It's not easy. But I have seen many passages of his writing and I understand that without dedication a good job can be lost.

After Thriller, *there was a time of sadness and feeling of depression. After taking part of such a mega show, big things don't follow soon. Here in Brazil, the arts do not have too much support. Even a talented artist has to make many sacrifices to evolve. Not having the money to invest in training is a problem. Taking classes in various dances, singing lessons, vocal preparation, speech therapist, everything is very expensive. But with the support and effort of my family, I kept fighting. I did another musical and then another play, so I kept singing in some places. Until the kids version of the TV talent show,* The Voice. *I was just at the age limit, but I signed up anyway, and I was called to audition. I passed the audition and went to what they call blind audition here, where I sang 'At Last' and all the jurors turned the chairs over to me. It was a career-defining moment, as I gained visibility in the media. I stayed part of* The Voice *until the semi-final. It was a wonderful experience. I met a lot of interesting people and I got in touch with very special professionals and I learned a lot. Gaining the respect of production professionals is always very good. I recorded a clip with new music made for me. It's still not enough, but I'll keep going. Then came an audition for a musical about the life and work of a great Brazilian composer and black singer, and I also passed. We are on the road for the second semester. We are on vacation due to summer and Carnival, but we resume the season in São Paulo in March. And we already have a new script approved in the announcement to be made in the second semester. I'm still studying, and dreaming of the Grammy. I'll get there eventually! I'll fight for it.*

Having participated in Thriller Live!, *[that] gave me a certainty that I can go forward. I know I'm going to have to fight, but I will grab the opportunities and make the best of me. But it was a great emotional and professional experience. I am grateful to the Sacred for having lived those moments. Thank you that you saw my potential and believed that I would be able to perform what they needed. Thanks to all who interacted with me, because they gave me a lot of strength and many positive energies. I am very happy to have been a Little MJ on the musical* Thriller Live! *Brazil Tour. Thanks, Gary, for everything and for being part of my story. It will always be a reference for me. I never forget it, it's always in my heart. Thank you so much!*

Pedro's Story

Pedro Henrique was the cutest little thing, full of personality and this adorable mock-American accent. Pedro was already an established TV child actor and was performing as 'Benji' in the Brazilian production of *Priscilla, Queen of the Desert – the Musical.*

Full of the confidence you would expect from a child with this experience, at the time of the audition, Pedro was probably the least 'MJ' out of the four boys we chose for the role, but this boy knew how to work!

On a rare evening off, myself, my assistant Jo and John, our MD, were invited to see Pedro in *Priscilla.*

We all knew the show well, having lots of friends who had appeared in the West End and Australian productions, so we were rather amused by this even bolder, brighter Brazilian version.

Pedro was really fantastic in the show, and shone as 'Benji', and although he was the most musical theatre-sounding of all the boys, we knew we would end up hiring him for the show.

At the time I had an agent and he told me about the audition. I was already a big fan of Michael Jackson so I got super excited and told him I wanted to do the audition.

In June 2009, when the news was given about his death, I started to get to know Michael better. I still remember that I was standing in front of the TV and did not want to miss anything because I was delighted to see his clips, listen to the songs and see him dancing. After that my mom bought me some of his DVDs and I kept watching and imitating.

Thriller's auditions were not easy, because it is a really big responsibility to be representing the King of Pop. It was also challenging, because all the stages of the auditions the audition were being filmed in the form of a reality show on TV.

I had so much fun, though, during the auditions. It was a little challenging at the beginning because of the number of people and also because of the jury being from another country, but every time I went in the room I took a deep breath and gave my best, having so much fun singing, and dancing, imagining that I was Michael Jackson himself.

When we opened the letter and and saw the words 'YOU ARE IN THRILLER LIVE! BRAZIL', my parents and I could not believe it, we cried a lot. It was a very happy, exciting and unforgettable moment, I could not believe that I had been chosen by an international jury to play my idol. It was a dream coming true.

Then rehearsals were very entertaining and intense as well, after all, it was a big responsibility for the whole cast to be able to perform like Michael and convey to the audience the same emotion that he did. It's not easy to perform like someone who is world-renowned and respected, so we had to work really hard, but it was a lot of fun too.

The directors were always very attentive to us, and they explained everything in a very slow and understandable way. I thought it would be more difficult, but since I was already doing English classes at the time, it was easier to understand what they said, and we also had a person who translated to us when we did not understand, which helped a lot.

Michael has always had a unique style that has always inspired me to want to learn to dance and sing! And as a person he also inspired me a lot, for example loving and caring for others and taking care of our planet, so much so that the music 'Man in the Mirror' is my favourite, because of its style and its message.

While I was still performing on Thriller, I was invited to participate in a TV series, and I also started dubbing movies and series for Disney, Nickelodeon, Cartoon Network, etc. After Thriller I continued to work on TV. I did two TV series, a sitcom, participated in several reality shows, and in the meantime

I kept on dubbing. I always dreamed of pursuing my career internationally and studying abroad at an arts school to improve myself, so in 2017 I applied to the Orange County School of the Arts, which is an Arts High School in California. After several stages of auditioning I got in, and now I'm in California, living my dream.

My experience at Thriller Live! was awsome. First of all for having the opportunity to play my idol, and secondly for having worked with an incredible team, with whom I learned a lot. This musical was one of the reasons that motivated me to study abroad, to seek fluency in English and better technical knowledge in the art industry. I learned a lot from this show, and it certainly influenced my life and career in a very big way, and mainly my achievements. I am currently living in California and studying in one of the best high schools in the state. I am very grateful for the opportunity to have participated in Thriller, because I would not be where I am today without this experience that opened many doors in my life.

Diego's Story

Diego Jimenez was probably the most 'MJ'. He was the least experienced performer but had spent years studying and performing Michael's choreography. This was not an unusual thing in Brazil and Diego was one of the new generation of hardcore fans. He was the one we had to work most with musically but each boy brought something special to the group and Diego's contribution was his innate knowledge of all things MJ.

I probably knew Michael Jackson before I was even born. My mother was a great influence, she always listened to Michael Jackson, so inevitably I ended up listening. But I wanted to go further.

When I was eight years old I started copying the movements and ways that Michael did and tried to sing along (I didn't understand English very well at the time, but I tried to sing even without understanding anything). It was from there that my mother saw that I really enjoyed doing this and started rehearsing and helping me with the dances, including, it was she who taught me the moonwalk.

I decided to show it to my friends and teachers at school, since then, I always attended talent shows and everything that involved dancing to the public. At first I was a little shy, but after I got used to it, I didn't stop.

The first time I heard about Thriller Live! was through a friend. She knew that I liked Michael Jackson and showed me a Facebook post that explained about the auditions, but they were only for dancers of legal age. But after a while, they opened the auditions for children, so I wasted no time and asked my mother to sign up.

Thriller Live! was my first audition, I had never played anything like it before and I had no idea what was coming. The registrations were online and I had to send some videos singing and dancing and that I had to spare, so the next day I was called to attend the auditions.

Arriving there, I did everything right, the nervousness was overwhelming, but I knew how to control it. The songs I already knew, singing I already knew, so I concentrated and gave my best. A curious moment for me is that one of the stages went really well on my birthday (24/10/2012), so moving to the final stage was like a gift.

With each passing day of audition, fewer people were still in the game, and that bothered me a little, because I could be one of those who were coming home. But I didn't, I gave my best and thanks to that I entered. It was a lot of pressure, but in the end everything worked out.

Getting that call was the realisation of a dream, because I enjoyed every second I was in this cast, if I had to do it all over again I *would, no matter the country. I met wonderful people, learned to live with people from different places and cultures, learned how a musical works and it made me grow a lot as a person and as a professional. But the best thing was to see my mother happy, because at all the shows, even when I was not singing or dancing, she was, and that already made me happy too.*

The rehearsals were very cool, well-explained and very dynamic, although it was something very serious, there were always jokes between us.

I loved working with an English team. I saw a great chance to train my English and to know better these people who were coming from so far to make a great show. I always liked to discover new things, it's important to take risks, and by the way, it worked out very well. I always had a fear of saying something wrong, or that people did not understand me, but that is part of the learning process.

I enjoyed working with everyone, because it was always a good and fun environment, everyone helped each other and made an effort to make a great presentation.

I have been influenced by Michael Jackson in the most positive way, because I always wanted to know more about his story, about his songs, the messages and the love he shared through art was impressive so I learned a lot from him. This intensified even more when he died, and to make things even worse, he died on my mother's birthday (25/06/2009).

After that, I could really see how influential Michael was, not just to me, but to the world.

After Thriller, for a while I did dance and singing lessons that I took as a hobby.

I also participated in a Coca-Cola commercial and since then I've been learning a bit about graphic design and photography.

169

And I also have parallel projects in the area of music production, I intend to start releasing some Brazilian rap/hip-hop and trap songs.

After Thriller Live! Brazil *ended, I gained great knowledge and experience about behavior, how to carry myself as a person and what it all made me feel. It was one of the best moments of my life, if I had to do it all over again, I sure would. Writing this makes me miss everything and everyone. But it was worth it, because it made me talk better, act better and live better.*

The boys were around the rehearsal room all the time. There was no discussion about schooling or tutors or keeping certain hours, they were just there. And it was wonderful, having that excitable energy around the place, these boys constantly rehearsing their show, practicing their spins and hearing, "Hee-hee!" from down the corridor. They stood in front of electric fans and screamed like Michael in front of a wind machine and eventually started learning the adults work too! It was just strange as in the UK (especially in the West End), we are beholden by so many laws as to how long we can work with the children. They come in, do their thing with strict chaperoning and go home. Of course there are very good reasons for this, but the boys in Brazil, by the time they hit the stage, were so immersed in what we were doing, they were some of the best boys we have ever seen.

Chapter Sixteen

This Time Around

13th January 2013.

I arrived back in Brazil, slumped on my hotel room bed and turned on my phone to discover two abusive messages sent to me on Facebook following the auditions for the latest touring production back home. These auditions happened right before I left for my flight to São Paulo heading back there to start rehearsals for the Brazilian production. Times once again were excessively eventful.

One of the messages was from an online troll who seemed to be using a fake photo. I guessed this because I didn't recognise the face of the user and after working with so many people in this job, I never forget a face! This wasn't just any troll but apparently someone who had just auditioned for the show. He was bitter he wasn't kept for a callback and decided I wasn't qualified to do my job. He also took the opportunity to call me lots of extremely offensive and infantile names, which I eventually found amusing, but not right after day of auditioning followed by a ten-hour flight! I deleted the message and blocked the user from my account and, eventually, from my mind.

Sadly, the second message was from someone who had been in the show previously, and at the same audition. He had shown interest in performing in the show again (five years after being in it before) so we arranged the audition but he didn't make the final cut. He was understandably disappointed but he ranted in his message that he was the best dancer in the room and better than most of the boys I had kept, questioning my judgement and suggesting I had wasted his time inviting him to the audition. This is a huge problem with social media where the user is able to explode and rant at the universe or an individual in that heated moment. The downside being that comment and sentiment is out there forever and can often be very damaging. The problem with this boy, like a lot of dancers these days, he forgot to look around and see how competitive our industry has really become.

After four and a half years working on this show, several cast changes later and many an amendment to the Act One setlist, we had it down to a fine art. We had found our groove and due to sheer repetition and often necessity when it came to budget and time restraints, we could teach this show and have a full company match fit and show ready in just three and a half weeks.

This production would be different for a number of reasons.

First there was the language. Little did I realise how few of these dancers spoke any English at all.

It was fine teaching an audition as the room full of trained bodies were taught to imitate, but trying to direct choreography and inspire through mine and Michael's work was a different challenge altogether when the majority spoke only Portuguese.

There was also the enthusiasm that drove the production, the producers and their barrage of ideas and requests for promo, filming and other little quirks that would distract from the work. All coming from a good place but quite often rather destructive to the process.

Junior was also incredibly hospitable and arranged lunches and meetings and wanted the cast and team to eat together every day and for me to attend all the meetings – for good reason – and to do all he could to sell the show. Theatre in Brazil was still a new art form and they have to work much harder to sell tickets and get those that can afford it, to sit up and take notice.

Then, and more seriously, there was the UK cast. During our time rehearsing in São Paulo, it turned out the guys from the UK had issues with visas and flights and after a huge hold-up, ended up arriving weeks later than intended and needed to work fully with the new company.

We spent weeks working with only the Brazilians, which was wonderful and really helped us shape the show and refine their work. The downside was that it meant we only had just over a week to integrate the Brits, both professionally and culturally.

During the rehearsal period, we rarely got an evening to relax. Junior felt it necessary to take us out to see sights, learn something about São Paulo or just experience the amazing restaurants, SP had to offer. Evenings were made up of long production meetings at the Future Group offices, followed by dinner and drinks at the latest star chef restaurant or the sky bar. Lunchtimes tended to be a more rustic approach where we ate Brazilian street food, one time being taken to the smallest of cafes to eat feijoada, a staple Brazilian meal paralleled to our Sunday roast, only eaten on a Friday.

Originally a leftover dish, feijoada is a black bean stew made with salted pork, sausages, loin, tongue and pork trimmings, all slow-cooked in a clay pot. It is served with rice, vegetables and farofa (a toasted cassava), a flour-like substance, apparently essentially to sprinkling over the stew. It was clearly a much-loved, traditional dining experience and to show our enjoyment, we drank a little cachaça (a sugarcane based liquer), despite having another half day of rehearsals to get through!

Regardless of our heavy schedule, we were getting the full cultural experience thanks to Junior.

One evening, we jumped in the car after being told we were going to a Samba School and to see their rehearsal for the famous Rio Carnival. Hearing the words 'school' and 'rehearsal', we only imagined a little studio or hall with maybe fifty kids?

After driving for miles into what felt like the ghetto, we turned a corner to see a long street with people setting up stalls and carrying equipment.

It was still daylight when we walked into an enormous warehouse. The space was huge and there were lots of people milling around, some lightly playing out rhythms on a multitude of surfaces.

There was a buzz in the air but this was definitely not yet a party.

It didn't register that a samba school is made up of hundreds of people of varying generations wh come together almost all year round as part of a very important Brazilian tradition.

As the evening warmed up and the giant space quickly filled, we started to see people with drinks in their hands. We all grabbed a beer and were taken upstairs to a balcony area which was apparently the VIP. At that point, the floor below was swarming with bodies, all of which were starting to get into groups. The excitable sound was almost deafening at this point.

Junior, continuing and winning in his mission to educate us about all things Brazil, explained to us that the Samba Schools' Parade was the highlight of the Rio Carnival. They all took it very seriously and the competition was always fierce and winning the title, extremely prestigious.

The preparation for the Samba Parades start months in advance. Every school is integrated from thousands of paraders, all from the community from which the school is stated.

First, each school chooses a different theme to the parade. It can be a celebration, a historical event or famous characters of Brazilian history, a special event, a place or anything that moves the audience's immagination. The school has to develop and remain within that theme during its parade.

Then, there is a contest to elect that year's samba song. This contest lasts a few months at each of the Samba Schools, while the Carnival designer creates the costumes and floats. In December, the rehearsals begin. During the month of December, the 'sambas de enredo' (that year's samba songs from every school) are recorded and CDs sold in the stores.

We were brought large bottles of whisky and bourbon and told to 'get ready'.

There was a sudden moment of silence and then... BAM! Everything came together and kicked off into this extraordinary demonstration. The chaotic world below us was suddenly organised and in sync, and all moving in an anti-clockwise direction!

There were different groups, drummers, dancers, breakers and bands all moving as one with some very well put together acts.

Some were in costume but as this was a rehearsal, others wore ordinary clothes. but we could still see the spectacle that this would become.

All highly choreographed, each section showed skill and a real love for what they were doing. And the sounds were incredible! The deafening beats of the samba drummers filled the air and drove this impeccably drilled crowd forward and around. We watched each section come round below us, again and again, getting better each time.

The different sections, or 'wings' as they are better known, were very specific. There was the drums section – the pounding heart of the school, composed by 250–350 drum players. This section provides energy and life along the parade. It's a community wing, so the costumes are paid for by the school. The drums director is the one who chooses the components of the group through various tests, rehearsals and discipline. The rehearsals begin months before the Carnival. Sometimes, the drummers' costumes are so big, it makes it difficult to play their instruments.

The Drummers' Queen – she is always a gorgeous, voluptuous woman, in charge of introducing the battery to the spectators. She is responsible for motivating and inspiring the battalion of musicians who follow her throughout the parade. There was no doubt who the Drummers' Queen was. She wore the most extravagant costume and was cheered by the spectators, everywhere she appeared.

The Samba Dancers are always the main attraction of the school. They are chosen through a competition that takes place every year, and it is certainly a great honour to be among the best.

Among the incredible capoeira, breakdancing and acrobatics and the colossal flags that swooped and filled the air, making as much noise as the drums, there was one group that caught our eye. A wonderful group of elderly ladies that were dancing a traditional folk dance, the 'Jongo' – a direct associate of the African culture in Brazil that heavily influenced the 'Samba Carioca'. They were all in traditional costume, flowing creamy white dresses with headdresses, and they ebbed and flowed in their own lyrical tempo, against the charge and madness of the pulsating samba. It was striking how content they looked, not tiring at all as the carnival carousel kept spinning.

The crowd swirled, the whisky flowed and we danced. This evening had come as a surprise but this atmosphere was exactly what I imagined Brazil to be and the reason I didn't hesitate to agreeing to cast the *Thriller Live!* dancers here.

The carnival rehearsal came to an end almost as abruptly as it started and we moved out of the warehouse. On the street were stalls with food and merchandise, almost like a mini festival. We danced our way through these stalls until Junior stopped us. "Okay," he said. "I have another surprise for you."

We followed him to yet another warehouse and walked through double doors to find hundreds of gigantic carnival floats all lined up one after the other. They looked just like brand new and really extravagant fairground rides. Jo and I immediately jumped into what we thought was a supersized Waltzer car, caught up in the heady feeling of this secretive surprise and giggling from all the whisky.

"No!" Junior shouted over from where he was showing Adrian another float. "No-one has seen these yet, they are hugely confidential and have their own grand reveal in two days' time. The owner has only let me bring you because of you who are."

We sheepishly staggered out of the float and into line with the others.

Following this enlightening and very cultural insight, Junior arranged for us, the *Thriller* company, to take part in one of the local 'Bloc Parties' (Blocos), a more intimate daytime gathering but no less atmospheric than the samba school rehearsal. He had special 'Thriller Bloc Party' tee shirts made with a mosaic-style image of Michael's face and the *Thriller Live!* logo. The dancers did a little impromptu performance, joining in on the already free-flowing atmosphere. We ate local pastel (pronounced *past-ow*), a light and crispy pasty filled with anything you wanted, both sweet and savoury. Everything in Brazil was so organically spontaneous and born out of a deep, soulful love of their own traditions.

A week later, there was a very similar feeling at the football ground when we were taken to see Corinthians play Palmeiras at the Arena Corinthians, São Paulo. In the stands, there was barely a feeling of competitiveness or aggression, only that of support and passion for the game. There was singing throughout and drummers playing the samba all the way through the match. I couldn't believe this was the same game I had avoided my whole life! I loved every minute, watching the huge flags being pulled from the top of the stands to the bottom and back again by the fans. But it was the players that really stood out for me. Passion, naturally soundtracked by all we were surrounded by, these athletes danced and slid up and down the pitch, showing nothing but love for the game and determination to win that ball.

177

They stealthily worked together, not letting up until the final whistle blew. To find out they were paid a small percentage of what we know footballers to earn felt tragic but yet again, filled me with inspiration.

Back in rehearsals, we were having a ball. One of the most exciting things about starting with a new cast of any show is seeing what each of them will bring once out of the intense and nervy audition phase and in a more assured working environment. I got to capitalise on each of the dancers' talents: Felix with his knowledge and flair for vogueing, Tiago 'Black' Dias's insane technique, Fernanda Fiuza's unique and very '80s gender fluidity, the other girls' attitudes, and the boys' B Boy personalities and tricks, some of which I have never seen the likes of. All wonderful stuff to draw upon when building the show. Each morning, most of the cast would gather an hour before warm-up to workout. Knowing how far some of these kids had to travel, this was most impressive.

Warm-ups were held by Jessica Powell Antonini, an Australian commercial dancer who had worked with me in the UK (she was part of the 2009 German TV promotion mentioned earlier in the book). Jessica now lived in Brazil after marrying a Brazilian hotelier, Rapha and was looking for work. We needed someone to look after the show as a resident director who could communicate with both the Brazilians and the British. There was no better solution and Jess did an outstanding job. So good, in fact, she went on to look after the Australian tour a year later.

With Jess's sunshine start-ups and the Brazilians' boundless energy, by the time we got started, the whole building was buzzing and made for a very healthy and happy rehearsal atmosphere.

I truly loved working with this team. As I was putting new material into the show, their attitude towards me and the work was infectious and I was able to reciprocate that love and respect with ease. It helped me create some great work and the show was already benefitting from such a positive start. As the weeks went on, there became a definite separation between the boys and girls' ability to retain and deliver. The boys were like machines, getting everything that was thrown at them and charging back at me, hungry for more. The girls became reserved and forgetful, almost blending into the background. In an already male-dominated show, they needed to work harder.

I called a meeting early one morning and this is where I began to understand the extent of the language barrier between us.

We all connected amazingly as a group of dancers but once we moved away from the stage of teaching the steps and into the motivation and direction of the show, language on a deeper level was imperative.

Demonstrating choreography to 'Blame It on the Boogie' and shouting five, six, seven, eight (or *cinco, seis, sete, oito...*) was fine but trying to direct and explain the political climate of the world when working on 'They Don't Really Care About Us' or discussing Michael's involvement with Brazil when shooting that video, it was near imposible to get that message across.

It turned out that more of the boys were able to understand a little English. It also transpired that the interpreter was delivering the translation of my direction both incorrectly and in shorthand and all of them, including the interpreter, were afraid to tell me.

The girls were feeling confused and alienated.

After this confession, the translators were swapped and I was given the lovely and talented Fernanda Rizzo who had been working with the young boys. Fernanda spoke perfect English and was also a psychologist. We became great friends.

It was then I decided to learn Portuguese. Our drive from the hotel was over two hours each way, a perfect opportunity to tune into some lessons. I got hold of a great course from Jessica and dove right into it. It helped immensely and worked almost immediately. I had already picked up phrases to get us through the simpler moments of the day, '*mais um*' meaning 'one more time', '*vamos fazer isso*' – 'let's do this' and the more obscure '*pau no gato*' meaning 'stick the cat' or 'go for it', taught to me by the ever-mischievous Eddy and Gustavo.

As the weeks progressed, so did my Portuguese and as we acclimatised to one another, the girls came up to the confident level of the boys.

When the Brits arrived, they were bowled over by the vibe and jumped right into the spirit of things.

We were all so relieved to see them and delighted to start piecing together this exciting part of *Thriller Live!* history.

As actors and dancers do, they fuelled each other with their energy, the Brazilians with their irresistable enthusiasm and by this point, wowing with their version of the show both with the choreography, and Leilah Moreno and Renato Max on the vocals. The Brits then coming back, captivating with their knowledge and slick delivery of the work they had performed for months and in some cases, years. It was a match made in heaven.

Leilah Moreno was a well-known actress and pop star in Brazil, very popular with the young kids. She was descibed to us as the Brazilian Britney Spears and was also a huge Michael Jackson fan, having written her own book about him. She has won two Latin Grammy Awards and a Latin Emmy for her recording and TV work.

Renato Max was a blessing of a singer we came across in the local auditions. A humble father, this man has the voice of a megastar and really added to our production with his awesome vocal talent.

Chapter Seventeen

Stranger in Moscow

There was never a dull day during this rehearsal period. Most days were a productive heaven with Junior and his team taking such a close interest in everything and providing help, creativity and promotional opportunities regularly. Some days were like being in a Brazilian 'novella' or soap opera and there are too many dramas for me to write about in this book.

Towards the end of our honeymoon rehearsal period, I decided we had worked hard enough.

The show was set and there was no more work to be done after hours. We had filled our extra-curricular schedule with photo shoots, film shoots, interviews and late-night translation meetings and now this was all complete. It was time for us to go out and enjoy ourselves. Thanks to Jess, we discovered there was a club called 'The Week' and I decided we should go after rehearsal one Saturday. Of course, this didn't even start until midnight so we had time to nap, change and have a light dinner before even setting off for the club. The club was part outdoors with a swimming pool and of course a great vibe. The music was uplifting with varying rooms playing deep house, trance and RnB. With a full day off the next day, we partied all night, completely satisfying our need to let our hair down, Jo and I both arriving back at the hotel after sunrise.

I woke to the blare of my hotel room telephone deafening me. I picked up the receiver and it was Junior. "Okay, Gary, I will pick you up in half an hour and we will go see the set."

It wasn't a question.

I rolled out of bed, still a little hazy, and rather cruelly called Jo.

"We are going to see the set," I announced. Her sleepy response was as expected…

Sunglasses on, we climbed into the back of Junior's jeep. Ricco, his co-producer, was in the front.

We actually felt okay but as the journey progressed, so did the hangover. We were in that jeep for about an hour and a half as civilisation started to disappear. The car jumped up and down over the rocky mountainous roads. "Where are we?" I asked, trying not to vomit. "Heading into the Amazon forest," replied Junior nonchalantly.

We arrived at the top of a very narrow hill after seeing nothing but breathtaking greenery for over half an hour when there before us was our show's set – bridge, steps, podiums, all right in the middle of the forest! I couldn't believe my eyes!

Next to it was a small hut with one man sitting outside who Junior went over to speak to.

I couldn't bring myself to look at Jo who was sulking behind her shades.

I jumped out to meet the solitary man who was introduced as the 'one who built it'.

This guy single-handedly built our set in his 'Amazonian back garden' and it was made mostly of wood.

I jumped up onto it to check its strength and stability. I remember this feeling bizarre, was it the hangover, or just the surreal fact I was about to give notes on the build of our set to a solitary smallholder in the middle of the Amazon forest?!

The health and safety of our entire cast rested upon this meeting so I jumped around a bit, performing 'Dirty Diana' and 'Don't Stop' to Jo, who was still resentfully sunk in the back seat of the Jeep hiding behind her sunglasses, my solitary audience member, unappreciative of all my efforts to entertain her!

I dreaded the journey back to São Paulo, rapidly eating into the remainder of our only day off. The only thing keeping me going was the the thought we were heading into our closing week of rehearsal. I sat in the back of that Jeep, focusing on the work left to do, aching for that last day in the rehearsal studio.

When that final day came to a close, all of us lively with exhaustion and overjoyed with our ultimate studio run-through, I spotted our wig designer, entering the building. She was guiding two men carrying boxes, about fifty of them, into the ground-floor studio. I felt Jo's eyes in the back of my neck as we descended the stairs, and turned to see her nervously smiling. "They've made a ton of wigs, haven't they?" I said to her. Grimacing, she nodded, fearing the worst. I grabbed a 'cafe con leche' and headed into the studio, greeting the designer in a breezy manner and looking at the wall of boxes all stacked up against the mirror. I was told to bear with her as she started to unpack. "But I told you, we do not have time to change wigs during the show, I was very clear it is MJ only, the Jackson Five, Leilah and Zoe." I was ignored and almost brushed aside as a mountain of plastic was pulled out of the first box.

Despite my instruction based on knowledge of my show rather than personal choice, they had gone ahead and created wigs for each scene for every ensemble member. There were ponytails for 'Hotel', bright coloured party mohawks for 'Boogie', individual short style wigs for 'Smooth', afros, up-dos and on and on it went. I felt sick.

The saving grace for all this madness was when the final box was opened containing the zombie masks. They were a triumph! Full head and hair, movie-quality prosthestics with so much detail, expertise and care put in, all moulded to each dancer's face and each one of them an individual character. I was astonished at how good they were and I could see the pride beaming from every face in the room.

I didn't have the heart to talk about how most of the other wigs would hit the dust once we got it into the tech, so I congratulated the team, hugged it out and helped re-pack the boxes.

When I came out of that meeting, slightly frazzled and the high from the day having lost its sheen, it amused me to see that most of the cast, including the boys, were still in the building, all hanging out on the foyer sofas that had become our lounge. All of them either lazing or goofing around together. I flopped down onto a spare edge of sofa, ready to think about getting back to the hotel and relaxing for the evening, when an urgent sound caught my ear. The sound of serious voices all talking over one another in passionate Portuguese got closer and I knew instantly something was wrong. A group of the dancers, mostly male, were ushering one of the girls into the sofa area. It was Samella. And she was crying hysterically. As part of the small crowd that naturally gathered around her, I asked around to see what had happened, was she injured, had she fallen or taken ill?

I asked Thiago Vianna who quietly but intensely informed me Samella had been dragged off the street and held up by two youths with a gun. She was distressed and in shock. We sat her down, got her water and I asked most of the group to give her some space.

The poor girl was terrified. The fact was, we had finished late on this day and after a certain time, the streets in Brazil can be very dangerous. The walk to the subway was over twenty minutes and despite finishing rehearsals in the studio during daylight, the timing of the cast actually leaving the building was not good.

Samella was shaken but not hurt. The youths had threatened her and taken her phone, but she was okay and starting to calm down. A couple of the boys looked at me and shrugged, and Eddy put his hand on my shoulder. This was Brazil, those that have nothing are happy, they work out so they can eat well and party. They carry toothbrushes around and clean their teeth at every opportune moment. The sun brings more joy than you can imagine but sundown can present much danger if one was not careful. Life here was full of extremes.

Samella was taken by the remaining boys to make that same walk back to the subway. This incident had certainly made me think. We were protected by our little drive into work and hanging out in and around the studio in our *Thriller* bubble. I watched the group leave, heading into another tropical rainstorm, the energy now subdued and all the boys on high alert, surrounding Samella like a protective troop.

I worried for Samella but knew they would all be okay and bounce back. Strange to say, but this was normal for them and they had built in strategies to deal with it.

Soon we would all be off to our opening location and I couldn't wait to see how all our work translated onto the stage. The vibe from the whole company was invincible and I had no doubt we would all remain one happy family.

Chapter Eighteen

They Don't Really Care About Us

That all changed when we got to Rio… Something about our arrival into this very different environment caused a shift in the dynamic. The atmosphere completely changed and despite the stunning backdrop and a lot of the cast being back home, things took a turn for the worst.

The first thing I remember was the heat. São Paulo was hot yet fresh due to the constant tropical showers. In Rio it was incredibly humid, day and night. So much so, there were mosquitoes everywhere, especially in the venue. In yet another concert hall, there were no windows in the auditorium and until open to the public, there was no air con, not in the front of house anyway. When loading in and starting to set up the tech before the cast arrived, every crew member including myself, was bitten on every inch of bare skin. That, paired with the insane heat, made for a very uncomfortable start.

When the cast arrived, all hell broke loose. The accommodation they had been put in was a building yet to be completed. Some of the cast had walked into a room with a missing outside wall and the whole place was a building site. This new resort had not yet been completed and yet, they were expected to stay there!

The Brazilians didn't appear to want to complain but the UK cast certainly did.

They were moved instantly to hotels, causing a rift between them and production. Unfortunately because most of them arrved so late, the same bond and trust we had wasn't quite there.

Not a great start.

I began to live for the early walks on the beach, the Rio sunrise giving me hope and the pure, clean air filling my lungs. I drunk in my frozen açai and granola breakfasts with Jo and Jess and the singular green apple still brought to me each morning by Gustavo always put a smile on my face.

The simple things making what was turning into a complex situation, more palatable.

The tech was tough. The stifling heat unbearable to work in and the hours long. Once songs were blocked on stage and perfected, we still had to do everything at least four times because of the kids.

Each one of those boys had, by this time, gained so much TV exposure, the pressure was on all of them. The dancers, although forever in great spirits, were not all used to having to retain so much information. There were daily clean-up calls to make sure the choreography did not slip and this took its toll.

The ecstasy we felt in the studio in São Paulo became work for the first time.

As we approached the date for our 'soft opening', I was called, frostily, into one of the large, unused dressing rooms.

I had the strong sense that something had happened and was about to go down, so I took Jo in there with me. Silent and heading towards exhaustion, we entered the room wondering what on earth the latest issue could be.

We sat together opposite Junior and Ricco and their expressions alarmed me.

Junior was stony-faced and I recognised the look. He was angry about something but lately he seemed to be wearing this expression a lot.

Ricco was almost glued to Junior's shoulder looking very shifty. It was only five minutes ago these two weren't working with one another anymore, and the whole of Ricco's team had left the production. Suddenly now Ricco (and his sidekick Fausto) were back on the scene.

Feeling their body language and the tension in the air, I braced myself.

Had someone been arrested? Or died?

This wasn't going to be pretty.

"We are unhappy with the way you are treating our star," Junior spoke in a very serious tone.

I had to think. "…star?"

We don't have stars in this show; Michael is the star and we are always very clear on that.

"Leilah." Ricco backed him up.

"Erm… okay," I offered, almost more of a question than in agreement.

"You do not have her joining in, she is not rehearsing enough and you do everything with Zoe."

Now you have to bear in mind Leilah had at least three weeks before Zoe and the other UK singers arrived. At home, the show would have been open by now and on the road.

She had plenty of time with the MD and ourselves and she was in a very good place.

Also Zoe had not performed in the show in years and had a lot of changes to learn.

Leilah was doing two shows a week.

I explained this in detail to the boys, who were clearly not interested in discussing the matter.

"She is very upset. You pay her no attention, she doesn't know what she is doing and you are not using her on the stage. We are very angry."

Alright, relax, I thought. The Brazilian facade, that was so inviting and intoxicating to begin with, was starting to fade and the drama that started to ensue on a daily basis was not at all pleasant.

They then also tried to insinuate that I was being mean and bullying her.

The disappointment, frustration and exhaustion raged internally as I tried to work out what had changed these people's view of me and my team…

This production was getting more and more difficult by the day and I started to understand why our producers in the UK liked to control everything themselves.

Discretion and tact are two qualities I possess in abundance, drilled into me by my father. I always know when to employ them and have always felt these, partnered with respect for everyone on my team, are crucial to getting a good result. This was one of those moments I had to compromise these qualities with some fight.

"Okay, enough." I sat upright. "First of all, Leilah is getting stage time. We are running everything several times and she gets at least one go every time we do it. This is a luxury where we come from. Zoe has a lot of catching up to do and is opening on Tuesday so she has to lead when we run things."

"We want Leilah to open for the press," Junior said gravely.

Oh, Jesus, I thought and looked at Jo.

"She is Brazilian, she is famous here and we want her to do the first show."

I took a breath.

"That's fine with me, Junior," I said. "However, I believe Zoe has it in her contract that she will do six shows a week and open for the press."

"I don't care," came the petulant retort.

"That's fine," I ventured again, this time a little more prudently, "but you may have an issue with our producers and most certainly Zoe herself."

"You put Leilah on and have her do the rest of the rehearsals." The tone was forceful and highly unnecessary. Jo and I looked at each other; what on earth was going on?

Were there issues behind the scenes we weren't aware of, or was this the true colours of these incredible hosts we had grown to love, coming out in the most ugly way?

It had been clear for days that the pressure of the show opening was getting to him and this conversation was proof.

I could only imagine what Ricco had been saying to Junior. Not two days before, he was barely on the scene and when he was, making comments how he would *love to see this* Thriller *show burn to the ground*. We all thought he had been demoted or removed from the production, but then here he was again, front and centre.

We left the room and I almost exploded.

The mood had changed so dramatically since arriving in Rio and the divide between Britain and Brazil continued to grow.

"What the hell is going on?" I impatiently spat at Jo. "This is all going very sour."

She just looked back at me, partly in shock and a little defensive on my behalf.

I walked out into the auditorium where Fernanda was waiting for me.

"Leilah wants to speak to you," she said quietly.

I sat at the production desk and waited.

Leilah came out of what appeared to be nowhere. Everyone had left for the day, producers included, and the theatre was silent.

The two of them approached me and Fernanda once again began to translate as Leilah spoke passionately (and seemingly a little sad) in Portuguese.

"Leilah says she has no problem with how you are working and is grateful for all the attention you have given her," Fernanda translated, completely contradicting the conversation I had just experienced. "They (the producers) want me to agree to more shows a week so they can promote the show in a different way and sell more tickets."

Ah, so this was about a higher issue, ticket sales. This was usually the reason behind any last-minute change of heart from the top. I wish they'd had the courage and the decency to just say that.

The girls continued in the same way to apologise (unnecessarily) and explain why this had all happened.

With opening night just two days away, I now needed to find a way to please everybody.

I also had to find a way to get the company through the rest of this tech without the whole thing falling apart.

After a couple of days of incredible time wasting and a lot of to-ing and fro-ing between the UK producers and Zoe's agent in London, we settled on the following and this is how we opened.

Leilah would act as a pre-show VIP guest and sing 'Who's Loving You' before the show began.

She would then come out during 'Earth Song' and lead the Rock section in the middle build of the song.

She did end up doing more shows in the week and the two girls split the promotion.

Zoe ended up becoming a star attraction in her own right, gaining a ton of fans in Brazil.

Leilah retained her dignity as a renowned artist in her home country.

That night, on her way home, Leilah was held at gunpoint at the open window of her car when stopping at a red light. Her purse and phone were taken but she was unhurt. Understandably very shaken, she did not come into rehearsal the following day. The second time in two weeks and in two cities, Jo and I started to count down the days.

***

The familiar sounds of 'heads up' boomed from above as lights were still being positioned and the set hung. The clashing sounds of clanging iron and drilling against shouts of, "Five, six, seven, eight!" made for the usual deafening chaos prior to the start of a show tech, all of this happening around our choreographic clean-ups, wardrobe checks and pep talks with the boys.

The first few sessions of tech were slow.

The change of environment combined with the urgency of production week had an impact of my working brain. As I shifted gear going into the tech, my mind solely on getting this show on and making it a success, most of my Portuguese had somehow disappeared, each direction having to be relayed by Fernanda over the microphone.

Each time we reached the end of a section we had to wait and then stop.

Ordinarily, this would be due to a quick change or technical problem but here, it was the wigs.

The wigs team were trying to place and style wigs on each of the dancers during every change. On this show, that was impossible, the quick changes were minutes, sometimes seconds long and attempting to pin and glue their 'perucas' after every song was really starting to hold us up.

My patience wore thin around session three and I quashed all the wigs except the necessary ones, the ones that we discussed in the meetings months ago and were given in the brief.

The bold Brazilian spirit remained unshakeable as the odd dancer kept appearing on stage sporting a wig instructed by the wigs mistress – just in case I liked it!

The final straw came two days later when working through 'They Don't Really Care About Us'.

Eager to see this number with our new drums and a more fluid Brazilian style of playing them, I waited, poised for their entrance. What completely shattered my excitement, breaking my attentionm were the wigs that came perched on each drummer's head. I hardly had to turn to Jo, who was already out of her seat and flying down the aisle, comedically waving her arms like a mad woman.

Each hairstyle was a different one, the most distracting being the one Eddy Lima was wearing. A knee-length dreadlock Rastafarian wig with Jamaican colours running through it. I understood this was a reference to the 'Olodum' and I got the sentiment, but it looked utterly ridiculous.

This was really starting to piss me off.

It wasn't until the music started and Eddy started drumming, stomping from side to side as part of the choreographed movement. His wig had other ideas and swung heavily in the opposite direction.

He looked like a deranged woolly mammoth, the movement getting bigger as he over-compensated, both Jo and I screaming (me over the microphone), "Take those f-ing wigs off now!"

The tech came to a standstill and the wigs all packed firmly in their boxes, never to be seen again.

I laugh at this now, in fact every time we teach this number I relive it, but at the time my sense of humour was dwindling away to zero.

'They Don't Really Care About Us' was directed by Spike Lee and shot in two locations in Brazil, in Pelorinho, the historic city center of Salvador, and in a favela of Rio de Janeiro called Santa Marta where the residents of the area were ecstatic to have Michael choose to represent them in his work.

The video showed Michael dancing with the favela community and the children of the Olodum.

Olodum is a non-government-funded organisation that develops activism to combat social discrimination and boost the self-esteem and pride of Afro-Brazilians. They also run a social project called Escola Olodum (Olodum School) where music is taught as a focus to keep young children, particularly boys, off the streets and away from drug gangs.

When Michael Jackson came to film here, the government tried to stop him; the favelas were not the face of Rio they wanted represented to the wider world. Even after he had left Brazil, there were claims that his visit didn't make any difference, even after the music video had appeared on television screens around the world. But that change did happen; the drug pushers and gunrunners were cleaned out of those favelas. Young and idealistic officers set up a special police force to ensure law, order and safety for the inhabitants and for visitors, as Santa Marta guaranteed attraction as the location of Michael Jackson's famous video. The mayor of Rio announced that a memorial would be created for him in Michael. That happened on the 26th of June, the very next day after Michael's death.

One of the most unforgettable days of this period was when the four children were taken to see this memorial. For us, this was fascinating tourism and another leaf in our MJ journal.

For them, the emotion was much deeper, all four of them fully understanding Michael's role as a hero to everyone in their country. With two of them coming from the favelas, the visit was solemn, yet celebratory and strangely mature. As their director, I knew this experience, along with the maelstrom of the last six months, would enrich each of their performance. On the eve of our show launch, I silently celebrated that.

Chapter Nineteen

Can You Feel It?

21st February 2013 – press night.

The warm-up that afternoon was even more hyped than usual. The girls were mostly going over their notes and checking choreography with Fernanda the dance captain and Jessica, my resident director, while the boys were all pretty much flipping, vogueing and battling one another in an attempt to keep their pre-show excitement contained. The kids, of course, were running around, copying the boys where they could and singing MJ songs at the tops of their lungs. If you could visualise pure, unadulterated joy, this would be it.

Feeling honoured and happy, I left them to it and made my way to the dressing room, where I had thirty-plus cards to write individual messages in Portuguese.

With all the problems ironed out, final dance cleaning and political issues solved, we all expected to have a really good show.

We gathered together at 7.15pm for a company circle where we all held hands. I said a few words to focus their energies, and Adrian, John and Junior said a few words of their own to inspire and remind them of certain notes and wish them all luck. Prayers and thanks were exchanged and we finished with a Brazilian chant and a loud, "*Merde!*" – this confused me as I knew it as a French expression but like our 'Break a leg!' or the German '*Toi, Toi, Toi!*', in Brazil, they use '*Merde!*' – and loudly.

There was an electric buzz in the air and the generous space backstage meant we could all run round to give notes, frantically get ready or in Eddy and Gustavo's case – goof around in their own 'special' pre-show style.

Then we waited. At 7.45pm, Jo and I decided to go through the pass door into the front of house and see what the hold-up was, only to discover there was no-one in the audience. No-one at all.

We ran backstage to find Junior.

"Don't worry!" he said calmly. "This is Brazil, no-one will arrive until at least 9pm."

I couldn't believe it. Junior's philosophy was that people in Brazil would probably leave around 7.15 knowing they had a two-hour drive. I should have known he was right – we had been here long enough and experienced those early-morning journeys to make it to rehearsal before anyone else!

My only issue was that we had warmed the company up way too early. But hey – we were in Brazil, it was roasting and this lot were so hyped, they didn't even seem to have noticed!

The auditorium filled up slowly starting from around 8.30pm.

When the show finally went up, it interrupted a building chant of, "Michael, Michael, Michael," and then a roar from the crowd as the lights went down and the overture started.

The whole show was a party, and the floor and balcony were lit up by mobile phones recording every second, with each member of the audience still able to dance and sing along.

Isacque was our Young MJ for this third performance, but the main press night, and he did not disappoint – the audience absolutely loved him!

The show that night was an almost flawless success other than a minor injury at the top of Act Two. Renan Tenca slipped and lost his shoe right before performing his back flip in 'Wanna Be'. His other shoe flew off during that flip and he landed on his head.

Undeterred, Renan came offstage briefly to put another pair of shoes on and went back on for 'Dancing Machine'.

Ironically, these replacement shoes were too tight and he almost missed his entrance out of the quick change into 'The Way You Make Me Feel'.

From this moment on, the shows in Rio went from strength to strength and the audiences full and close to riotous by each finale. Backstage though, there was more continuing weirdness taking place.

On three occasions, one of our 'Dirty Dianas' had issues with her costume. This wasn't just a fitting thing or a problem with how something had been made, it seemed she was being targeted. The first problem was during previews. Ana was very meticulous and always set her costumes and props, checking them several times. On this particular show, her shoes were removed, making it impossible for her to enter the stage. 'Dirty Diana' was a solo that day and Ana very unhappy with it.

When her shoes returned, they were miraculously two sizes too small. She didn't discover this until the quick change prior to the number, so once again she was unable to perform.

The last incident was less curious and a little more divisive. On arriving to her station to change for the song, everything was there, shoes were fine but when Ana went to put on her headdress on, it had been slashed in two! Nobody could work out what had happened or where this was coming from but it made for a very uneasy atmosphere backstage. The costume designer had walked off the production, but because of the language difficulty, it was hard to fully understand why that happened. After Ana took some time off with an injury, she thankfully returned to better judgement from her perpetrator.

As always, the cast were able to rise above any negativity and there were smiles all around. And although production may not have got everything right or managed things in the same way we were used to, there was plenty to smile about. There was a constant flow of food and candy for the cast and crew, and Junior insisted on having a masseur backstage at all time. I've never seen the likes of dancers running off stage at the interval and straight onto the massage table but this was the norm here on this show! Junior's generosity didn't end there and the kids and cast were showered with gifts, Miu Miu shoes for Zoe, Xbox consoles for the kids, you name it. One beautiful gesture that will stay with me was seeing images, shortly after we left, of a special matinee performance Junior had organised for Children with Cancer on May 16th 2013. The auditorium was full of carers and sick children and the stage filled with them as they joined the cast to sing 'Heal the World'. It was very moving indeed and something Michael would have wholeheartedly embraced.

There were understandably still lots of issues that followed once Jo and I left for the UK, but the production drama did plateau; the team found their groove, learning what it takes to exist together as a theatrical touring company. Relationships were healed and the show, after touring to Brasilia and finishing in São Paulo where it all began, became a huge success for Junior, this unforgettable group of people and for Brazil.

I am very happy that the connections with many of my Brazilian family are still strong, particularly with the male dancers. Eddy Lima has played MJ in our UK/Europe touring production and I brought five of the boys over to London in December 2013 when directing a stadium spectacular, *The Tina Turner Experience* for the Gelredome in Arnhem, Holland.

I call these crazy talented, very special people in my life my 'Minions'. They call me 'Papi'.

Junior and I are also still in contact, a mutual admiration for one another's creativity and drive maintaining that initial bond. A brilliant photographer – many of the shots of the show, documenting the journey throughout, were taken by him. Junior was kind enough to let me feature some of them in this book.

After such an intense few months I was more than ready to get home. But to leave Brazil was to leave the innocence of these beautiful people, the culture, its weather, the complexity and splendour of the samba, their football, and its unique and graceful dance. The danger, gratitude and genuine zest for life, I will always miss.

Six years on I still have those indelible memories and qualities that live within me and my every day, and those people are still very much in my heart and in my life.

Written by Edson 'Junior' Cabrera:

Working alongside Gary Lloyd to create Thriller Live! *Brazil was an experience that gave me great respect for his work as a director. His ability to take a production like* Thriller Live! *across multiple countries capturing the intricacies of each culture was awe-inspiring. His focus was solely to give the Brazilian audience an experience that was one hundred per cent theirs.*

Equally impressive was the sincerity in the care he gave to the entire cast from the auditions, throughout the rehearsals, to every show. This was extremely critical in identifying the young boy to play the adolescent Michael Jackson. Gary's dedication and support for all helped to ensure a brilliant cast bringing a depth to each performance that would remain in his audience's memories forever.

In Conversation with Zoe Birkett

Zoe was the winning female of the original *Pop Idol* TV talent series. She is now a global musical theatre and TV star.

GL: What was the first MJ song you remember hearing?

ZB: *The first MJ song I believe I ever headr was 'Rockin' Robin'. I used to be a disco dancer and I used to compete. I was the under fourteens disco dancing champion… of the world at one stage which was amazing. And we used to do rock and roll as one of the competitive dances and the song I always chose to do my rock and roll dance to was 'Rockin' Robin'.*

GL: You were the original female lead in the first tour of *Thriller Live!* and kept developing the role on many tours after that. How was that?

ZB: *Being part of* Thriller Live! *and originating the role many moons ago was such a huge thing for me and my whole family, especially my dad. I remember speaking to my dad and saying, "I've got this part!" and over the years, when I've come in and out and done various productions all over the world, I've always found new challenges within the music, within the choreography and new things about Michael Jackson that I didn't really know. His artistry, as a musician and a performer, and each time I've come back to* Thriller Live! *I've learned more about him. It's never felt like doing the same thing again; I've always learned more every single time. Even working alongside the other singers who are all MJ fans, they have taught me things.* Thriller Live! *is somewhere I always like to call home.*

GL: You have seen quite a few changes to the production over the years. What is your favourite MJ song to perform?

ZB: I've got two from different productions. 'The Way You Make Me Feel' is definitely one of my favourite numbers to do. It's a classic for me and one of my favourite MJ songs, along with 'Jam', actually, my other favourite song of all time. But where ['The Way You Make Me Feel'] fits in the show, the production, working with the boys, the choreography and me as a performer. I love anything that's sassy and a bit diva-esque. It's one woman on that stage, feeling that power with these men around her and a brilliant part of the show.

So that was definitely one of my favourite numbers to perform in the show.

But when we took the show to Brazil, you [GL] put in 'Human Nature'.

Performing that song out there was something else. As soon as it started, the Brazilian fans went absolutely crazy and again, I fell in love with that song and that definitely became one of my favourite parts of the show. So every single night I couldn't wait to get out there and sing 'Human Nature'. Oh! And also 'Jam' – when that opened the show, that was an awesome opening.

GL: You took your role out to Brazil [as one of the few Brits] and came back with quite a fan following. How are the MJ fans in Brazil different to the UK and Europe?

ZB: The fans in Brazil were hardcore! The fans in the UK are a little bit more reserved. We love his music and we will buy a ticket and go see the shows. The fans in Brazil... I mean, I left there with such a huge Brazilian following, that at one point I considered relocating to Brazil. I met with a manager, which was crazy, and they were all so supportive of me.

But MJ fans in general, and I have been to South Africa and Europe as well as Brazil, are all really dedicated and really dedicated to you as an individual. Some of the MJ fans I have took with me over the last ten years over the last ten years from the very beginning who still come and see me in shows now. So it's not just the MJ fans that are fantastic but also the Thriller Live! fans and that's all down to Michael Jackson.

But the Brazilian fans would follow, they would write, they would turn up at the TV stations. It felt like something out of the '80s when you would see that on the TV with the legends when the fans would camp outside. It was definitely that type of feeling in Brazil, they are all so emotionally involved. I have Brazilian fans that come to the UK to still see me in shows! That's just unbelievably crazy. They are so, so passionate about Michael Jackson.

Also I think because Michael filmed the 'They Don't Really Care About Us' music video in Brazil, that just set a benchmark for the country. With everything that Brazil goes through with the poverty and the passion. You would never know what these people go through, living in the favelas [etc.] as they are the most wonderful humans you will ever meet. So I think for Michael Jackson to choose Brazil to film the video for this song there, they are such proud people, I think it's an important thing to add, that out of all the places in the world, Michael chose them – he chose Brazil.

GL: What was your experience of doing the show in Brazil?

ZB: I grew up a lot in Brazil. I experienced a lot of different things. As one of four British singers, with a whole Brazilian production team, it was a challenge. I remember arriving late and you guys were already there. I remember getting off the flight and meeting a girl who didn't speak any English, lucky she had a translator with her! I got driven straight to rehearsal – I'll never forget, straight to rehearsals after a ten-hour flight. There was another translator with you translating to the dancers what you wanted them to do and I was literally like, "Whoah – there is nobody that speaks English!"

Then for the six months we spent there, we were just left, having to fend for ourselves.

Luckily, I spoke a bit of Spanish which is kind of similar to Portuguese. But we had to learn really quickly how to communicate with these wonderful people. My dresser, Paula, the loveliest woman, she actually did not speak one word of English, even up to the day that I left! We used to translate to each other through Google on our phones and that's how we got by. But for all of the madness that we had on that tour, the connection, despite not speaking the same language as each other, was phenomenal. The production team, the sound crew, stage management and the dancers, with everybody, it was such a lovely team. All the Brazilians were so happy to be part of this production and they felt so honoured, and they absolutely slayed the whole show every single day.

It was something I looked at and thought each and 'every one of these people are absolutely fantastic and super talented'. The talent in Brazil was just off the scale!

So much so, you [GL] brought the boys over to do the Tina Turner show because they were just so sensational, there's no denying that.

But I got to know some of them and we would go back to their houses. Some of them would live in a favela and it would take four packed buses to get to work. The culture was so different for us English. We would walk around with our nice things and they had absolutely nothing. It was an eye-opener and I left with so many wonderful friends who I am still connected with. It was a wonderful, life changing experience.

GL: Where were you when you heard about Michael's passing?

ZB: *I was with you! I was doing [The Showgirls] gig at the Arts Theatre. I was in Priscilla at the time. And I came and sang for you at your concert. I remember being in the wings and all the dancers were saying Michael had died and I thought it was one of those silly hoax things. But then you mentioned it and that whole night now just seems a blur. The main thing I remember my dad calling when I was on the train home and he was in bits. And I think he stayed up and watched the news until around 5am to find out what was going on.*

I them came down to Thriller *the next day and there was so many flowers and candles, letters and cards as a tribute to MJ outside the theatre; it was beautiful but a very, very sad night.*

Part Four
Victory

Chapter Twenty

Looking Through
The Windows

Being a director, part of a creative team or management of a long-running show, carries a responsibility that can sometimes be twenty-four seven. *Thriller Live!* has toured constantly since 2008, visiting a staggering 230 cities!

Sometimes, the producing partners in these cities are new to the game and the experience can be tough or, at the very least, a learning curve for both parties. Then there are the long-standing relationships with the established and thriving promoters like BB Promotions in Germany, who run a very tight ship and make our job so much easier. We have a ten-year relationship with the guys at BB and the show still sells out all over Germany to some of our biggest and most loyal fans.

Naturally, problems arise on tour, so when you have more than one production on the road as well as the mothership running in the West End, it can sometimes feel non-stop. We receive calls and emails constantly about behaviour, technical faults, epidemics, injuries and cultural issues. Of course, we are not always on the ground having to deal with these issues face to face, they are dealt with daily by the unsung heroes, the company managers, resident directors and dance captains.

But we do hold the responsibility to provide the solutions to a lot of the problems.

Of course, this is what we sign up for, dream of, even. That one of the many shows you put your heart and soul into, runs and expands, playing to millions around the world.

Here are just a few examples of the kind of thing I am talking about, amusing anecdotes and some more serious issues we have all had to deal with:

We have often seen mixed-gender performances, especially in the early days, with Britt Quentin (2009–present) singing the female's songs (namely 'Blame It on the Boogie' and 'The Way You Make Me Feel'), and Miranda Wilford (2009–2013) taking some of the male ones, most memorably 'Beat It'. This is where you rely on stellar individuals within a cast, able to jump in and save the day.

Of course Michael sang all of these songs, so a male jumping in to save the day doesn't sound that odd. In the context of the show's design and knowing how high these keys are to sing in, it is no mean feat.

One of our male leads became renowned for getting a frog in his throat and violently coughing into his microphone for the duration of 'Show You the Way to Go'.

On a different night, that same performer decided to jump off one of the podiums during 'Beat It', misjuding his landing and dislocating his knee, this time continuing to sing while writhing around in agony on the floor. The dancers around him were so (unsympathetically) in the moment, they proceeded, in character, to mime kicking him down as part of the action! This became another example of Miranda grabbing the mic and finishing the vocal in front of this faux-violent scene, putting the audience ahead of the actor.

There was the time we discovered Ricko Baird, our only MJ at the time, had locked himself in his apartment an hour before the show was due to start. This was one of the most panicked sixty minutes I can remember, as we would have had to cancel the show, a catastrophic decision for the theatre, producers, and a would-be huge disappointment for that night's audience.

It took for Adrian Grant, our production manager Andy Sharrocks and producer Derek Nicol to go round there to try and get him out. In the meantime, Adrian arranged for Suleman Mirza from *Britain's Got Talent* act 'Signature' to come to the theatre. Amazingly he was in London and around the corner, and turned up within minutes of that call.

Wardrobe got to work finding costumes to fit Suleman. While hoping Ricko would still miraculously appear, I started working with him on stage. There was only so much he could do, pretty much just 'Billie Jean' and 'Thriller', but even this was a great help as we had no understudies in the building. The thing is, in these situations, it's not just that artist you have to work with. Each of the numbers that affected this track had to be reblocked, meaning the choreography and positioning that the cast performed every night had to be reworked in minutes to accomodate this problem. This can often be a daily task, to this day putting major stress on the resident director's and dance captain's shoulders. That night, dancers Jordan Darrell and Richard Smikle took on 'Smooth Criminal' and 'Dangerous respectively' and we somehow made Suleman's appearance a coup for the audience, who lapped up the surprise special guest appearance that evening.

Each of the boys did a fantastic job and Ricko eventually got out of his apartment, able to perform the next day...

Sean Christopher, one of our first touring MJs, was put into the show with very little time to rehearse, doing an incredible job and staying loyal to the show for a number of years.

His first show, however, will go down in our history books, not for wowing the crowd with his performance of 'Billie Jean' but for not putting his Jacksons wig on properly. When performing 'Show You the Way to Go', he knocked his wig off his head, watched it fly downstage, making no attempt to pick it up or put it back on his head. Poor Sean spent the rest of the medley, which I think at that time also involved 'This Place Hotel' and 'Another Part of Me', sporting a stocking cap, looking bald against the other boys in their pristine and glossy afros.

Two cast members, who shall remain nameless, thought themselves clever, setting up injuries in advance, one of them even going to the trouble of wearing a neck brace for a few days prior to them both going off sick. That night, they were both seen front and centre on the televised Brit Awards dancing behind a major artist in a particularly 'hair-whippy' routine. Needless to say they were both fired from the show.

This has happened on more than one occasion...

A story from the front of house team that always shocks and amuses is the one about the couple who were asked to leave after they were discovered having sex in the balcony during 'Beat It'.

This begged a number of questions, not least how did they physically achieve that in such narrow seats at the Lyric, and did they wait specifically for that song?!

Security were brought in on an early tour in Glasgow when at the end of the show, groups of drunken revellers would try and join the cast on stage for the finale.

Jo Dyce, associate choreographer, 2008–present, remembers:

In the early days of the West End production we started off only having four male dancers, although randomly there were five girls. We never had enough boys to play The Jackson Five so there was this one show where I had to go on as a boy for the J5 medley. This also happened in a later show on the tour when in Trieste, Italy. I looked kind of cute as a boy and with my natural afro, it worked playing a young Jackson but on this particular show at the Lyric I also had to go on as an older Jackson for the 'Show You the Way to Go / Shake Your Body' section. Those costumes were super-tight, though, so I wore a sock in my trousers to theatrically enhance my manhood. The looks I got from the audience were hysterical, especially when the front few rows saw me reappear in the next number as myself!

A memory that really jumps out for me (and still makes me laugh) was when Zoe Purpuri, mid-show, slipped and almost fell down the back of the bridge from the top, almost landing on the band. The band were all playing 'Blame It on the Boogie' at the time so couldn't help her and she was left flailing, holding on for dear life with one hand and half a leg! Oli, our bass player, and John Maher tried to help her playing one-handed and somehow managed to stabilize her. We now have a barrier in place to stop this from happening again!

Britt Quentin, tour resident director, 2010–present:

Macau 2017

Half the cast and crew caught what the locals call 'the Macau bug', leaving us to do a show with just two singers – myself and Shaquille – and quite a few hefty reblocks for the dancers. In the same period, we did two three-singer shows, and a couple of two men only, two women only shows. Eleven of us caught the bug, including our drummer, and some were off for two weeks or more.

Also quite a few shows were cancelled because of two separate typhoons. The theatre, which was inside the hotel, was flooded, the brand new hotel and surrounding resort had water everywhere.

Tree branches had blown in through the corridors because all the windows in the resort popped open during the storm – a safety measure put in place to prevent the wind blowing the building over... that's literally what we were told! The grounds were all ruined with uprooted trees, fallen lamplights, and the emptied pools were full of debris and patio furniture. The AC in the resort was off for four days, as were the lights, only a few emergency lights left on. It was a pretty traumatic experience.

South Korea 2013
We performed on a huge stage, but not on our set. The set had been built too small (they had done the conversions wrong) and the whole thing very unstable. So... we did four completely redesigned shows without using the set at all. But, there was no time to move it from the stage. We literally performed around and in front of the set, and couldn't use it. It really was awful and it took Lauren Gore (the dance captain at that time) and me hours to come with a presentable show.

When it came to the props, they provided us with one red sofa (for 'Smooth Criminal'), and it was a second-hand sofa, probably from the late '60s – it really smelled, it was stained, it was absolutely huge with a tall high back. And again, totally unstable, as it only had two legs.

Arena Tour Germany 2009
One of the most memorable parts of these shows was – the White section.

Seeing literally thousands of people in giant arena spaces turn their lights on their phones and sing along to 'Man in the Mirror' at the top of their lungs, waving those lights – almost every show without fail. A very magical, memorable atmosphere which always reminded us of the impact his music has on people all around the world... in whatever language.

Poland 2017

Unfortunately, on a string of one-nighters, the power supply hadn't been sourced properly in one arena. There was a popping noise in the PA system... literally like the sound of popcorn in the microwave... throughout the entire show. The show went up more than forty minutes late as the sound team tried to get rid of it, but were unsuccessful. The constant, loud, popping noise was also in all the singers' in-ear monitor mixes. The decision was made by producers and local promoters to put the show up anyway. Singers had to sing the show without in-ears in an arena, and the dancers had to dance to 'many beats'! The singers were miserable, many of the audience members had their fingers in their ears, and the dancers just tried to keep a straight face – it just became comical in the end!

Dancer Liam Lawrence in 'They Don't Really Care About Us', on the bridge far stage left somehow, during the rock-out section, lost his balance, slipped and fell into one of the lighting towers. The only way he could get down, was to climb down the tower. It must have looked pretty funny from the audience.

One of the zombies coming through the auditorium, Gabriela Hernandez, was attacked by a patron because she was so frightened. The woman was literally beating her on the head screaming out of fright as though she was a 'real' monster!

Another Gabriela story, she hit her head in 'Dirty Diana' during her opening solo, leaving a pretty deep cut. She was bleeding quite profusely but didn't come off stage. Penny Smart, the second 'Diana', then entered, and tried to tell her she was bleeding, Gaby thought she was sweating. She couldn't hear anyone because of the head piece. Everyone was telling her to go off because she was bleeding so badly down her face and costume. Even the bass player in the pit was trying to tell her at the end of the song. She did the whole number without coming off!

Kuwait 2019

After spending two days re-structuring the show for a strict Muslim audience, as well as months of preparation on costume re-designs, we arrived in Kuwait pretty pleased with ourselves at the outcome, convinced we had thought of everything. We got into the dress rehearsal where the very excited local promoters lined up to watch.

When it got to 'Shake Your Body', Trace Kennedy and I launched into the audience participation section completely forgetting the build up was to encourage the audience to shake their hips like the Jacksons, a foot-stomping, hip-grinding moment that was bound to offend. As we hit the first 'grind' we stopped looking at each other like, "How do we get out of this?"

We just called the band back in and awkardly went straight to the last chorus.

Phil Watts, touring company manager of the last eleven years, writes:

'Eleven Smooth Years.'

It was 2008, and I had an established working relationship as a tour manager with the producer/promoter Flying Music when they asked me if I would like to look after this new show they were launching... Thriller Live! Of course I said yes, little thinking that I would, eleven years later, be penning these words before another performance.

It's well documented how many shows have been performed, countries visited and people entertained in that time; for me it's more measured in bus calls, airport lounges, hotel rooms and frantic calls for emergency cover from literally all around the world!

Stand out memories include:

A one-nighter in Pune, India, December 2011. This was a private client who chartered the show for a private party for 1,200 guests in a private residence. The only issue was, when we arrived, there was a huge tree in the middle of the stage that could not be moved!

Yasmin and the cast spent most of the day re-blocking the show around the tree.

The audience were slow to come to the stage area at the top of the show, but soon came forward and mostly stayed in front of the stage for the whole performance. As most of the audience did not know what the show was (we were asked to keep the Thriller *logo off the screen until five minutes prior to performance), there were a few confused faces at first.*

The crowd certainly warmed up as they recognised the intro to 'Beat It'.

There were great cheers for 'Smooth' (and for the lean) and they particularly enjoyed 'Man in the Mirror' and the finale.

The client sent down his congratulations after the show and there was praise for the cast as they mingled after the performance.

The production was all supplied locally with the exception of the video control gear.

After that, the two-hour journey back to the airport took five hours and somehow forty people made the flight. I didn't make many friends amongst the Indian army personnel that day.

Our first arena show, which was in Cologne in 2008. The reaction of 6,000-plus people that night made it clear there was something special happening.

Performing the show the day after MJ passed – a crazy day during which we all went through every possible high and low imaginable.

We often think 'it's just a job' but Thriller Live! *has become more than that – so many of us have shared personal and professional highs as well as the usual dramas which are better kept on the road – or possibly on Facebook, if you're unlucky.*

I'm glad I said yes.

Sharon Speirs, West End company manager, 2009–2016:

My best emergency rescue story is the day Britt was performing Man 3 and he had a glycaemic episode and could not carry on just after we started the show (this was the one and only time he has been sick). We had no cover in the building due to holiday and sickness. I asked Beth [Minter – wardrobe mistress] on the way to stage and asked, "Whose Man 3 costumes do we have in the building?" and she replied Alex Ko.

Shit, I thought, *he lives in Manchester, but we called him anyway, just in case.*

*He just happened to be in London and was around the corner at the Hospital club with another ex-*Thriller *cast member Oggie Iwo.*

He said he'd been drinking but I said, "Can you sing and dance?" He said, "Yes," and over he ran. We were all waiting for him, got him in costume and he went on for 'She's Out of My Life'. We didn't even have to stop the show. Not the most responsible fix to a problem but we had no-one else. Alex was great, although he did say he was a little sick in his mouth during the song!

A more serious memory was when the roof collapsed at the Apollo theatre, next door to us.

The Curious Incident of the Dog in the Night-Time has been running in London since August 2012. On the 20th of December 2013 The Apollo's ornate plasterwork ceiling collapsed and brought down part of the lighting rig.

Firefighters worked really hard in very difficult conditions...

they were rescuing people from the theatre and making sure no-one was trapped.

The theatre had been almost full and 720 people were watching the performance.

There were children – it's a family-friendly show, of course – who were crying, and there were adults leaving the building, covered in dust and plaster. We heard the commotion and it was very frightening. We thought we would have to stop the show but the police advised us to continue with Act Two of the show as they felt it was better to keep everyone inside and off the streets.

The Prime Minister David Cameron tweeted: "I've been updated regularly on the Apollo incident. I'm grateful for the fast work of the emergency services in helping the injured."

Chapter Twenty-One

Whatever Happens – The Casting Process

Casting is the first stage in our process of putting it together. In over twenty years of being on a panel, casting *Thriller Live!* is single-handedly the hardest thing I have ever had to cast. This is purely down to the incomprehensibly challenging material that Michael has created and the standards we have set ourselves and have adhered to for the past ten-plus years.

The show is a juggernaut that relentlessly charges non-stop through the Jackson catalogue, giving neither actor nor audience member time to breathe. With this comes a demand on all of the performers that this has to be assessed very early on. We sing most of the songs in Michael's keys, bringing only a handful down a tone. The choreography stays at arena level throughout and involves hip-hop, breaking, acrobatics, partner work and technical jazz. We put any singer or dancer who wishes to to be seen through their paces in several rounds of auditions held by John Maher and myself. The bit we don't see is in the hands of casting director Debbie O'Brien. Prior to any audition she wades through thousands of submissions for each of the roles, carefully choosing eligible candidates that have experience or promise in the right fields for us. The final decision for each auditionee is always made by the three of us together with creator Adrian Grant and producer Paul Walden. I truly believe this attention to detail and the fact we are all so heavily involved even after all this time, is the secret behind the show's continued success.

As you read in the previous chapter, a long-running show that is constant high impact song and dance, maintaining that cast and their level on stage is a full-time job. It requires a hHrculean tenacity from both cast and creatives and an immeasurable trust between us.

There is the travel, their stamina and health, illness, injury and all of this is hard to predict even over three or four sessions with our auditionees.

Usually, we get it right and most people make it through their contract.

Then of course the unexpected can happen: injuries or vocal problems that require surgery or long recovery periods. There is also the issue of mental health that can strike anyone deriving from a number of things, both show-related and personal. More than a handful, though, have stood the test of time and gone on to become our emergency covers that we are forever indebted to.

The Singers

Our principal front line have to fit within the slimmest of casting briefs and are the most difficult part of the cast to find. As musical director John Maher will explain later in this chapter, this music is so very complex, our auditions with these almost always supremely talented singers, merely scratch the surface with what we need them to achieve.

I watch in wonder even now at how our singers can perform this material, not only at night in the show but sometimes at a 10am rehearsal when putting in a new cast. The sacrifices they make are fuelled by an unwavering passion for getting it right and being the best which is what we require from every performer.

Firstly, the voice is king. Quite simply, if they cannot hit the notes or show signs that with a little vocal wizardry you can find your way around a certain part, there is very little point pursuing the audition process any further. Once we find that voice, there must be some understanding and connection to the way MJ and the Jacksons sing that material. We rehearse them on the phrasing and their vocal delivery and once they have passed that test, they have to be able to back it up with some performance dynamics. Sounds obvious but quite often we have found the most incredible voices belonging to session singers, who also look fantastic but are not used to being out front or sometimes seen by an audience at all.

This is where their audition may fall down and it is a devastating loss for both us and them.

Getting the job for these guys really is step one, as the work on the show presents the start of a huge growth period for all the principals. Piecing together the microscopic detail of the music side while learning, retaining and attacking the movement at a satisfactory level make for a demanding few weeks, sometimes months, early in the process. Not all of them are able to connect with it and embrace it fully, others may take a while but the final result is always a great reward, particularly for the actor themselves.

All of this applies to the many young men we see to play Michael at age eleven. It's a tough gig for them and although we now have to compete with shows like *Motown*, *The Bodyguard*, *Kinky Boots* and *The Lion King*, for these children, *Thriller Live!* is vocally the most demanding.

The Children

Like the singers, each child has to be a triple threat – someone who can sing, dance and act. These boys have to be believable as Michael, and that is quite a tough brief to begin with.

We look for instant charisma, strong voices (that don't sound like they are about to change) rhythm and an ability to move. Quite often the great movers or performers have voices about to break and the best singers can be just too young and inexperienced.

We set up the Young MJ Academy in late 2012 and the first graduates performed their final audition on Friday the 8th February 2013. Since then, any young hopefuls are entered into the academy and learn all the show material ready to perform to the creative team upon graduation.

The best of the best make it into the show.

The Dancers

We see dancers in their hundreds.

Over the years, *Thriller Live!* has progressed from being a show that only attracted commercial/hip-hop dancers to a show that ALL dancers want to be a part of at one time in their career. More and more apply each year to try and make it through the door and the demand on the casting department has probably tripled in our ten years at the Lyric, not to mention the touring casts we have put together over the ten plus years.

The show itself has also developed so much that I now require more from my dancers within the choreography. So, as a result, we look at dancers from all walks of life possessing talents in all styles.

The dancers in the show are all athletes and treat their bodies, their diet and each other with the same discipline. This strenuous and regimented environment pulls the company together and manifests in some great friendships but it takes some training and even the strictest of body worshippers may fall foul to the constant injuries that occur. Broken wrists, slipped discs, concussions and dislocated knees have all featured as common mishaps over the ten-year run and various companies performing around the world.

Original cast member Emily Rumbles forced her way through the whole of 'Smooth Criminal', despite slipping a disc in her neck, which resulted in her being carried out of the theatre on a stretcher and several weeks off the show. Nathan Graham made it all the way through the gruelling rehearsal period as one of the fittest in his cast, only to rupture his achilles when learning the 'lean'.

Nathan, to this day, has not performed the show.

A *Thriller Live!* contract is like a marathon that in some cases can last years, but I need to somehow assess that mental focus and physical endurance as much as possible at audition stage.

Musicality – as a dancer, Michael Jackson was a terpsichorean, walking metronome. I never once saw him miss a beat. Even when he made the odd error in the choreography of some live performances (yes, he was a genius but also a human being!), his rhythm and accuracy of musical detail never ever faltered. As a creator of music, the heartbeat of every track comes from (not leads) the dancer in him. Listen to the way beats two and four not only land but are forced, almost mechanically, in songs like 'Billie Jean', 'Beat It', 'Dangerous', 'The Way You Make Me Feel', to name a few. The relentless four to the floor infectious thump of 'Can You Feel It' and the militant, authorative crunch in 'They Don't Really Care About Us'. If a dancer cannot adhere to these beautifully structured guidelines, be carried along and controlled by this driving force and show precision in his/her audition, I cannot even consider them for the show. This is rule number one.

One thing I established very early with my first touring cast that has become the show 'brief' is an all-individual look, particularly with the girls. We pride ourselves on always leading the way to celebrate diversity within the cast and being true to Michael's unique way of putting all looks, colours, shapes and sizes together.

This means that rather than the ensemble having an overall identity, each member has to be distinctive, both in their skills and presentation and especially in their look. My desire was to try and ensure that the audience went out at the end of the show not only knowing the 'MJs' and the singers but having a clear idea of who each of the dancers were.

Finding these individuals comes down to the long process of casting and to each of the ensemble member's uniqueness when they get on that stage.

It all starts in the audition room. You have to stand out.

It goes without saying that you need talent to get through that door. But just like casting the singers, this material and the demand of the choreography and its vast profusion needs a specific kind of ability. The audition process is long and arduous but always vital to go through with such a critical examination.

There are dancers that come in and you can see they are 'almost ready'.

The look, the style may be there but technically they need more experience. "Maybe next year," is said and we always remember, putting them on a list to recall when the time for cast change quickly rolls round again. Then there are those who desperately want it and try year after year, changing outfits and hairstyles, hoping this may make them more 'right'. Some are just naturally too relaxed in their movement, lacking in dynamic, others not sophisticated or advanced enough to handle all the different styles.

I would advise any dancer wanting to audition for any of the *Thriller* productions to be solid and content enough in themselves to stand strong in front of me when showing their strengths. Whether that be technique, tricks, commercial or a hell of a personality, know who you are and don't second guess what you think may get you the job. Despite the content and the rigid structure we have, this show builds and morphs with its performers and I have been known to cast dancers based on intuition and something special being displayed in that audition room.

The auditions that stand out for me were Suzette Brissett (2010 cast) from the open audition in 2009 and Kamilah Beckles (original London cast), who I first saw as a third year graduate student at 'Move It!' an annual dance conference held at Olympia, West London.

I have never known any dancer catch my eye like Kam.

This attraction is a special gift she possesses and everyone who witnesses her on stage says so.

Simeon Henry, 2009 cast and MJ understudy:

Sim was brought in by two dancers, Daniel Uppall and Mikey Frome, who had been recommended to me by Jordan Darrell from the original London cast. All three boys went to Cambridge Performing Arts (Bodywork Studios) and Sim was a B Boy/breaker they danced with outside of college.

Sim and Daniel had already performed as extras in the opening week of *Thriller* – bringing their incredible tricks to the 'Beat It' number but I hadn't seen them dance.

Simeon was not a trained dancer but I asked him to 'give it a go'.

He really struggled with the routine, barely able to put one foot in front of the other and certainly not able to turn. I remember we taught the 'Remember the Time' combination, which is very intricate. Sim was all over the place but there was something about his focus and determination that caught my eye.

Then he showed his tricks which were out of this world.

All three boys were given roles on the 2009 tour and we spent four weeks giving Sim extra tuition.

Sim stayed with the show for years, playing MJ in many countries on the tour. This was a rare gamble of mine that truly paid off.

Leslie Garcia Bowman (2017 West End company), a New Zealander and graduate from my college, Laine Theatre Arts, showed his passion for MJ in a beautifully executed version of the 'Smooth Criminal / Bad / Dangerous' combination. With so much personality and confidence, he sailed through the routine, making his audition a memorable one to this day.

He unsurprisingly went straight into the first London company of Lin-Manuel Miranda's *Hamilton* after *Thriller*.

Gabriela Hernandez, a Venezuelan firecracker who would not look out of place on a Beyonce tour, blew me away with her attack and instant understanding of the choreography. Gabriela is still to this day, one of the most exciting 'Dirty Dianas' we have had.

Fabrice Labrana (Arena tour 2009), a dancer from France, brought over for the open auditions by cast member Joel Elhadj, wowed us all with his lyrical movement and unparalleled freestyle. He struggled when learning the routine but had all the technical dancers heading for the door when he came forward to show his individuality as a dancer.

From a 2017 press release:

> *Gary Lloyd, Thriller Live!'s award-winning director and choreographer, said, "Dancers are the beating heart of our production, and with over thirty Michael Jackson song and dance routines, Thriller Live! is one of the most physically demanding productions ever seen in the West End. We work hard to maintain the highest of standards as I deliver choreography based on iconic moves created by the greatest entertainer of all time, who himself always strived for excellence and pushed the physical limits of what his body could produce. I am thrilled and excited at the quality of our new dancers whose energy and committment to the memory of Michael Jackson is inspirational. This show is a gift to anyone that lives to dance and for anyone that loves to entertain or be entertained."*

John Maher – 'ON THE MUSIC':

If there's one thing I enjoy even more than playing and conducting the show, it's the process of putting each new production together. 'Building the monster', I like to call it. And for me this starts with finding the right singers. On this show, that's harder than it sounds. I've been MDing shows for most of my adult life, and I can testify that Thriller Live! is without any shadow of a doubt, and by some considerable distance, the most difficult to cast of all the shows I've worked on. I know Gary feels the same way. MJ had an extraordinary vocal range. (If you've ever tried singing along you'll know this, no matter what gender you are.) We do the bulk of the show in Michael's original keys, so the vocal range alone rules out perhaps ninety-five per cent of the male candidates, and a surprising proportion of the female ones, as well as more than half of the children. But what set MJ apart as a vocalist even more than his remarkable range, in my opinion, was the incredible rhythmic feel of his vocals. This was true even when he was a young child, as he had a groove any great drummer or bassist would be proud of.

Every now and again, someone comes in who is vocally brilliant and so obviously right for the show; they sail through the audition process and win the entire panel over in almost no time. Sometimes this happens with incredible timing, when we're on the edge of despair. I remember a long audition day in the early years when we were looking for Young MJs. It was late afternoon, and after dozens of candidates we'd hardly seen anyone worth recalling. We were in a dark underground room that wasn't doing anything to help the mood. In a rare show of frustration, one of our producers exclaimed, "Why is this so hard?" I remember trying to smile, and saying, "Because we're trying to find a twelve-year-old who can sing like Michael Jackson." It's a big ask. MJ was an incredible singer throughout his life, but he was perhaps never more out-of-this-world-astonishing than when he was a boy. A few minutes after the producer's frustrated comment, another kid walked in, in his school uniform. We braced for another disappointment, but our jaws collectively hit the floor as this incredible, angelic voice came out. That boy was Mitchell Zhangazha, who became one of our best ever Young MJs, and when he grew up went on to play Stevie Wonder in Motown: The Musical. *I also remember a Friday afternoon during auditions for one of the early tours. We had most slots filled but hadn't quite found everything we needed. It was 4.40 in the afternoon on the final day of auditions, and there was just one last candidate left on the list. John Moabi walked in and blew everyone in the room away, singing up a storm and coming closer than anyone we've ever had to MJ's incredible rhythmic feel and delivery. Very serendipitous timing! He's been with the show for most of the eleven years since, never any less brilliant than he was when he lit up that audition room like a supernova. Of course it's wonderful when those people turn up, and we're lucky to have several who, like John, have been with us for many years. But in a funny way, I'm more proud of the cases where it took a bit more digging or a bit more time and probing to find the magic an auditioning singer would eventually bring to the show. I'd never presume to take credit for anyone's talent – that's partly God-given and partly the product of their own hard work – but I do love it when we're able to develop what someone initially presents and together turn it into something really special. One of our current lead singers first came to us straight after graduating from a course for singing actors, so the voice was heavily embedded in a musical theatre style. That's great for* Oklahoma! *or* Phantom of the Opera, *but it's not so much use for* Thriller Live! *At the first audition it was just me and Debbie O'Brien, our wonderful casting director, and we talked for a while afterwards about this singer, as we felt there might be a soulful instrument lurking deeper down. We decided a callback audition was worthwhile, and told the singer exactly what we wanted, being frank that we wanted them to move away from the 'MT' style and to capture more of MJ's rhythmic attack. When the singer returned for a work session a week or so later the change was unbelievable, and this exponential improvement continued over several more sessions. Indeed there had been a soulful voice within, and it was quite fantastic, ideal for Michael's songs. The entire panel was won over at the recall audition, and that singer is now a very highly esteemed member of our cast. It's very satisfying and rewarding when things unfold that way.*

People often ask what we're looking for in the auditions. "Square One," as Debbie has heard me say to many hundreds of vocalists, is, "your voice, MJ's phrasing." In other words, if you come in to audition, we want you to sing in your own voice, and not try to impersonate Michael. But we do look for people who 'get' MJ's style, and can capture some elements of his incredible phrasing. Phrasing is a very personal thing though, and MJ's was particularly idiosyncratic. So no-one will ever get all of it. But that's a good thing – if you could imitate his phrasing perfectly you'd be the world's best MJ impersonator. You'd never be out of work, but it wouldn't be with us. We want you to study MJ's style (we'll do loads more of that if you get into the show) and get your head around his particularly rhythmic approach to singing. Some elements will 'land' with you and osmose into your singing, and some of it just won't be organic to you. That's cool, because we need you in there too, bringing your own special sauce. What we want is to hit that sweet spot where a great singer imprints him or herself on a song, but in a way that is sympathetic to MJ's original, and which shows an understanding of what makes the song tick. Most often, that comes down to rhythm.

A lot of singers like to sit behind the beat, as they find it really helps them express themselves in a song. That works perfectly in a lot of styles of music, but if you're auditioning for this show my advice would be – don't! I reckon that MJ back-phrased maybe half a dozen times in his entire career. Most of the time he sits tightly with the rhythm section. And in his later stuff, he sometimes sings literally as a member of the rhythm section. Not many vocalists can do that – some can't break the habit of a lifetime sitting back on the beat, and others just don't have the rhythmic chops to nail it. So if the range knocks out almost all of the auditioning men and many of the women, the demands of the style knock out most of the rest. And that's before we start thinking about the look, style, charisma, experience, chemistry and other qualities that Gary and our producers require on top of the sensational voice. Like we say – it's a hard cast, and it's a hell of a tough gig for a singer to score.

Because the musical style of the show is so particular, I'll often do a few 'work sessions' with the singers between their preliminary audition and their call-back in front of the rest of the creative team. These are like rehearsals for their second audition. In those sessions we'll discuss the style in some detail and try the songs in various ways, working out the best approach for that particular singer. Very often I'll play the candidates a recording of The Jackson Five song 'Never Can Say Goodbye'. I have an a cappella recording of Michael's vocal from that track. It's a clean, unaccompanied recording of a twelve-year-old child singing a light, mid-tempo song, and you can dance to it. In fact, it makes you want to dance. Just the vocal, by itself. I play that track to the recall candidates because it tells you just about everything you need to know about how to sing Michael Jackson's songs. Make the vocals dance. Make us want to dance, with just the groove of your singing. Sounds easy, huh? If you try it, you'll find one more reason why MJ was a once-in-a-generation talent.

Another trap a lot of singers fall into is thinking they should 'riff' all over the songs, or in other words, deviate from the original melody by decorating it so constantly that it becomes almost unrecognisable. This style of singing became very popular in the nineties and noughties, particularly via singers like Mariah Carey and Christina Aguilera. While those women both have extraordinary gifts which they used to more or less create a new style, it's not an approach that sits comfortably with MJ's songs, for the most part, as by its very nature it makes the vocal line less rhythmic and less punchy. Listen to the way MJ relentlessly pounds the repeating chorus lines in 'Dirty Diana'. A riffy approach might have been more ostensibly 'impressive', but it wouldn't have captured the haunted, hunted feeling of the lyric the way Michael did. And that's what makes the song work so well. There are places in the show where we cut the singers loose and encourage them to go completely nuts, but most of the time we want them to keep things strongly rhythmic, the way the songs were originally conceived. It always seems a little presumptuous to me when a singer goes off on a riffy tangent in the first lines of their first song at their first audition, almost a little bit rude even, and it raises a red flag that they may not be able to sing with the kind of discipline and respect for the originals that we're looking for. MJ could riff like a monster, but he very, very rarely did. That's a pretty major clue.

Once we've found enough brilliant singers who can handle the songs and actually bring some of their own magic to them, it's then about combining them into a (no pun intended) harmonious team. We also have to find some equally brilliant and even more versatile singers to be their understudies. The male understudies, or 'swings', have to be able to sing all three male roles. That's a very tall order indeed, and performers with the requisite skill are very few and far between, so much so that I think of them as one of the show's most precious assets. Once everyone is assembled and we get into a rehearsal room the fun really starts. There's nothing quite like rehearsing great songs with a great singer. It's intense and exhilarating. But if there's anything I enjoy even more, it's rehearsing a whole bunch of great singers together. The back end of the show gets progressively more ensemble-based, so the vocal arrangements grow in size accordingly. Teaching each new company the intricate harmonies of 'Man in the Mirror', or the soaring wails and gospel-infused call and response of 'Earth Song' – those are some of the best times I've ever had at work. The final icing on the cake is watching that new company take to the stage, learning and growing under Gary's guidance as they embark on this challenging but richly rewarding musical journey.

Chapter Twenty-Two

Remember the Time

I met Peter at the stage door of the Lyric. It was so good to see him after all this time and he greeted me with his usual warm smile and a huge hug. "Gaaa… ry!" he said in his recognisable Australian drawl. As we both embraced, you could feel the massive amount of respect we had for one another. We had a brilliant and very creative time working together, the last time being seven years ago.

I first came into contact with Peter Andre when I was hired to direct and choreograph his big comeback tour in 2010.

Actually, that's not quite true… and here comes a confession!

In 1995, I was part of a boy band with two of my fellow actors, Gary Forbes and Darryl Paul. We were all performing in the West End long-running show Starlight Express *which is where I met the boys; they had been friends for years before that. The band was managed by my lifelong and best friend Keith Cox (who I met at Stage One theatre school) and we all wrote and produced the songs ourselves. We were called 'Access All Areas'.*

The whole thing was determined, driven and very exciting but a rather naive operation.

This was in the days of the mid-'90s where the record industry was still booming and the charts were poptastic. The days of Take That reaching their peak (the first time round) and many copycat boy bands emerging to try and achieve the same heights amidst the emergence of dance music and the excitement of these pop records being remixed by the kings of house, Todd Terry, CJ Mackintosh and the like, particularly Michael and Janet Jackson.

*Access All Areas became one of the best known touring bands in the UK **not** to get a record deal!*

We toured the country on every pop tour, radio roadshow and club gig and had a huge fan following. We also supported every act going but never quite got that break. We even performed alongside *NSYNC on a dreadful roadshow stage in the Midlands, with hardly anybody watching, in their days before any major success. We also played alongside the Spice Girls the week before 'Wannabe' hit and changed their lives forever. This was one in a long line of life lessons that really taught me everything really does happen for a reason, and every failure really comes into play at some point later in life, becoming not so much another frustrating defeat but a re-direction and a guide for what lies ahead.

Five years later, along with bestie Keith Cox again, I went on write, produce and manage another pop act, BOOM! After having offers thrown at us, including legendary Nile Rodgers wanting to write with us, we achieved an album deal, a number eleven UK hit and the experience of making that album. We spent a good year and a half collaborating with Lucas Secon, who has gone on to write and produce for (among others) Kylie, Britney Spears, Olly Murs, Toni Braxton, Mos Def, Snoop Dogg, Christina Aguilera and Travie McCoy.

Before the finished album was released, we were stunned to be dropped from the label (along with All Saints and Sugababes) when the big record giants merger thing started to happen. Again, not a huge success, but all that experience has paid dividends when dealing with various clients and contacts in the industry. To work at this level, you have to be more than a little spiritual... BOOM! struggled to get re-signed due to the birth of reality talent shows on TV, starting with Popstars *and followed swiftly by* Pop Idol, *which I became a creative on both in the UK and Germany as well as working on the first three seasons of* American Idol.

So each of these 'failures' had a part to play and most certainly had a hand in steering me towards Thriller Live!

So after meeting Peter initally in 1995 when he was a headliner on the MIZZ *magazine tour (along with Haydon Eshun when he was thirteen and in Ultimate Kaos!), our paths crossed again when I was hired to direct and choreograph his big comeback tour in 2010.*

The album was called Accelerate, *so we named the tour 'XLR8' using what was then the fresh acronymic style that was starting to become popular with the kids!*

Peter wanted a big show and he certainly got it. I came up with the creative concept and directed the show, and on the choreography, worked alongside Kenrick Sandy. Kenrick was, and still is, a wonderfully creative force who has managed to succeed in this ever-exploitative industry by remaining true to himself and his vision. This resulted in him deservedly being awarded an MBE for services to dance and the community in 2017.

The creative team also included Vince Foster, who had designed the lighting for Janet Jackson's recent 'Rock Witchu Tour' tour. We even got to use the moving bridge from Janet's tour at the rear of the stage in our design for the 'XLR8' show.

We presented the best songs on the album opening with the single 'Defender', which Kenrick choreographed. We did some old hits and I created some mash-ups with new album tracks and old favourites. Each section of the show had a concept. TEAM ANDRE – a tough militant section that showed Peter and his dancers as a unified defence force. This section included the single 'Defender'. The other sections were called FANTASY, NATURAL (a section dedicated to Pete's children) and ICON. I put together a fun and colourful section called '90s REVIVAL that used Pete's old hits 'Turn It Up', 'Natural' and 'Flava / This Is How We Do It' together with a medley of 'She's Got That Vibe / Ain't Too Proud To Beg / Two Can Play That Game'. Pete loved performing all of these songs and had his brother Michael onstage DJing for this section.

The reason I am writing in such detail about Peter's show is because of my discovery of what a huge MJ fan Peter is. We explored a lot of material as he really wanted to pay homage to our hero, and we had to get it just right.

After much discussion, Peter performed 'Human Nature', which was beautiful, and we fused 'Dirty Diana' with his song 'Outta Control'. He also did his version of 'Billie Jean', complete with a beatbox breakdown and the full dance break.

We probably spent the most time rehearsing this as he really wanted to do a good job, and he absolutely did.

Peter works so, so hard and the process of putting the show together was a very focused and enjoyable one with an amazing team, the best musicians, fantastic dancers, including my assistant, Jo Dyce. The only major issue was when we lost Pete for a couple of days when he collapsed during a production rehearsal very close to the first show. The issue was a kidney stone and we had to down tools while he rested and received treatment. Like the trooper he is, though, Pete performed that first show, missing out some of the more physical stuff, but he would not let his fans down.

Later that year, Peter was asked to sing 'Man in the Mirror' for the incredible annual televised fundraiser Children in Need, which I staged. It went down a storm.

We'd had a fantastic time working together but like everything in this business, life and other projects get in the way, so despite almost working on another tour, our paths didn't really cross professionally again after that.

So Peter coming to guest at *Thriller* was our third meeting but really chapter two in this story of our collaboration on Michael's work.

After meeting Peter and enjoying that first moment seeing him again, I took him through the stage door and down into John Maher's room where a keyboard lived permanently. John and I had gone through my thoughts of what Peter should try for the show, alongside what would work dynamically for the gala.

Pete stepped in and I introduced John. As a fellow Aussie, they naturally had a moment discussing where they were both from, how long they'd been here in the UK, etc. It was the perfect ice breaker.

We got on to what we should try out and Peter gave us his pitch: "Okay, so I was thinking, and tell me if this is crap. I thought we could do a medley of bits of songs, start with 'Billie Jean', then go into 'Rock with You', maybe 'Man in the Mirror'…"

He tailed off as he saw mine and John's expressions.

"Okay," he laughed. "Crap."

It wasn't crap or even a bad idea at all, but I went on to explain to Peter that the show is incredibly technical and with the timeframe (the show was less than a week away) we had very little time to create anything new, as much as we were up for doing so.

We decided the best idea was to talk through the show's running order and Peter could tell us what he was familiar with.

We started with 'History' and Peter proceeded to sing through every song, and brilliantly. He knew every lyric, every vocal lick and was clearly having the time of his life singing through this material. He could have quite easily appeared in every number in the show but as excited as I could see John and I were becoming, we had to choose wisely. The first choice was 'Rock with You'. A great groove, the perfect melody and feel for Pete and a relatively easy one to start with.

As I explained how we get into the *Off the Wall* material in the show, Peter then told us a lovely story of how he discovered Michael and became a lifelong fan.

At age six, the Andre family moved from the UK to Australia and to Peter's horror the music that everybody seemed to be listening to there was rock, and not just rock... Australian rock! On his next birthday, his dad gave him some money and he says he remembers running down to the record shop and buying *Off the Wall* on vinyl. He says he literally wore the record out, playing it over and over and singing along to it. During this rehearsal, there was no doubt how true this story was, as Michael's spirit came through Pete's vocals in every song he sang.

We worked through each song in order and it was so clear we could pick any of them and it would work fine for Peter.

The range was no problem (and these songs are high!) and he truly understood the style.

Despite his success, Peter is a really underestimated singer and seems to have become more of a celebrity than as a perceived artist. And in my opinion, trying to survive the industry in these times, more power to him. We live in an age where you have to find what works and stick to it, and I believe success comes to those who walk through the open doors of opportunity rather than those who insist on banging on the closed ones. This is exactly what Peter Andre has done, and standing with him, watching him work again and feel these songs, some of the most incredibly difficult songs to sing, I appreciated his talent more than ever.

Looking at John, I could see he felt the same way and after singing through 'Billie Jean' and 'Thriller', as we reached the end of the show, we had a plan.

Before working through the chosen songs in detail, John and I left Pete to warm his voice up. I brought some hot water down from the company office and Peter had brought his own lemon and manuka honey to make a tea for his voice.

Pete would sing 'She's Out of My Life' – a perfect choice to bring him out and have that moment in the spotlight, a great way to introduce the star of our show for that evening.

Continuing in the *Off the Wall* section of the show, he would then join the dancers for 'Rock with You'. This would be a thrill for the audience and for Peter, as he loves to move!

The second half would see him performing 'I Just Can't Stop Loving You' and leading 'Man in the Mirror', which, when the atmosphere was right, could really stop the show.

The session went well and we all looked forward to Peter coming back on the day to learn the staging and work with the cast. I say 'all', as the crew, who are never easily impressed, all commented on how great he was and what a good show it was going to be.

Moments after leaving the theatre, I received a message from Peter. It said, *"Love you brother, thanks so much for this. I'll make you proud."*

Tuesday came around quickly and the dancers, who are always called first, arrived early and ready to work. In the theatre, there is always an electricity in the air when working on something new, especially if a guest appearance is involved.

We started with 'Rock with You' where I taught everyone the restaging to incorporate Peter's performance, as well as adding a new section for the girls I had re-choreographed only a couple of weeks before for the tour.

The two-hour call came and went in a flash and before we knew it, Peter had arrived.

I introduced him to the cast on stage and it was amusing to see the dancers (mainly the girls, but not all!) go weak at the knees as Peter addressed them in his usual charismatic style.

It was strange to think that he (and I) are now nearly twice the age of some of these very talented kids.

After Peter has finished filling them up with positivity and love, the dancers took a break and Pete and I got to work. We had very little time to put this together and make it work.

Pete was nervous and now we were alone, it started to show.

"Do you think I should do 'I Just Can't Stop Loving You'?"; "Maybe I shouldn't do 'Rock with You'."; "How about I just do 'She's Out of My Life'?"

"Peter, you'll be fine," I reassured him. "You know this stuff like the back of your hand, I've kept the staging really simple for you and it's gonna be great." I patted him on the back and steered him towards the keyboard where John was sitting.

The other singers had started to arrive and as soon as Peter was introduced to them, he wanted to jump right in.

We started with the duet, which he would sing with the wonderful Vivienne Ekwulugo.

They launched straight into it with the band and it was beautiful. I could see Vivienne was a little nervous but as always, she held her nerve and showed nothing but assurance to Peter as they sang together. It really was a moment.

We then walked through 'She's Out of my Life', and Pete really understood all the drama within my staging, a very simple movement track but really telling the story conversationally and in an intimate way just like the record.

I then brought the dancers on and Pete was in his element. Again, I had kept this really simple for him so he could concentrate on his vocal. I brought on the stunning Sophie Usher, one of our dancers, to lead him around the stage and anchor him when we got to choreographed choruses.

She was pictured with him in the show and of course the most flirtateous looking photos were featured the next day in *OK* magazine and the tabloids.

Daily Mail: "*Peter Andre dances up a storm with Emily MacDonagh lookalike during* Thriller Live! *debut… as his wife watches in audience.*" *The Mirror*: "*Peter Andre sets pulses racing with energetic performance with female dancer – who looks just like wife Emily*," and so on.

We raced to the end of the rehearsal and after congratulating Pete, sent him off to wardrobe to run through his outfits for that evening and for him to have a well-earned break.

I then turned my attention to our guest hosts, Jon Culshaw and Russell Kane who had both just arrived and were standing with Ginette. What I haven't mentioned is that this particular performance was a special performance in aid of The Prince's Trust. Jon, Russell and Peter are all affiliated with this amazing charity, hence the importance of their involvement.

Prior to them arriving, I had spoken with Jon a fair bit and he had come in to see the show so I knew he was pretty well prepared. Russell, on the other hand, was hyper and bouncing around like a very likeable blue-arsed fly. He explained, in his excitable manner that he hadn't been told anything and had no brief whatsoever. Ginette and I handed him the cue cards that had been made in anticipation of this, and they contained the links that I had written for the pair of them.

"Listen, guys," I said. "Use these as a guide but put it all in your own words and do your thing with it."

We took them up to the stage and Russell immediately started dancing around.

"Can I do the moonwalk?" He looked at me with wide puppy dog eyes, almost panting, as he pulled the bottom of his trousers up to show off his white socks.

"Sure," I laughed as he was halfway across the stage.

We worked in a couple of little gags and ran the basic blocking, which included a poignant and very moving video from The Prince's Trust and the work they do for young disadvantaged people.

Both Jon and Russell embraced being part of this event with the same warmth and excitement as Peter and once we had run their links and they were happy, they went off to get ready for the show.

The show got off to a great start with loads of energy from both hosts and, despite calling Jon a 'bell end', some great ad-libbing from Russell.

The cast, band and crew were all psyched, of course, and they delivered nothing less than a stellar opening performance. Peter paced up and down behind me in the wings, watching each number from either the side or on the monitor on the prompt desk. I guided him on for each appearance he made but he needed no more support than that. It was like he had performed with us for the last ten years, and singing these songs like he had been singing them his whole life. Of course, the latter was true.

He made all the cast and each audience member feel special when he was out there, a gift he is blessed with, and this Michael fan was clearly having the time of his life performing his idol's songs on our stage.

The reviews were all extremely positive the next day, all calling Peter's performance, 'heartfelt', 'on point'. "***** *Peter Andre was flawless, after delivering a very moving 'She's Out of My Life', he had the audience at fever pitch with an incredible rendition of 'Man in the Mirror'*," and praising the show itself more than ever before: "***** *5 stars for Thriller Live #4000. Thriller Live is the experience of a lifetime. The passion, the intensity and true love for this show from all involved… There is nothing that needs to be perfected it cracks it every time. I'm not sure it could ever be beaten.*"

We were all ecstatic at the response and hoping that the enthusiasm Peter had to come back and perform some more shows with us wouldn't wane so we could jump on that opportunity with him.

His presence had such a positive effect on the cast and the show, it would be a shame for it just to be a one time only affair.

Peter had an offer to play Billy Flynn in *Chicago* at 10am the following morning.

Needless to say, he will be appearing as our special guest on certain shows throughout 2020.

Chapter Twenty-Three

Blood on the Dance Floor

Shortly after the 4,000th gala and the hype that surrounded us, we were all in again, this time filming something for BBC's *Strictly Come Dancing*.

It was Halloween week (always a good week for us!) and we had been asked to put something together for Oti Mabuse, who was the pro dancer and Graeme Swann, ex-cricketer and Oti's celebrity contestant this year. They were, of course, performing 'Thriller'.

It was yet another early start for the team but everyone involved arrived less than zombie-like to work on another version of the 'Thriller' routine.

The camera crew were already setting up and I caught up with the director about what he wished to achieve in this rather short shoot.

The *Strictly* dancers have the most insane schedule, spending every day of the week rehearsing with their celeb partner on whatever dance has been allocated to them that week. This has to fit in with their schedule and sometimes they rehearse well into the night. On top of this, there are rehearsals with their pro partner and the rest of the pros for the group dances and various performance slots.

The further they get in the competition, the bigger the workload and therefore the longer the rehearsals.

As another hero of mine, Debbie Allen, famously said, *"You want fame, well, fame costs and right here's where you start paying... in sweat!"*

A mantra most dancers are more than familiar with.

The shoot was a ligh- hearted one. The dancers were really on it and once Oti and Graham arrived we were ready to shoot.

They were in great spirits and Graham spent the whole time goofing around and having fun.

You could see they were both tired. The show was mid-season and the rehearsals and all the extra B-roll filming was taking its toll. Nevertheless, Oti made him show us their routine which received a huge response from our enthusiastic cast and then we got to work. We got some great shots of the two of them learning the main elements of the Thriller routine and a fantastic final shot with Graham, as Michael, hitting the air as the zombies all fell to the floor around him.

Off camera, I gave Oti some pointers on some of the moves to ensure they were a little more authentic, which I was pleased to see them execute really well on the night.

Unfortunately, it wasn't their best performance. The 'scene' began in the cinema with them eating popcorn and looking up at the screen. They then jumped up and went straight into the ('Thriller') dance break, peppering in elements of the cha-cha and over the top reactions to the lyrics.

Graeme did a rather impressive moonwalk right before the chorus but seemed to be concentrating more on the Michael/zombie elements rather than any of the technical elements of the cha-cha. They landed in the bottom two 'dance-off' for the first time, really highlighting how difficult it is to deliver a technically precise Latin dance when trying to stay in such strong, specific characters.

Thankfully, they stayed in the competition for another couple of weeks and we got some fantastic exposure for the show.

Chapter Twenty-Four

Invincible

The conversations around what we would do for our upcoming tenth anniversary came thick and fast. The recent 4,000th gala had become a vehicle to try and achieve many things. Building on our relationship with The Prince's Trust, lining up the best guests we could and having The Prince's Trust ambassadors Jon Culshaw and Russell Kane, with Peter Andre performing, meant we sold some tickets to support an exceptionally worthy charity and got some serious press exposure, but it also took some organising!

It was a wonderful event and it kept the excitement in the theatre for quite some time, even getting everybody through the heavy Christmas show schedule which is a gruelling time in any West End show's calendar. But when asked about the tenth anniversary, I really wanted to do something that was about the company – the people in the show, in front of, and behind the curtain.

We had the most exciting cast on stage at this time (*see cast list at the back of the book to see the 2018/2019 company*) and they were seriously dedicated to the show and all these milestones they were honoured to be part of. None of us creators have ever taken a day for granted on this show and this cast followed suit.

I spoke with Ginette, head of marketing at Flying Music. Ginette and I usually started the process together on these mega dates in the diary, plotting and planning what incredible feats we would suggest and hopefully achieve. We very rarely ticked every box on our wishlist, but this time we were both in agreement, this one had to be about the performers… the *Thriller* family.

We started with the original cast. What a coup to get everyone back together, a photo op of that original line up, and while researching this, started to build a list of everyone that had ever been in the show *(again, see cast lists at the back of the book).*

We soon discovered that not everyone from the original cast was around and we had Kieran Alleyne, our very first Young Michael, out on tour playing the adult lead.

Still we had a few thoughts up our sleeve. I reached out to Layton Williams, one of our first four boys who played Michael as a child. Layton had just played the first black Billy Elliot in the West End and came straight to us from that show.

To my delight, Layton responded almost instantly with a really enthusiastic, "I would love to be a part of this, count me in!"

It was crazy to think that ten years had passed since Layton appeared in the show.

Unfortunately, Layton did not have the best time. Our big press story, coming from *Billy Elliot* as the first black boy to play the role and who was wowing us in the rehearsal room, got a cold over Christmas right before we went into technical rehearsals.

We have come to learn that boys of a certain age, when their voice is ready to break, a virus or cold can literally cause the voice to start changing, and this is what happened to Layton.

The poor boy suddenly started finding it hard to sing almost any of the material and we were forced to think about a plan B.

Little Sterling Williams opened our first preview and Kieran Alleyne, the least experienced and the underdog in this race, became our opening night star.

Previews were tense as we tested out each boy in front of our new West End audience. Layton became increasingly nervous as we delicately rehearsed his material each day.

We decided we had to put him on stage to ease his anxiety and perhaps find out once and for all whether his voice may be breaking, which was all our prediction.

We gave him a Saturday matinee and took great care getting him ready, both practically and mentally. Having already had such massive exposure on *Billy* and tons of experience in successful British TV comedy *Beautiful People*, Layton knew how to prepare for a show and presented with great confidence and bravado through warm up and the build up to the show.

"Are you ready?" I put a gentle yet supportive hand on his shoulder as we stood in the wings waiting for his cue. Layton nodded, still staring out on to the stage, a steely determination taking over him as he prepared to discover what lay ahead.

He got through the first number, the sweet 'Music and Me', fine. OK – we're off!

I stayed in the stage wing for support and to be there in case Layton froze or the voice just didn't come out of him.

Kieran was fully dressed and on standby. This was normal procedure with the children who covered each other.

'I Want You Back' started and Layton looked fantastic performing that iconic opening few steps.

The song started and the vocal once again was okay, a little husky but good. As the song progressed and we moved into 'ABC', I could hear there were problems. Layton's voice began to dip and drop, and he was clearly struggling.

I was on the opposite side of the stage to Kieran and his chaperone, so although I was thinking about swapping them over, I couldn't really do anything about it.

At that moment, I glanced back to the stage where Layton began to dance, and not the choreography from the show. It was like Billy

Elliot had possessed him and he pirouetted and leapt around the stage like a beautiful ballerina. Trouble was, it just wasn't Michael.

I ripped a sheet of A4 from my notebook and grabbed a Sharpie from the crew table.

'COME OFF STAGE – KIERAN ON FOR BEN (the song)' I wrote in huge letters and waved it around so Layton and Yasmin the resident director, the chaperone ... anyone, would see it!

Back in those days, the boys sang a lot and all in one section of the show, it was incredibly challenging for them.

By the time we got to 'The Love You Save', Layton was singing everything down the octave and still dancing around, albeit brilliantly, to cover how embarrassed he must have felt that he was sounding more like Jermaine than Michael.

High kicks, backbends (and can this boy high kick and backbend!) and spins across the stage. This had now become more Baryshnikov than Jackson!

We managed to get Layton off the stage and swapped with Kieran for the song 'Ben'.

Layton slumped onto the stairs as he came off. "Was it awful?" he cried.

The poor boy was devastated.

That day Layton left the building and I didn't see him again for what must have been at least five years. However, not a day went by in that theatre where I didn't think about him and those early days.

The wonderful end to this story is that Layton has had the most buoyant and successful career and on this day was rehearsing to take over the leading role of 'Jamie' in the latest West End sensation *Everybody's Talking About Jamie*. This followed a string of leading roles in *RENT* and TV's *Bad Education* and the brilliant comedy *Benidorm*, written by my old friend Derren Litten, among other hit shows.

On arriving at the theatre, Layton and I literally bumped into each other, had huge hugs and I thanked him for agreeing to take part. He had just finished a rehearsal with John Maher and was vocally ready for his guest appearance but yet to do his staging rehearsal.

He held on to me, looked me square in the eye and said, "Thank you, this has given me closure like you wouldn't believe."

My heart broke and my eyes filled with tears. The thought that he had been carrying that experience for ten years was devastating to me. But of course it made sense. A born performer like Layton, to have to go through something that, which must have felt more humiliating than it actually was, is devastating. Experiences like that stay with you forever.

We hugged again and said we would see him at 5pm when his *Jamie* rehearsal next door at the Apollo theatre had finished.

My next stop and original member to contact was Ben Forster.

Now quite a celebrity, not many people realise that Ben began his West End career as a leading man with us as our original Man 3. *(He appeared at twenty years old in the ensemble* La Cava, *a musical written by Larry O'Keefe who I collaborated with recently on the European premiere of* Heathers the Musical, *so we were not quite his West End debut.)* And fewer people know that I met Ben while teaching and choreographing at the famous Italia Conti stage school in the mid-'90s.

Ben did his three-year musical theatre training there.

I remember his first day, which happened to be an audition for an end of term production of *FAME* we were doing, and a show I went on to direct and choreograph twice after that. He could not put one foot in front of the other!

I remember the studio full of determined young dancers, each one giving their all and I could see over the sea of heads, all whipping and turning in perfect synchronicity, a dark headed figure at the back of the room by the window, several beats behind and looking terribly confused. It was Ben.

I fought my way through the sweaty crowd and looked at him. He smiled that famous smile.

"Are you okay?" I said.

"Nooo!" he sang in his Geordie lilt. "I'm not, I can't dance!" he said, still smiling.

We spent some time breaking it down and he still struggled, but his good humour and determination got him through that audition, through that three-year course and got him where he is today.

Needless to say when we finally heard that voice, no-one had to ask why he had been awarded a place at the college.

He has come a long way since those days in Goswell Road.

Also during that time, one of my students was a young Daniel Mays, who has since gone on to enjoy an incredible career as one of our finest screen actors. A list that is way too long to mention, the star of *Vera Drake*, *Made In Dagenham*, *Mrs Biggs*, *Line of Duty*, *Rogue One* and more recently *Fisherman's Friends,* would kill me for spilling that my strongest memory of him was his impersonation of Michael Jackson which he busted out in class one day. Not just an impersonation, Dan, (and he won't mind me saying this) while at college was not the best dancer at all and 'played' Michael in my recreation of the 'Blood on the Dance Floor' music video in another end of year show at Italia Conti.

To see him go on to such great heights makes me very proud to have worked with such a lovely guy and I am impressed he has kept his moonwalking past a secret... until now.

In the meantime, Ben has spent the last six years enjoying the spotlight after winning Andrew Lloyd Webber's *Superstar* talent show on BBC TV. This followed a string of similar shows where Andrew produced new productions of *Oliver!*, *The Sound of Music* and *Joseph and the Amazing Technicolour Dreamcoat*. These shows were designed to 'discover' young unknowns to launch in these shows and did make stars of Lee Mead, Jodie Prenger and Danielle Hope, all of whom have enjoyed very successful theatre and, on occasion, TV careers.

Superstar was the latest and a much slicker, tougher version of the aforementioned.

All males were competing for the role of 'Jesus' and featuring ex-*Thriller* singers, Roger Wright, Nathan James and Ben Forster, who all made it to the final five.

The two left in the final were Ben and Rory Taylor, an incredible vocalist who is now touring as Man 3, Ben's original role on our tour, and has been for a number of years and made the role completely his own.

In *Superstar*, Rory and Ben were both audience favourites, clearly good guys as well as insanely talented.

I was personally so happy these two made it to the end and even more thrilled that Ben won the crown. It wasn't until the other night, when watching the first half of the show with Ben, I discovered the winning song 'Who Wants to Live Forever' by Queen was designated to Rory.

When Ben showed dislike for his song, 'I Don't Want to Miss a Thing' by Aerosmith, Rory simply turned to him and said, "Okay, mate, I'll swap with you."

I was shocked to hear this so long after the fact, but it didn't surprise me of Rory, a really genuine, warmhearted guy who is generous to a fault. I guess they will never know whether it was the song choice or the performance that did it on that final night.

Rory went on to play 'Simon Zealotes' in the Australian tour of *Jesus Christ Superstar*, along with Ben playing 'Jesus' and the Spice Girls' Mel C playing 'Mary Magdalene'.

Ben went on to play Jesus for two years around the world, the leading role in *Elf – the Musical*, 'Brad' in *The Rocky Horror Show* and probably his greatest role, the coveted 'Phantom' in Lloyd Webber's *Phantom of the Opera*. The boy has done better than good and I am immensely proud of him.

Ben responded to my email almost instantly:

Gary!!!!!!

Sorry for the delay. I'm in Japan. Been crazy busy doing the first show.

Of course I'd love to come and be involved... can you remind me what the white section is!??? Oh god. It's been too long. Also I just want to add I had a broken leg and back this year so it's hard for me to be physical or dance. Is the white section just walking on and singing!!? Haha sorry to be old and fussy. I just don't wanna say yes get there and find out it's too difficult and annoy everyone !

Hope you're well!!!! X x

I smiled. This was so Ben, but I was horrified to hear about the broken leg and broken back.

Apparently the leg was so badly broken, the doctors didn't check for anything else and the back repaired itself while Ben was laid up recovering from the broken leg!

He still has lower disc issues but thankfully has made a full recovery.

Anything to get out of dancing!

We continued chatting and Ben made it back from Japan in one piece and into the theatre to work with John Maher.

The plan was for this evening to be as low maintenance as possible. It had been a busy year with the 4,000th among other things, so we planned to rehearse everything (apart from 'Ben') on the day.

On my way into the theatre, I noticed a flurry on social media from the fans all talking about our show and wishing us luck but also simultaneously discussing an upcoming documentary to be shown at the Sundance festival called *Leaving Neverland*. Michael's nephew Taj Jackson was leading a very strong campaign against this HBO-made documentary which features Wade Robson and Jimmy Safechuck coming out to tell 'their truth' about years of so-called abuse by Michael.

There has been much added to the dialogue within this campaign showing the contradictions Robson and Safechuck have displayed since defending Michael in court previously.

At time of writing, the documentary is yet to be released and so the global response is unknown.

However, knowing this was about to surface, it was yet another affecting moment walking into the theatre that day.

The rehearsal was made up of soundchecking Ben into 'Man in the Mirror' and 'Heal the World'. 'Heal the World' hadn't been in the show for quite some time so we had to teach the song and its simple staging to the current cast ahead of the ex-cast members arriving later that afternoon.

I also had to rehearse with John, the vocal that would be split with Layton and Mitchell, introducing three of our young MJs, the third being Eshan Gopal. Eshan was with us for probably the longest period of time as a young MJ and even went on to play Michael around the corner at the Shaftesbury Theatre in *Motown the Musical*. Eshan has always been a shining light of a boy, able to master the performance of Michael at eleven years old, but can also give our older male dancers a run for their money when busting out the 'Billie Jean' dance break. While at *Thriller*, he hardly ever grew and his voice, which always rang like a bell, remained pure and untouched throughout his time with us. Imagine my shock, then, when I opened John's door to walk in and witness this tall teenager, dressed in a black track suit and sporting the start of some growth on his top lip.

"Wow! What happened to you?" I exclaimed as I walked in. Poor Eshan smiled uncomfortably like any teenage boy going through these changes. I wasn't used to seeing this usually over-confident boy embarrassed by anything. I teased him about his facial hair and we talked briefly about what he was up to and then we got down to business. His voice was breaking so we had to be careful about which part he sang as his range had definitely changed. Eshan could, however, still really sing, and John and I gave each other a knowing look. We couldn't wait for him to grow and develop vocally so we could get him in to see us as an adult when his voice had fully developed.

The rehearsal on stage continued as we took Eshan to join the rest of the company to run the whole thing with the band.

When we got out on stage, Aisling Duffy, our long-time resident director was running 'Heal the World' with the current cast in her usual calm, collected manner as all the ex-cast members started to arrive.

It was so weird and wonderful to watch all these faces arriving in the very building we opened in ten years ago, each face sparking a different memory. It was also interesting to see which ones gravitated towards one another and who had done the show with who. There was an almost kinetic energy already starting to fizz in the air.

This part of the day-long rehearsal consisted of a mini reunion and staging the ex-cast members onto the stage. They were as unruly as they always were and naturally falling back into old habits and dynamics, particularly the boys. It was wonderful to see but curious to have that energy back in the building as, over the years, discipline has become much tighter and something we have become really proud of.

The current cast watched on in amazement while going over their staging, as 'Heal the World' is no longer in the show. A new experience for them for this one-off performance. The singers, including Ben, arrived from their vocal call and got into their microphones, band were in position and we got ready to begin. Lastly Mitchell and Eshan joined and the band played the opening chords of 'Heal the World'.

Our current cast line up was made up of John Moabi and Haydon Eshun, both male leads with the show since 2008 and 2009 respectively, David Julien and Vivienne Ekwulugo.

John Moabi started to recite the new intro I had written for him:

We have had the privilege to stand here for the last ten years paying tribute to this amazing artist we all hold dear to our hearts. Over 200 performers have graced this stage with their talent and on this very special night, we would like to share that stage with them once again.

Please put your hands together as we give you, from the past ten years, the companies of Thriller Live!

John and Haydon looked at each other, and then at me. I could see they were both already feeling emotional. Both of them have invested so much in the show with a lot of the people standing around them and these moments always elicit a myriad of feelings and memories. Every time we did anything like this, there was an unspoken throwback to the night Michael passed, where we all performed this song for him.

We rehearsed the song a couple of times with Mitchell and Eshan, Mitchell singing in for Layton who had not yet arrived from his tech rehearsal for *Jamie*.

The boys were great, as always, turning out a performance in one 'take'.

We continued to run it gratuitously, as we waited.

When I got word that Layton had arrived, I ran round to the stage entrance and escorted Layton, who was breathless and sweating from his rehearsal, through to the stage.

It was like a scene from a fly on the wall film documenting an artist running through the backstage, passing each of the key individuals, from the sound department handing him his microphone, stage management guiding him through to the centre of the screens where he would his entrance, and lastly myself, taking Layton out onto a full stage of people he either didn't know at all or hadn't seen for a very long time.

I paused as Layton took a breath, scanned the area and processed very quickly what he had to do.

We had no time – the call was about to end on stage and Layton was needed back next door to complete his own *Jamie* rehearsal.

The moment was palpable, Layton's senses on overdrive as he took in the space, a stage he had not stood on for over ten years in one of the most traumatic chapters of his life, suddenly realising this journey was to reach completion in a matter of hours.

"Let's do this," he said.

We took a brief moment to talk through the staging, then we got to it.

Like the other boys, as well as being a fighter, Layton was a true pro and this last run went as smoothly as the rest.

During this one though, I happened to look over to see that Sterling Williams, another of our original Young Michaels had arrived and joined on one of the lines.

I almost didn't recognise him having not seen him since he left the show in 2011, but then he grinned at me and I saw those glistening green eyes. Unmistakably Sterling.

The rehearsal came to an end and after hugs and a few tears, Layton ran back to the Apollo and the other alumni and current cast went their separate ways and onto their break.

Noise came from the dressing room as everyone arrived outside. There were crowds of friends, family and fans at the stage door and out the front of the theatre. The atmosphere was electric but so full of warmth as the feeling of this celebration was spread throughout the waiting audience. This atmosphere was made only more special by the unexpected appearance of – snow!

The waiting crowds gleefully dispersed as the pure white feather-like jewels fell, turning everyone into children, their joyful shouts and squeals spilling into the theatre creating a pre-show soundtrack like no other. This moment in time was already one to cherish and the show hadn't even started yet.

Ordinarily, on one of these performances, I would feel frantic by now, worrying about our guests, their whereabouts and would they remember all we had rehearsed?

This time, the decision to only use the fabric of the show itself, our cast – past and present – meant I could actually watch the show from out front, along with the rest of our audience.

This night's audience was made up of other cast members, their family, friends and, of course, fans of the show.

On my way to my seat I saw and was able to greet many familar and friendly faces (the satisfaction of this reunion just kept on giving), and this included seeing Adrian and Denise Pearson. Adrian and I shared a congratulatory hug and a brief discussion about our speeches which were to happen later on during the show. I turned to Denise and we held each other tight, always so happy to see one another. Denise looked at me with that ever-enthusiastic look. "So, do you want me to sing 'Man in the Mirror'?" I could have killed her. It was 19.25. The show started at 19.30. I had been asking for weeks and my dream was to get our original line up (or as close as possible) on stage to sing 'Man in the Mirror' together. Truth be told, for me (and most of the performers that shared a stage with Denise), Denise WAS *Thriller*. She was the closest thing to Michael and the Jackson family we had ever had performing their material and she had god-like status.

"You are kidding me, right?" I said, laughing, "It's too late. We have spent all afternoon rehearsing and I can't do that to everyone involved, I'm sorry."

Denise could have gone on that stage, no rehearsal, winged the performance and absolutely brought the house down, but the amount of other people it involved, it just wouldn't be fair to drop this on them.

"Enjoy the show," I sang as they took their seats, followed by a huge sigh and then under my breath, "Damn…" as I ran up to my seat.

The show began to huge anticipatory whoops and cheers from the stalls where the *Thriller* 'family' were all seated. This ricocheted up through the circles and balcony and sitting in one of the boxes, I was able to see all of it.

Looking down on the sea of faces from our rich history, hearing and feeling their enjoyment at the onstage performance but also the shouts and cheers to those things in the show that triggered nostalgic reactions, made me very proud. I found Denise and Adrian in the stalls, who were clearly loving the show, Denise mouthing every word. This cast were once again putting on a hyped yet perfectly controlled show despite their nerves and the distractions of a very rowdy crowd!

Little did they realise, in my eyes, they were really showing how this show should be done. This cast could not be a better group for us to celebrate and promote our tenth anniversary in the West End and I sat there feeling immense gratitude towards each and everyone of them.

Ben Forster, who had been sitting in the box next to us, suddenly appeared around the 'corner', holding up his champagne glass for a 'cheers'. "It's amazing," he yelled over the music, like we were in a nightclub, during 'Shake Your Body' – a part where the audience are asked to stand up and share their groove. He was able to watch the first half from out front as his appearance took place only in the second half.

When we got to the White section and in particular, 'Heal the World', I was emotionally transported back to June 26th 2009. An echo of the night where we all paid tribute, in shock, to Michael Jackson and his passing. The night where we sang this song in tears, filling the stage with love for Michael and each other. This night was no different and, although a more jubilant celebration, we were still able to recognise that feeling of loss.

Producer Paul Walden started the speeches by thanking everybody on stage and involved in the production.

I spoke after Adrian but went on for quite a while, continuing to thank the team, the family and the audiences for all their contributions to the last ten years.

Adrian's speech, however, was about Michael, and as a parting note to us all on our tenth anniversary celebration and on the eve of what Channel 4 were about to air, could not have been more poignant.

This show is thanks to a twenty-one-year relationship that I had with Michael Jackson, working with him since I started a fan magazine in 1988 – Michael was the most giving person I know, he was the kindest person I know [breaks down – audience cheered]. He opened his doors to me and his world when I was just twenty-one, the first time I went to Neverland.

This may take a few minutes, this story, but Michael gave me his time so we are going to give our time to him because we're all here because of Michael Jackson.

Like I said, I started the fan magazine back in 1988 and I sent it to Michael's management, they loved it, they said Michael loves your magazine, I sent it to him regularly, he gave his feedback. And in 1990 I was invited over to Los Angeles where he was recording the Dangerous *album. And I went to Westlake studios. Michael walked into the room – he was wearing a fedora, shirt – he looked incredible. He was singing acapella, he sounded incredible. He walked into the room. He thanked me for producing the magazine – I thanked him for being Michael Jackson [audience laugh] and from that point on we got on really well. I sat down in the studio with him, he played me some songs from the album he'd recorded, I interviewed him. I asked if I could take some pictures – his management said, "No, you can't take any pictures." Michael said, "No, it's fine, you can take some pictures for the magazine." 'Cause Michael was understanding that, [you know] he had a fanbase, he had people that loved him since the age of eleven, and he wanted to give back to them. And the work I was doing was giving back to his fans, so Michael was very supportive of the work that I did.*

I'll just tell you a couple of stories about that time.

New York when he was recording the HIStory *album. There's me in the studio, there's Jimmy Jam and Terry Lewis, there's Janet Jackson, there's Lisa Marie Presley and Lisa says, "Who's he?" and Michael says, "He's the guy. He's the one that puts my fan magazine together, and he supports me through all this and he puts these books together." [holds up his books and opens the front page of* The Visual Documentary *showing a written note from Michael – audience cheer]*

This is a book that I wrote in 1994 about Michael. And Michael signed it and he said, "Adrian, with heartfelt appreciation, [Adrian has to look at the writing, getting another affectionate laugh from the audience] for all your hard work on my behalf, love Michael Jackson."

The key thing here is 'hard work'. Everyone here has worked really hard to get where they are. All the dancers, all the crew, all the musicians, all the singers have worked really hard. I worked hard for twenty-one years to get to this point to create a show about Michael Jackson. When I first came up with the idea, people said I was crazy, people said it wouldn't happen and it wouldn't work. I put the first show on at the Dominion theatre had a great team – with Kerys Nathan who's not here, thank you, Kerys, for being the director of the first show. Thank you, Jonathan Park, for the set idea. I had a great team of people, Yasmin, who was involved with the first production and we worked really hard for four weeks to put the first production together. It wasn't perfect but we put everything into it. I put everything into it and the end I had nothing left. Flying Music were in the audience, they loved the show and from 2007 we started touring the production together.

The last story – I could go on for ages, I met Michael so many times, he was such an amazing, giving person. He was like, so supportive, but the last time I spoke to Michael, I said, "Michael, y'know people are writing these stories about you, why don't you be open and honest and come out and say something about all these negative stories about you," and he said, "No matter what I say, no matter what I do, they are always gonna write bad stuff about me." And I remember having conversations like, one time we were in the studio together and he had a pimple on his skin and he was really embarrassed about it and I said, "Don't worry about it, Michael, you look great," and he said, "Do I?" and he cancelled his photo shoot just for that day and then he said, "Sorry about this, Adrian." And then a few months later he flew me back out to Chicago and we did the photo shoot and that's the kind of person he was. So [looking up] thank you, Michael Jackson. I just want people to know that he was down to earth, he was kind, he was funny, he was intelligent. I miss him. But every day I'm reminded of his brilliance because of this fantastic cast that we have, and thank you for your support.

Adrian Grant – January 22nd 2019

Conclusion

This book has taken ten years on the road, building the memories of each story and then a good two years to compile these stories and sit down to write it. I could have written a book about directing *Fame the Musical, Grease,* or any of those other shows I have worked on, had great fun with and been truly invested in at the time. But the reason people who do my job don't write books about everything they work on is because they are just jobs. Those of us lucky enough to work on wonderful shows created by the best to last the test of time are still only fulfilling part of the director's job description. A show is a show, some more life-impacting than others, but you very rarely get given the gift of a project where you already have a lifelong affinity and passion for its subject. That's what makes *Thriller* different to anything else I have ever worked on and why being IN the show is different to anything else any of us have worked on before.

You could write a fascinating book about *Les Miserables* the musical because it has such an emotional history as a show and such alluring, record-breaking success, but none of us can personally relate to the French Revolution.

I feel that *Thriller Live!* connects pop culture with theatre in a way that a lot of the other jukebox musicals cannot do. *Mamma Mia!,* for instance – a show that me and my family adore for its soundtrack, its story and its sing-a-long entertainment value – doesn't achieve that same connection, because it is not about ABBA. *Thriller*, although not quite a musical in it's fullest form, allows the audience to experience Michael Jackson's legend within it's mini-musical content and all the different characters and fantasies that he created.

For lovers of his music, for those that want to relive every moment shared with Michael, whether live or through record player or Sony walkman speakers, it is complete and stands shoulder to shoulder alongside the other jukebox staples that have come and gone over the last ten years. The heart of *Thriller Live!* is the rich fabric of Michael's work, his songs, the production, his style and the outfits, the hairstyles, all created by every fibre of Michael's being and with us, the fans can share this with their families and sing the songs that created the sound of their youth.

We are the positive, representing Michael as an artist, not a superstar wacko or weirdo, and using every day this show is still running to perfect his iconography and maintain his legacy. This music and all its characters create a musical show of its own that is more relevant to Michael's life and what he left behind than any biography could.

Working as a director and choreographer in this industry that is ever-progressively fusing commercial with classic and 'legitimate' art is difficult, and presents what I call the 'music lover's lament'. I have spent my life collecting, loving and listening to music, but when you work with artists or on their material for long periods of time, it can really create a vicious counterpoint that is not always welcome.

Having worked with certain artists that are not that pleasant (no names mentioned in this book) you sometimes just don't want to listen to their music anymore. Thankfully, working with some of my heroes such as Paul McCartney, Giorgio Moroder and dear friend Jennifer Hudson, this was not the case. Alternatively, working as a creative for years on shows like *X Factor* and *American Idol* (for which I am extremely grateful), there are only so many times you can hear 'Ain't

No Mountain High Enough' without wanting to close your iTunes account, change course and become an accountant!

Working on *Thriller Live!* and on Michael's material, there is no counterpoint. It is a harmonious parallel, a relationship of pure sync and a journey of discovery. The train is still running and we are all very much still on it. Learning, loving and collecting, carefully transferring that knowledge with the gentle precision and control of a seasoned stamp or butterfly collector. Those things we never heard before, soaking up that production and listening or looking out for something new. Those delicate petals of gold, floating naturally into our ether and deep into our psyche. After ten-plus years of the conscious and the more 'by osmosis' method of studying Michael, the Jackson family and all that comes with it, I am still hungry for more.

I would love for us all to experience another ten, twenty, thirty years on *Thriller Live!* but whatever happens, I still consider my role blissfully complicit in representing this legacy and all I have learned, a gift. A gift never to be taken for granted.

I look back at myself and my mission statement to the original cast.
    "…enjoy every moment as it may only last a couple of weeks."

Since the 25th of June 2009, I have felt nothing but gratitude and love to the fans and families who come to appreciate our work and to all my *Thriller* family that make it happen.

Thriller Live! has performed around the globe in thirty-seven countries, five continents, to five million people, achieving 7,000 performances and £120 million at the box office

However there will only ever be, one Michael Jackson.

Our History

16.08.2006: *Thriller Live!* – the first-ever show at the Dominion Theatre, London.

18.03.2007: First official tour of *Thriller Live!* hits the road.

27.03.2008: First tour of *Thriller Live!* directed and choreographed by Gary Lloyd.

02.01.2009: *Thriller Live!* opens at the Lyric Theatre, Shaftesbury Avenue, London.

04.03.2009: Michael Jackson announces 'This Is It', a run of ten concerts at the O2 Arena, London.

25.06.2009: Michael Jackson dies.

07.07.2009: Michael Jackson memorial, held at the Stapes Center, Los Angeles. Original *Thriller Live!* 'Young MJ', Shaheen Jafargholi, sings 'Who's Lovin' You'.

12.07.2009: T4 – *The World's Greatest Popstars: Michael Jackson*. Presented by Ne-Yo.

This was probably the first of many featured TV appearances we have been asked to do over the years. Pop star Ne-Yo was to present the hour long tribute to Michael Jackson as part of the T4 show *The World's Greatest Popstars*. Together with Ne-Yo, we were to rehearse and record a thirty to fourty-five second edit of the 'Thriller' dance break with zombies around the stage trap. Ne-Yo appeared coming up through the trap, and introduced the show as well as performing various links in different locations around the theatre. Ne-Yo interviewed Ricko Baird about his connection with Michael.

Kieran Alleyne also appeared as young Michael.

Dancers who appeared were: Jo Dyce, Kamilah Beckles, Christabelle Field, Samantha Jackson, Yasmin Yazdi, Lee Alexander, Jordan Darrell, Lewis Davies, Elliot James.

October 2009: *Thriller Live!* first UK arena tour.

28.10.2009: *This Is It* premiere.

13.03.2010: In March 2010, we were asked by the Make a Wish Foundation, on behalf of Hollywood actress Eva Longoria, to appear at their benefit fundraiser at the Dorchester Hotel in London.

20.06.2010: Unveiling of Michael Jackson memorial at the Lyric Theatre.

To honour the first anniversary of Michael's passing, GMTV approached us to perform for their item on the show. We filmed from the theatre and performed our Jackson Five medley as well as Ricko Baird performing a segment of 'Smooth Criminal' to include the moonwalk.

Written by Thriller Live! PR Kevin Wilson at the time:

A big thank you from GMTV and from myself for everyone's hard work and early start this morning.

I have watched back the tape and we had sixteen name checks for Thriller Live! *at the Lyric Theatre between 6.00am and 9.20am, two full performances of 'ABC', Ricko teaching Kate Garraway to moonwalk and two splendid interviews by Rick and one with Adrian – we even had the TV review on our sofa with the cast of* Thriller *joining in!!*

The programme opened on the street and followed Kate into the foyer as she revealed the memorial to the TV audience.

The memorial was unveiled by myself, Adrian Grant, Mitchell Zhangazha and Perri Kiely from Diversity.

This also from Nekesa Mumbi Moody – *Associated Press.*
Published in the *San Franciscio Advertiser*:
Memorials, vigils and parties planned for King of Pop one year later.
By: Nekesa Mumbi Moody
Associated Press
06/24/10 9:05 PM PDT

Performers from the Thriller Live! *show pose for photographers next to the commemorative plaque to mark the anniversary of the death of US performer Michael Jackson, as it is unveiled at the Lyric Theatre in London's West End, Thursday, June 24, 2010. After his death on June 25, 2009, the Lyric Theatre has become a focus for fans who created a shrine of flowers, candles, and tributes as it is the home to the* Thriller Live! *show celebrating the music of Jackson and the Jackson Five.*

13.03.2011: The 2011 Olivier Awards.

Thriller Live! was nominated for the Olivier Awards Audience Award and we got involved in the promotion for this alongside the other major West End nominees: *Phantom of the Opera, Les Miserables, Wicked* and *Jersey Boys.* We were nominated for this award for the next four years.

27.05.2011: Boy band Blue appear on the show to help celebrate our 1,000th performance.

I spent the early part of 2011 working together with the BBC and boy band Blue, putting together their creative and choreography for our UK Eurovision entry performance that year.

Blue were to represent and the song was called 'I Can', written by Duncan James and Lee Ryan with Ciaron Bell, Ben Collier, Ian Hope, Liam Keenan and Norwegian production team StarSign.

We came eleventh in the competition (not bad going, compared to some) and the single peaked at a disappointing number sixteen in the UK Top 40 chart. After already selling fourteen million records globally, the band were not too disheartened.

What most people don't realise is how consuming the Eurovision machine is. There is an incredible amount of pre-production and promotion that has to happen in the UK, which is nothing compared to the schedule when you reach the country hosting the contest.

In the week leading up to the big event, there are constant personal appearances, a multitude of daily interviews and a million rehearsals! The pressure builds, the team gets closer and closer and after all that work it is remarkable, yet understandable how attached you get to the idea of doing well, even winning, after all the work put in. Of course, for a lot of the other countries involved in the competition, doing well affects more than just their pride and can be quite a political experience for some.

After the bubble burst and we returned to the UK, I continued working with Blue on their next tour.

Back at *Thriller*, when looking for something different to commemorate our 1,000th performance, I suggested Blue.

They were up for it and the producers liked the idea so away we went working on some stuff.

Blue were to perform 'Man in the Mirror' – a relatively easy song to hand to special guests and an easy one to stage.

What we didn't expect was the response. The boys were revealed behind the screen and when they were introduced, the audience screamed for what must have been the whole of the intro.

The problem was, none of the boys could hear the music. None of us thought of them using their in-ear monitors and the intro to 'Man in the Mirror' is a simple solo keyboard sound, which nobody could hear over the screams. Duncan was first to sing and missed the pick up. Simon tried to take over but was struggling to hear the key. Thankfully the screams covered all of this, only the looks on the boys faces (and Duncan checking the first verse lyrics written on his hand) gave them away.

As the boys walked forward (and the screams got louder), each of the band were able to pick up the monitors hanging in the wings as well as the band coming in. As they hit the chorus, Lee took over the vocal and the magic happened. Suddenly they were back in sync and once they saw the crowd, they all relaxed and suddenly were loving being out there. Despite the bumpy start, it was a huge success and each of the boys did a brilliant job, paving the way for enabling us to introduce pop stars and celebs into our gala performances.

Summer 2011: *Thriller Live!* released new artwork featuring cast member and long-running 'MJ', Michael Duke. This artwork was included on our new front of house signage, taxis, buses and billboards across London, as well as national and international poster campaigns.

This year, 2019, is the first time we have used a different image to this (to commemorate our ten years in the West End and using images of Stefan Sinclair as 'MJ'), however the sign at the front of the theatre is still the same.

17.04.2012: Longest-running show at the Lyric Theatre.

On the 17th of April 2012, *Thriller Live!* officially became the longest-running show at the Lyric Theatre in 125 years, beating *Five Guys Named Moe*, Cameron Mackintosh and Clarke Peters' production of the Louis Jordan musical, the previous record holder.

25.06.2012: Onstage vigil at the Lyric Theatre.

Last night the West End cast of *Thriller Live!* paid an onstage candle-lit tribute at the Lyric Theatre to mark the third anniversary of Michael Jackson's passing. At the start of the show, the entire cast assembled on stage bearing candles. Against a rolling montage of images, and Michael's distinctive fedora hat on a microphone stand picked out in a single spotlight, the near-capacity audience were told, "Every day he created history. Every path he took, he left his legacy. And although Michael Jackson has gone too soon, his music lives on forever. Tonight we're here to celebrate his life. And as we take a moment to reflect, we're reminded why he is the greatest entertainer of all time."

15.11.2012: *BBC's Children in Need*, 'Pop Goes the Musical!'

Children in Need has made over a whopping £1 billion since its birth in 1980. As an annual televised celebrity fundraiser, famously hosted by the inimitable Sir Terry Wogan until his death in 2016, it has raised awareness and vital funds for childrens charities all over the UK and around the world.

We got to play our part in 2012 by being asked to take part in 'Pop Goes the Musical!', where five of the West End's top musicals played host to very special performances by pop stars.

"Will they be able to hold their nerves in front of a packed house?" Geri Halliwell performed with the cast of *Singin' in the Rain*, Alexandra Burke with *Les Miserables*, Blue with *Jersey Boys*, X Factor finalist Amelia Lily with *Shrek the Musical*, and with us, Macy Gray, X Factor winner Joe McElderry and girl band Stooshe.

Rehearsals with Stooshe took place over a number of weeks. They wanted to perform 'The Way You Make Me Feel' and as there were three of them, there was some restaging needed. The girls were talented, very enthusiastic and showed a real love for Michael and his music. The team all enjoyed working with them as they were a great laugh but also worked hard.

The hard work paid off as they were brilliant on the night.

Joe was to perform 'She's Out of My Life', learned it really quickly and did a sterling job on the night. Macy chose 'Rock with You' and both were turning up on the day to learn their staging.

I re-worked 'Rock with You' to ensure Macy had clear space around her, as well as freeing up the dancers so she could feed off them when on stage together.

When she arrived, Macy was incredibly shy and found the rehearsals difficult. She was nervous about being out of her comfort zone and kept wandering off – every time I gave a direction to someone else, when I turned around she was gone! I would find her in the stairwell and had to coax her back on to the stage.

We got through it but I was terrified about what might happen that evening.

When it came to the performance, Macy was brought down to the stage. While waiting for her cue, she sat on the stairs by the band at the back of the set. I went round to assist her to her position and when she stood up, she had on the highest heels, making an already Amazonian Macy Gray even taller! She seemed much more relaxed than earlier which was a relief, but in those heels there was no way she would make it under the bridge where the screen was due to open to reveal her. Before I had the chance to change plan and walk her to the wings to send her on from side of stage, she was off! Macy had remembered what happened musically going into 'Rock with You' and took off 'a hair' early (so she was listening!) into her first position. The screen opened, she hitched up her skirt and ducked under the screen with ease, walking downstage and asking the audience, "Put your hands together, c'mon!" I exhaled and went to move quickly towards the wing to watch the performance, only to spot something Macy had left on the stairs. With my director's sixth sense always spotting a backstage hazard, I went to remove it only to discover it was a bottle of Cointreau! Picking it up and shaking my head, I laughed to myself and went to watch the performance we had all been looking forward to. Macy had come alive on that stage and turned the song into her own, making the show feel like a Macy Gray concert.

That half-drunk bottle of Cointreau still has pride of place in the company office.

13.11.2012: Mo Farah music video – do the 'Mobot'.

'The Mobot' – conceptualised by James Corden on his show, *A League of Their Own*, this video was produced between May and November to help raise money for the Mo Farah Foundation, a charity set up by Mo with the aim of providing aid to people affected by the drought and famine in east Africa, particularly in Somalia, specifically using some money towards the building of an orphanage in Somalia where he was born, and *'life inspiring projects for the public in the UK'*.

The video involves firemen and women across the country, postmen, schoolchildren, cheerleaders, swimmers, community centres and children in Africa, as well as Fearne Cotton, David Haye, Jack Whitehall, Mr Motivator, Tom Daley, Richard Branson, Boris Johnson, Phillip Schofield and Holly Willoughby and the cast of *Thriller Live!*

Sadly, the foundation closed in 2016.

21.02.2013: Opening night of the Brazilian production in Rio de Janeiro.

08.02.2013: The first Young MJs graduate from the inaugural Young MJ Academy.

11.10.2013: To celebrate our 2,000th performance in the West End, we were awarded a slot on *The Alan Titchmarsh Show* – a very popular daytime magazine show.

We performed 'Smooth Criminal' led by David Jordan, Haydon Eshun, Andrae Palmer and Zoe Birkett.

08.12.2013: The show was invited to perform on BBC's *Strictly Come Dancing* with Kevin Clifton and Susanna Reid. They were to perform an Argentine tango to 'Smooth Criminal' on the show itself and wanted our guys to coach them in an item to show before the performance. Our understudy MJ, one of our dancers, Rob Anker, was chosen to do the coaching and appear alongside Kevin and Susanna in the item.

We sadly lost Rob on 27th July 2017. He died in a tragic car accident in Canada where he had relocated with his girlfriend and young son. Rob was a beautiful boy and an incredible talent. Originally an acrobat, he became a very sought-after commercial dancer in the UK. I met him on the set of Peter Andre's 'Defender' video in 2010, where he showed huge promise as an up and coming talent.

He became one of the 2013 cast members of *Thriller Live!* and was a huge MJ fan. His star was rising as a choreographer, fitness guru and business entrepeneur after relocating to Canada when his life was tragically cut short. May you rest in peace, Rob.

24.06.2013: Madame Tussauds reveal new waxworks of Michael.

Thriller Live! cast members come face to face with their idol!

Thriller Live! cast members today unveiled Madame Tussauds' newest wax figures, not one, not two, but three stunning Michael Jacksons. David Jordan, Britt Quentin and ten-year-old Eshun Gopal were given a sneak peak of the figures before they take up residence in the attraction from Tuesday 25th June.

The figures, which portray Jackson as a young boy in his Jackson Five days, a more mature King of Pop in his 'Dangerous' era and in his later 'This Is It' incarnation will remain united in the attraction for three months. Fans can also see unique archive materials from his long relationship with Madame Tussauds.

"We were extremely lucky to enjoy a very special relationship with Michael Jackson and he was a big fan of Madame Tussauds," said Nicole Fenner, PR manager for the world-famous attraction. "He gave sittings to our studio team and as well as personally unveiling a figure at the height of his fame in 1985, he paid private visits to the attraction also. These figures span the breadth of his career and we hope fans will agree they are a fitting tribute. And where better to reveal them for the first time than on the stage of Thriller Live! *– the ultimate celebration of his music!" she added.*

26.09.2014: *Thriller Live!* becomes the twentieth longest-running musical in the West End, overtaking *My Fair Lady.**

25.01.2015: After 2,530 shows, *Thriller Live!* reaches nineteenth place in the running for longest-running musical in the West End, surpassing the Dominion production of *Grease.**

12.04.2015: *Thriller Live!* overtakes *Oliver!* as the eighteenth longest-running musical in the West End, beating their 2,618 performances.*

14.07.2015: We introduce a new opening and more new material to the show.

'Don't Stop 'Til You Get Enough / Billie Jean Remix', 'Who's Lovin' You', 'Rockin' Robin', 'Remember the Time' and 'Earth Song' are brought in, as well as shortening some songs (to allow for the additions), new costume designs and updated choreography.

16.06.2015: *Thriller Live!* perform on ITV show *Surprise Surprise* hosted by Holly Willoughby.

MJ: David Jordan. Dancers: Jordan Darrell, Lindon Barr, Janiere Williams, Austyn Farrell.

07.10.2015: It's a $150 million *Thriller!*

A ten-month UK and European tour opens in Blackpool this week with an updated version of the show – including new songs, videos, costumes and special FX.

A new West End booking period to September 2016 opens on Thursday as the new version premieres and extends *Thriller Live!*'s record-breaking seven-year London run.

May 2016

Egypt to become the thirty-second country to premiere *Thriller Live!* Long-running, record-breaking West End concert spectacular, *Thriller Live!*, has now taken in excess of $150 million at the global box office.

16.12.2015: *Thriller Live!* becomes the seventeenth longest-running West End show, overtaking Andrew Lloyd Webber and Tim Rice's *Evita*.*

05.10.2016: Rod Temperton – writer of 'Thriller', 'Off the Wall', 'Rock with You', 'Burn This Disco Out', 'Baby Be Mine' and 'Lady in My Life' – dies.

18.12.2016: *Thriller Live!*, the concert spectacular that was created to celebrate the career of Michael Jackson and The Jackson Five, has now become the sixteenth longest-running musical in the West End. On 18th December, the cast performed the 3,304th show at the Lyric Theatre, overtaking *Me & My Girl*, which opened in 1985.*

04.02.2017: *Thriller* smashes another West End record!
Thriller Live! plays its 3,358th show at the Lyric, when it will topple the legendary 1972 rock opera *Jesus Christ Superstar* to become number fifteen in the official West End Hall of Fame.*

05.03.2017: *Dancing with the Stars* Ireland.
Thriller Live! performs 'Man in the Mirror' on their ICONS show. Singers: Chevone Stewart, Shaquille Hemmans and Rory Taylor.

26.03.2017: After already overtaking *Evita*, *Me and My Girl* and *Jesus Christ Superstar*, *Thriller Live!* now overtakes *Jersey Boys* to become the fourteenth longest-running show in the West End.*

20.03.2017: *Thriller Live!* takes part in the BBC Radio 2 '24-Hour Danceathon' 2017 with DJ Sara Cox in aid of Comic Relief.
Led by David Jordan as 'MJ' and also including dancers Ebony Clark, Jacinta Seivers, Leslie Bowman and Arnold Mabhena.

04.09.2017: Tito Jackson mentors the candidates at the Young MJ Academy.

11.10.2017: Once again I spent a birthday filming a TV special for *Thriller*, this time at Pinewood Studios for the BBC revamp of *The Generation Game*. After spending two days rehearsing a special version of 'Smooth Criminal' and filming the contestants' versions for the show's camera script, it was discovered that the 'powers that be' had not cleared the rights to the song and we were no longer able to use it.

We turned up to the studios with nothing to present but having decided, out of the list we were given, 'P.Y.T. (Pretty Young Thing)' would work. So, right on set amidst the crew and the producers I set to work creating something new for this song. The staging contained a mix of 'Smooth' (including the lean), the fun interaction and sass of 'P.Y.T.' and 'Dancing Machine' and it actually turned out pretty good. When the contestants joined and the whole thing was filmed, it was a really fun piece and enabled them to 'freestyle' – hilariously. I was one of the panel judges toegther with comedian Rob Beckett and Olympic Gold medal winner Denise Lewis. The show's revamp received mixed reviews.

Performers were David Jordan as 'MJ'. Singers: Ina Seidou, Reece Bahia, Haydon Eshun. Dancers: Jason Gray, Lindon Barr, Myron Birch, Joe Drum, Charlotte Bazeley, Penny Smart, Savanna Darnell and Ebony Clarke. Assisted by Aisling Duffy.

19.10.2017: BBBA Awards.

Adrian Grant won the Image Award at the Black British Business Awards. The award was for creating *Thriller Live!* and for the significant and positive contribution he, and the show, have made to the standing of people of African and Caribbean heritage in Britain.

December 2017: 'One Chance to Dance'.

In December 2017, we were asked to appear in the Naughty Boy featuring Joe Jonas 'One Chance to Dance' viral music video. With the references to Michael Jackson in the song, Naughty Boy (having seen the show) wanted to use the cast. We shot the video on stage using costumes and choreography from the show as well as adding extra choreography, slow motion glamour shots and stills throughout. We never turn down a chance to dance!

MJ: Florivaldo Mossi. Dancers: Shakara Brown, Jorgia Vaughan, Emma Jane Smith, Ella Durston, Ella Redhead, Joel Ekperigin and Florivaldo Mossi. Additional choreography: Aisling Duffy.

28.06.2018: Reece Bahia wins Eastern Eye Emerging Artist Award.

Reece Bahia wanted to be a dentist but dropped the idea to pursue his love of music and went onto study performing arts at Stratford College. Bahia featured in Simon Cowell's *You Generation* commercial and also appeared on *The Voice UK* in 2014. He won the lead role in Michael Jackson's *Thriller Live!* at the West End after five gruelling auditions – *Eastern Eye*.

29.08.2018: Happy birthday, Michael!

Thriller Live! performed on *The One Show* for MJs sixtieth birthday and travelled around London singing songs from the show on a double-decker bus.

12.09.2018: 4,000th performance gala.

A host of celebrities will join the cast of Michael Jackson musical *Thriller Live!* for a gala performance in aid of The Prince's Trust.

The evening, which is being held on 12th September to celebrate the show's 4,000th West End performance, will feature Peter Andre, Russell Kane, impressionist Jon Culshaw and original *Thriller* cast member Kieran Alleyne.

The special guests will host the evening and perform Michael Jackson tracks alongside the West End cast, with all proceeds from tickets sales donated to The Prince's Trust.

02.01.2019: *Thriller Live!* celebrates 'Ten Years at the Lyric Theatre'!

Spring 2019: New ten-year artwork across London.

02.04.2019: *Thriller Live!* extends at the Lyric Theatre to September 2020.

07.04.2019: West End history was made on this day when, after 4,625 standing ovations, *Thriller Live!* overtakes *Miss Saigon* to become the thirteenth longest-running West End musical of all time!*

This Sunday (7th April), the 4,625th West End performance of *Thriller Live!* will see it overtake *Miss Saigon* to become the thirteenth longest-running West End musical.

Jackie, Marlon and Tito Jackson told Encore Radio:

"Thriller Live! *is such a cool celebration of Michael's music and the music of the Jackson Five we made together. We loved the show when we saw it, and fans in the audience were 'thrilled' with the performances. It's great they've extended their run so more fans can have an opportunity to dance to Michael's music, the Jackson Five music, and to have a great night out." – Encore Radio*

*As recorded by officiallondontheatre.com

Acknowledgements

My family: our tragic losses over these past few years have been more than traumatic bumps in the road. But out of the darkness comes a strength, fuelled by everything taught by those we have lost.

Mum, this book is dedicated to you. You taught me to keep going, to always look ahead and go for that goal, whatever it was and I have always felt you behind me pushing me forth. And Dad, both your ever-supportive love allowed me to achieve everything I put my mind to, including this piece of work.

To my husband and son, RJ and K-Dawg – 'Team TJ'. Three is a magic number. I love you both. Thanks for putting up with me when chained to my computer, following this dream. You are everything to me and we will always dare to dream together.

Joanne, my sister and dance partner. Without you at the beginning of this story, there may have been a different ending. Thank you, I love you.

With special thanks to: the Jackson family, especially Tito, Jackie, Marlon and La Toya, for being so wonderfully human.

Thank you, Chris Newlands, for making me do this.

Deke, Jill and Jamie Arlon, for making me believe I could do this.

Ginette Sinnott, for all your patience and endless generosity with this book and with me in general.

Keith Cox, for a lifetime of friendship and all the advice.

Yasmin Yazdi, Philippa Iliffe, Rosie Lowe, Lauren Bailey, Hannah Virk, Jack Wedgbury, and all at Troubador and the Book Guild.

Andy Fickman – just for being you and making me feel like a superhero.

For all the anecdotes and conversations – Adrian Grant, John Maher, Kieran Alleyne, Zoe Birkett, Mitchell Zhangazha, Ricko Baird, Haydon Eshun, Yasmin Yazdi, Britt Quentin, Phil Watts, Sharon Speirs, Edson Cabrera Junior, Jessica Powell Antonini and Jo Dyce – your words and creativity are vital to this story.

Love and thanks to Peter Andre, Jon Culshaw, Russell Kane, The Prince's Trust, Gloria Jones, Kenny Ortega, Ne-Yo, Chris Brown, Giorgio Moroder, Ben Forster, Layton Williams, Eshan Gopal.

The Liga Solidaria, Daniela, Maria Louisa, Rodrigo and all the children we met that day. May your beautiful work continue.

My inspirational teachers: Janice Sutton, Chris Pearson, Sue Miles, Richard Dring, Anne Lister, Pat Dennison, Barbara Evans, Richard Glasstone, Nigel Brooks and Betty Laine. This story would not exist without all your faith in me and how that has motivated and shaped my career.

To my agent, Bronia Buchanan, and all at BBA Management.

The incredible *Thriller Live!* team:

Adrian Grant – the creator; Paul Walden and Derek Nicol – the believers; John Maher – the music maker; Ginette Sinnott and Kevin Wilson – the marketing wizards; Mark Strange – for managing the impossible. My associates – Jo Dyce, Rose Wild and Yasmin Yazdi.

None of this would happen without you, I love and appreciate you all more than you could ever know. My incredible creative team: Nigel Catmur, Chris Whybrow, Jonathan Park, Rob Jones, Catherine Teatum, Jessica Ma and all at Shooting Flowers, Colin Rozee, Mandy Smith and all at Potion Pictures, The Twins FX Illusions. Our casting teams, Debbie O'Brien and all at DOB Casting; Benton Whitley, Duncan Stewart and all at Stewart Whitley Casting.

Company managers: Caroline Stroud, Phil Watts, Sharon Speirs.

Resident directors: Britt Quentin, Aisling Duffy, Jessica Powell Antonini, Miranda Wilford. Dance captains: Danni Rothman, Jordan Darrell, Jordan Palmer, Stefan Sinclair, Fillippo Coffano, Ebony Clarke, Jason Gray, Kofi 'Game' Prempeh, Danielle Hampson, Rachel Kay, Mikey Frome, Lauren Hearnden Mayer, Gianni Arancio, Kevin Heatherson, Katrina Ridley, Lewis Davies, Lauren Gore, Fernanda Fiuza, Thiago Vianna, Sophie MacDonald, Leslie Garcia Bowman, Danny Bradford, Shakara Brown, Florivaldo Mossi, Penny Smart, Peter Cleverley, Stevie Mahoney, Michael Lin, Shae Carroll.

I have never underestimated the difficulty of your job and the power of your patience. So much thanks to you all.

All at Flying Music: Andy Jennings, David Drury, Belynda Galliard, Carina Milligan, Imogen Burgess, Tony Rex, Liam Hogan, Charlotte Denny and Andy Sharrocks.

Nica Burns, Laurence Miller, David Holder and all at Nimax Theatres; Adam Ellacott, Darren Coogan, Paul Mount, Tony Priestley, Kate Garratt, James Huxstep, Emma Jennings, Glen Keane, Andy Young, John Herbert, Michael Edwards, Paul Lewis, Nolan Meetings, David Mansell, Maria Da Silva, Mark Bennett, Ian Brown, Mikey Barr, Gareth Eldriff, Kevin and Manuel.

Thanks to all those who have given us space over the last ten years: Espaço 10 x 21 São Paulo, Pineapple Dance Studios, Husky Studios, Dance Attic Studios, Dance Works Studios London, WAC Arts, Marylebone Music Studios, Urdang Academy, Rambert Studios, Alford House, The Courtyard and the Umbrella Rooms.

Thank you to each member of the cast and crew over the years, most of whom are listed below.

Anyone missing is certainly not forgotten.

2009 – Original London Cast:

Ricko Baird, Ben Foster, John Moabi, Denise Pearson, Roger Wright, Earl Perkins.

Kieran Alleyne, Sterling Williams, Layton Williams, Ashton Russell, Sean Williams, Yasmin Yazdi, Jo Dyce, Dannii Rothman, Richard Smikle, Kamilah Beckles, Jordan Darrell, Lewis Davies, Christabelle Field, Elliot James, Emily Rumbles.

BAND: Musical Director, Keyboard 2 & Guitar 2 John Maher; AMD, Keyboard 1, John Rutledge & Mike Guy; Guitar 1, Damien Cooper; Bass, Oliver Latka; Drums, Mike Bradley; Percussion, Keyboard 3, Accy Yeates.

2019 – Ten-Year Anniversary London Cast:

Florivaldo Mossi, David Julien, John Moabi, Haydon Eshun, Vivienne Ekwulugo, Sophia Mackay, Charlotte Berry, Wayne Anthony Cole, Jonah Mayor, Joey James.

Triple Calz, Isaiah Mason, Xhanti Mbonzongwana, Christian Posso, Jay Jay Prince.

David DeVyne, Aisling Duffy, Ebony Clarke, Filippo Coffano, Matt Vjestica, Eliza Hart, Oskarina O'Sullivan, Zinzile Tschuma, Leona Lawrenson, Mari McLeod, Daniel Blessing, Joel Ekperigin, Simone Moncada, Vivien Gayle, Arnold Mahbena.

BAND: Musical Director, Keyboard 2 & Guitar 2, John Maher; AMD, Keyboard 1, Ryan Alex Farmery; Guitar 1, Damien Cooper; Bass, Oliver Latka; Drums, Mike Bradley; Percussion, Keyboard 3, Adam Kovacs.

2019 – Ten-Year Anniversary Touring Cast:

Kieran Alleyne, Britt Quentin, Rory Taylor, Letitia Hector, Ina Seidou, Nick James, Trace Kennedy, Daniel Bradford, Shakara Brown, Savanna

Darnell, Danyul Fullard, Amelia-Annie Layng, Rishard Kyro Nelson, Zec Luhana, Lee Pratt, Nadia Robinson, Penny Smart, Mitchell Eley, Sian Nabbs.

BAND: MD & Keyboard 1, Andy Jeffcoat; Guitar 1, Allan Salmon; Assistant MD, Percussion & Keyboard 3, Tom Arnold; Drums, Matt Arnold; Keyboard 2 & Guitar 2, Rob Minns; Bass, Johnny Copeland; Alternate Bass, Jo Phillpotts.

Aaron Buck, Aaron Witter, Abigail Swain, Accy Yates, Adam Bernard, Adam Kovacs, Adam McClelland, Adriana Louise, Aisling Duffy, AJ Lewis, Aled Jones, Alex Buchanan, Alex Burke, Alex Ko, Alexander Jackson, Alexander James, Alexandra Bryan, Ali van Ryne, Alice Nuttall, Alice Rhodes, Alice Ross, Alishia Marie Blake, Allan Salmon, Amanda Amielle, Amelia-Annie Layng, Amira Gemei, Amy Brand, Amy Johnson, Ana Zgur, Andi Mac, Andrae Palmer, Andre Faulds, Andrew Derbyshire, Andrew Holton, Andrew Lyle-Pinnock, Andrew Sloane, Andy Chisholm, Andy Jeffcoat, Andy Smith, Angela Riddell, Angelica Allen, Anna Edwards-McConway, Anna Newton, Anna R Edwards, Anna Tremain, Anthony Best, Anthony Earls, Antony Morgan, Arnold Mabhena, Ashleigh Cherry, Ashleigh Frost, Ashley-Jordon Packer, Ashton Russell, Austyn Farrell, Beccy Jones, Becky Hicks, Becky Potts, Ben Forster, Ben Harrold, Ben Mason-Foster, Ben Sherratt, Ben Webster, Bernadette Brennan, Bernice Jauncey, Beth Minter, Bill Dimeo, Blake Slater, Blaze Ellis – Porter, Brett Baxter, Brian Robert Junior Kotelo, Britt Quentin, Brittany Woodrow, Bryn Pedrick, Busola Peters, Cal Hawes, Caleb Stewart, Carole Stennett, Caroline Stroud, Caroline Tyndall, Caspian Moyo, Cassandra Rogers, Cassie MacMillan, Cassie Rogers, Chad Wilder, Chante Simpson, Charity Jones, Charlie Smith, Charlotte Bazeley, Charlotte Berry, Charlotte Buonaiuto, Chelsea de Carvalho, Chevone Stewart, Chloe Ferns, Chloe Hollingsworth, Chris Arias, Chris Gordon, Chris Jackson, Chris Whybrow, Christabelle Field, Christian Posso, Christian Sharrier, Christina Hunt, Claire Carter, Claire Harrison, Claire Wincott, Clare Bonsu, Claudimar Neto, Clementine Lar

N-Jones, Cleo Higgins, Cordell Mosteller, Courtney George, Craig Garratt, Craig Steward, Crystal Hantig, Cyrine Anderson, Daisy Woodroffe, Dak Mashava, Damien Cooper, Danni Hampson, Daniel Blessing, Daniel Bradford, Daniel English, Daniel Hunt, Daniel Louard, Daniel Odejinmi, Daniel Uppal, Daniel-Terell Toorie, Danielle Hampson, Danielle Mooskos, Danni Rothman, Danny Barlow, Danyul Fullard, Dário Gomes, Darren Holt, Darryn Farrugia, Dak Mashava, Dave Lamb, Dave Loughran, David Devyne, David Jordan, David Julien, David Olaniyi, Davide Giananinni, Dawn Harvey Kerlen, Dean Lee, Deborah Dada, Demelza Fry, Denise Pearson, Denzel Daniels, Derry Glover, Diane Noorlander, Diarmaid O'Kaine, Dominic Daly, Donna Calvert, Dwayne Wint, Dylan Debuitlear, Earl Perkins, Ebony Clarke, Eddy Lima, Elaine Morris, Elijah Crossley, Eliza Hart, Elizabeth Ford, Ella Bolton, Ella Coghill, Ella Redhead, Ellen Dawson, Ellie Muscutt, Elliot James, Esme Cruse, Emily Bailey, Emily Golding-Ellis, Emily Gould, Emily Grace Radjen, Emily Jane Bailey, Emily Rumbles, Emily Smith, Emma Leigh Rose, Emma Rowe, Emma Sheppard, Emma Smith, Emma Stillman, Emmanuel Sakyi, Eric Santos, Eshan Gopal, Esma Frances Kirk, Fabiana Figueiredo, Faye Young, Felix Pimenta, Fernanda Fiuza, Fernanda Rizzo, Fillippo Coffana, Fiona Samways, Fiona Shepard, Florivaldo Mossi, Frances Williams, Gabriela Hernandez, Gareth Sizer, Gemma Bishop, Gemma Hanley, Gemma Hoff, Gemma May Johnstone, George Lumpin, Georgina Mannifield, Gerald Wooding, Gianni Arancio, Giulia Scrimieri, Glaucia Fernanda de Oliveira, Glenn Jenkins, Grant Du Plessis, Gustave Die, Gustavo Della Serra, Hannah Reymes-Cole, Hannah Wing, Harriet Van Reysen, Harry Butcher, Haydon Eshun, Hayley Evetts, Hayley Kharsa, Helen Parsons, Helen Shrimpton, Holly Jackson, Hope Vivins, Ian Pitter, Ian Turner, Idney De'Almeida, Idriss Kargbo, Ina Seidou, Inca Jaakson, Isaiah Mason, Isobel Rush, Isobelle Wild, Israel Donowa, J Rome Wayne, Jacinta Seivers, Jack Saundercock, Jackie Ellis, Jacqui Green, Jade Albertsen, Jade Hill, Jag Souldeep, Jaime Barr, Jamal Crawford, James Anderson, James Hassett, James McKeogh, Jamie Davies, Jamie

McCredy, Jamie Trowell, Janiere Williams, Janine Summerhayes, Jasmine Eccles, Jason Gray, Jay Brock, Jay Jay Prince Lothian, Jayde Nelson, Jaydon Noel, Jen Clarke, Jenine Agymange, Jennifer Goodheart-Smithe, Jenny Trent, Jermaine Johnson, Jess Broadbere, Jess Taylor, Jesse Smith, Jessica Craft, Jessica Edkins, Jess Ma, Jessica Powell, Jessica Warne, Jim Bob Woods, Jo Burgess, Jo Conlon, Jo Dyce, Jo Hunnisett, Jo Philpotts, Joanna Jones, Joe Drum, Joe Francois, Joel Ekperigin, Joel Elhadj, Joel Lundgren, John Bettison, John Grainger, John Maher, John Moabi, Jon-Jo Inkpen, Jonah Mayor, Jonathan Lynsey, Jonathan Shaw, Jonny Buck, Jonny Copland, Jordan Alexander, Jordan Ayoola, Jordan Colls, Jordan Darrell, Jordan Palmer, Jorgia Vaughan, Joe Drum, Joshua Cameron, Joshua Daley, Joshua Ivey, Josiah Choto, Jovanny Pichardo, JRome Wayne, Julia Saunders, Julie Colbert, Justin Kielty, Kamilah Beckles, Karleigh Williams, Karli Van Heerden, Kathryn Louise Wilson, Katie Bradley, Katie Oropallo, Katie Roddy, Katie Weatherly, Katinka Hutchinson, Katrina Ridley, Kayla Lomas Kirton, Keenan Munn-Francis, Kelvin White, Kemi Durosinmi, Kevin Heatherson, Kieran Alleyne, Kieran Rogers-Bedminister, Kim Hill, Kim Murry, Koco Zaveleta, Kofi Agyemang, Kuan Frye, Kwame Kandekore, Kyle Johnson, Laura McNaulty, Laura White, Laura Wilson, Lauren Gore, Lauren Headon, Lauren Mayer, Laurence Russell, Laurie Delaney, Laurie Kay-Hue, Lavinia Holland, Leah Hill, Leanne Whitehead, Lee Alexander, Lee Caulfield, Lee Pratt, Lelo Alves, Leo Tierney, Leona Lawrenson, Leilah Moreno, Leslie Garcia Bowman, Leslie Pierce, Letitia Hector, Lewis Davies, Lewis Hector, Lewis McIntyre, Liam Lawrence, Libby Hall, Lindon Barr, Lindsay Hill, Lisa Gilby, Lisa McConville, Lisa Mitton, Lisa Spencer, Llinos Lloyd (Tink), Lorenzo Dizel Cubuca, Louis Murton, Louisa Reece, Louise Murphy, Louise O Daly, Lucinda (Lucy) Moore, Lucy Bell, Luke Sabatini, Lunna Gomes, MaByn Aita, Maddy Johnson, Magnus Einang, Mandy Ashley, Manuela (Ela) Schmid, Marcellus Virgo Smith, Mari Macleod, Maria Akpan, Maria Gibbons, Maria Lawson, Mariella Spotto, Mark 'Robbo' Robinson, Mark Deighton, Mark Robinson, Mark Wheatley, Marlena Johnson, Marlon

Villa Nova, Martin Guppy, Martin Meachem, Martina Gumbs, Martina Isibor, Marvyn Charles, Mary Weah, Matt Doidge, Matt Lee, Matt Smith, Matt Vjestica, Matthew Giles, Matthew Jrbanek, Max Ephson-Clarke, Maxine Hughes, Melinda Tzambazakis, Melissa Burton, Melissa Lye, Melissa Rose Gumbs, Messiah Unsudimi, Mica Townsend, Michael Duke, Michael Guy, Michael Henderson, Michael Kavuma, Michael Lin, Michael Whyte, Mig Ayesa, Mike Bradley, Mike Lindup, Mike Osman, Mike Pensini, Mikey Frome, Mikhael Baque, Miranda Wilford, Miriam Power, Mitch Peters, Mitchell Eley, Mitchell Zhangazha, MJ Mytton Syanneh, MJ Mytton-Sanneh, Molly Ward, Monica Kabasomi, Myron Birch, Nadia Robinson, Natalie Brook Reynolds, Natalie Morton, Natalie Young, Natasha King, Natasha McLean, Natasha Selwyn-Smith, Nathan Graham, Nathan James, Neil Pettit (BJ), Nia Evans, Nick James, Nick Pamment, Nicky Caulfield, Nicky Chisholm, Nicky Ives, Nicola Hill, Nikki Whitlock, Oggie Iwo, Oli Latka, Oskarina O'Sullivan, Owen Jordan Mugowa, Page Barrington Bobb, Paris Green, Paris Johnson, Paul Bond, Paul Mason, Paul Thomson, Penny Smart, Peter Barnett, Peter Cleverley, Peter Eldridge, Petra Jolly, Phil Clarke, Phil Watts, Phillipa Ratcliffe, Poppy Ballon, Prinnie Stevens, Rachel Bevans, Rachel Garrison, Rachel Gossan, Rachel Schofield, Ramon Mariqueo Smith, Ramona Acrom, Ramona Ocran, Raphael Martinez, Rebekah Bridges, Reece Bahia, Reece McConnell, Remi Black, Remi Gooding, Renan Tenca, Renata Carvalho, Renato Max, Renee Harriott, Ria Dawson, Ria Horsford, Rich Hoxley, Richard Herrick, Richard Pattison, Richard Porter, Richard Smikle, Rick Bhullar, Ricko Baird, Rishard-Kyro Nelson, Rob Anker, Rob Minns, Rob Smith, Rob Summers, Roger Collins, Roger Wright, Rory Taylor, Rosa Prados, Rose Wild, Roshawn Hewitt, Rosie Stroud, Ross Sands, Russell Young, Ryan Alex Farmery, Ryan Josiah, Ryan Lawrence, Ryan Shaw, Ryan Tate, Ryene Oliveira, Sally Miura, Sam Fleet, Sam Johnson, Sam Vincent, Samantha Jackson, Samantha Johnson, Samella Nathielle, Sammi-Lee Jayne, Saphira Kelly, Sara Marwick, Sarah Dean, Sarah Dobbs, Sarah Jones, Sarah Linn Taylor, Savanna Darnell, Scarlette Douglas, Scott Maurice, Sean

Christopher, Sean West, Sean Williams, Shae Carroll, Shakara Brown, Shanay Holmes, Shane Keogh-Grenade, Shanice Steele, Shaquille Hemmans, Sharon Porter, Sharon Speirs, Sian Nabbs, Simeon Henry, Simon Brockwell, Simon Dixon, Simon Doe, Simon Holroyd, Simone Moncada, Sophia Mackay, Sophie Bond, Sophie Cathersides, Sophie MacDonald, Sophie Robyn, Sophie Usher, Stefan Sinclair, Stefanie Gruen, Stephanie Colburn, Sterling Williams, Steven Robertson, Steven Thompson, Stevie Mahoney, Sue Bennett, Suzette Brissett, Suzie George, Tamsin Pearson, Tania Chant, Tanisha Spring, Tariq Olajorin, Tariq Wooding, Tarnya Neil, Tasha Turan, Taylor Lockhart, Theresa Carey, Thiago Vianna, Thomas Cassidy, Thomas Remaili, Tia Sackey, Tiago Dias, Tilly Stokes, Tim Scott, Timothy Stapor, Todd Holdsworth, Tom Arnold, Tom Cox, Tom Pickering, Tonia Mia Vernava, Tony Azzopardi, Tony Ben Azouz, Torann Opera, Trace Kennedy, Tracey Fahy, Travis Blake-Hall, Trenyce Cobbins, Twinnie Lee, Ty Reece Stewart, Tyler McLean, Tyrone Henry, Valerie Munn-Francis, Victor Rounds, Victoria Lamm, Victoria Pasion, Vivian Gayle, Vivienne Elwulugo, Wayne Anthony-Cole, Wayne Robinson, Will Cottrell, Will Fry, Xhanti Mbonjongwana, Yasmin Yazdi, Zak Haywood, Zak Maguire, Zayn Johnson, Zec Luhana, Zinzille Tshuma, Zoe Birkett, Zoe O'Sullivan, Zoe Purpuri, Zuriel Kabasomi.

Countries *Thriller Live!* Has Toured

Abu Dhabi
Australia
Austria
Belgium
Brazil
China
Czech Republic
Denmark
Dubai
Egypt
Finland
France
Germany
Greece
Holland
India
Ireland
Israel
Italy

Japan
Kuwait
Latvia
Lithuania
Malaysia
Monaco
New Zealand
Norway
Poland
Singapore
Slovakia
South Africa
South Korea
Sweden
Switzerland
England
Scotland
Wales

Touring Dates

UK Spring 2007
UK Autumn 2007
UK Spring 2008
Germany Autumn 2008
Holland Autumn 2008
UK Autumn 2008
UK 2009 incl. Spring Autumn
and Arena
Poland Spring 2009
Czech Republic Spring 2009
Rotterdam Spring 2009
Germany Autumn 2009
Austria Autumn 2009
Italy Autumn 2009
Switzerland Autumn 2009
Germany Autumn 2009
CSE Europe Autumn 2009
BB & CSE Spring 2010
Greece June 2010

South Africa Summer 2010
China Summer 2010
UK tour Autumn 2010
UK tour Spring 2011
BB tour Spring 2011
Monaco Spring 2011
Scandinavia Spring 2011
Singapore Spring 2011
Abu Dhabi
UK Autumn 2011
BB tour Dec 2011–2012
Japan Dec 2012
Brazil – Rio 2013
Brazil – Brasilia 2013
Brazil – São Paulo 2013
UK Spring tour 2013
South Korea 2013
UK Autumn tour 2013
BB Spring 2014

UK Spring tour 2014
Japan June 2014
UK Autumn tour 2014
Australia & NZ 2014–15
Malaysia
Germany Autumn 2015
Scandinavia Autumn 2015
UK Autumn 2015
UK Spring 2016
Egypt 2016
Israel 2016
Macau 2016
UK Spring tour 2017
Munich 28 March to 9 April

Macau 2017
UK Autumn tour 2017
UK Spring tour 2018
Germany Jan–Feb 2018
Scandinavia Feb 2018
Germany April–June 2018
UK Autumn 2018
BB Autumn 2018
Amsterdam & Ghent 2018
Poland Autumn 2018
Germany Spring 2019
Kuwait & Dubai 2019
UK Spring/Summer 2019

*We have harmonised around the world for over a decade,
leaving nation to nation singing the music of Michael Jackson.
As we continue to turn yet another page in the book of his legacy,
we create our own HIStory.*

References

Page ix – 'O2'

Referring to the O2 Arena, London.

Page 5 – Nimax (theatres)

Nimax Theatres Ltd. is a theatre group owned and operated by Nica Burns and Max Weitzenhoffer.

Page 10 – 'VT'

'Video tape', an industry expression used to describe a video clip.

Page 22 – New Bounce

New Bounce were a boy band made up of Mitchell Zhangazha, Kuan Frye, MJ Mytton-Sanneh and James Anderson (aged 12–16) who all met working as the Young Michael Jacksons.

Page 27 – Studio 54

Studio 54 is a former nightclub, frequented by many stars, including Michael Jackson around the *Off the Wall* period. It is currently a Broadway theatre, located at 254 West 54th Street, between Eighth Avenue and Broadway in Midtown Manhattan, New York City. The building, originally built as the Gallo Opera House, opened in 1927, after which it changed names several times, eventually becoming CBS radio and television Studio 52.

Page 38 – Jennifer Batten

Jennifer Batten is an American guitarist who has worked as a session musician and solo artist. From 1987 to 1997 she played on all three of Michael Jackson's world tours.

Page 38 – Five Star

Five Star are a British pop group, formed in 1983 made up of siblings Stedman, Lorraine, Denise, Doris and Delroy Pearson. Between 1985 and 1988, Five Star had four Top 20 albums and 15 Top 40 singles in the UK. Like the Jackson Five, Five Star were masterminded by their father, Buster Pearson.

Page 47 – 'swinging'

A term referring to the role of 'swing' – someone in a theatre show who understudies more than one part. Often not on stage until needed, their sole job is to cover those that fall ill or become injured or on longer contracts, take holiday.

Page 49 – Kym Mazelle

Kym Mazelle is an American singer-songwriter. She is regarded as a pioneer of house music in the United Kingdom and Europe. She is credited as 'The First Lady of House Music' and has had many hits as a solo artist.

Page 49 – Shaheen Jafargholi

Shaheen Jafargholi is a Welsh actor and singer. In 2009, he finished in seventh place on the ITV competition series *Britain's Got Talent*. Since then, he has portrayed the roles of Shakil Kazemi in *EastEnders* and Marty Kirkby in *Casualty*.

Shaheen played the young Michael Jackson in the early tours of the show and sang at Michael Jackson's memorial.

Page 49 – Aaron Renfree

Aaron Renfree was the oldest member of S Club 8 and starred in BBC's *I Dream.* He is now a successful dancer and choreographer.

Page 50 – Sinitta

Sinitta Malone known professionally as Sinitta, is an American-born British singer. She is known for having success in the mid-1980s with the single 'So Macho' and had several other hits during the decade. In the 2000s, she became known for television appearances, including *Loose Women, The Xtra Factor* and *This Morning*. She took part in the ITV show *I'm a Celebrity... Get Me Out of Here!* in 2011.

Page 50 – Zoe Birkett

Zoe Birkett is a singer from County Durham, England. She was one of the youngest contestants on the first series of the ITV talent competition *Pop Idol* in 2001, being only sixteen at the time. She released a single, 'Treat Me Like a Lady', in 2003, has had a successful theatre career and was a contestant in *Big Brother* in 2014.

Page 50 – Noel Sullivan
Noel Sullivan is a Welsh singer and actor. He was a member of the British pop group Hear'Say who won the ITV talent competition Popstars. He is now a successful TV actor and musical theatre performer.

Page 56 – The Electric Boogaloos
The Electric Boogaloos are a street dance crew responsible for the spread of body popping and electric boogaloo. The name 'Boogaloo' came from a song called 'Do a Boogaloo' by James Brown, which was also adapted as a Boogaloo street dance done from Oakland, California. They were founded by Boogaloo Sam in Fresno, California in 1977.

Page 57 – The Little Prince
Director / choreographer Bob Fosse performed a song and dance in Stanley Donen's 1974 film version of Antoine du Saint-Expuréry's *The Little Prince*. This has been credited as the inspiration for Michael Jackson's *Billie Jean* choreography.

Page 57 – The Band Wagon
The Band Wagon is a 1953 American musical-comedy film directed by Vincente Minnelli, starring Fred Astaire and Cyd Charisse.

Page 65 – American Bandstand
American Bandstand is an American music-performance and dance television program that aired in various versions from 1952 to 1989 and was hosted from 1956 until its final season by Dick Clark, who also served as the program's producer. It featured teenagers dancing to Top 40 music introduced by Clark and at least one popular musical act.

Page 66 – Motown 25
Motown 25: Yesterday, Today, Forever is an award-winning 1983 television special, produced by Suzanne de Passe for Motown Records, to commemorate Motown's 25th anniversary.

Page 79 – Ultimate Kaos
Ultimate KAOS were a British boyband successful in the 1990s, and formed by Simon Cowell. Its original members were Jomo Baxter, Jayde Delpratt, Ryan Elliott, Nick Grant and the then nine-year-old Haydon Eshun.

Page 80 – Damage
Damage are a British R&B boy band who achieved success in the 1990s with eleven hit singles, including four Top 10 successes on the UK Singles Chart. They have sold 2.5 million records worldwide. The band consists of Jade Jones, Rahsaan J Bromfield, Andrez Harriott, Coreé Richards and Noel Simpson.

Page 80 – Reborn in the USA

Reborn in the USA was a British reality television show broadcast on ITV, in which ten British pop acts were transported to the US, where they were supposedly unknown in the hope of revitalising their music career.

Each week, the American audience voted for their favourite act. The two acts with the fewest votes would then face the vote from the British public, where the following week the act with the fewest votes was eliminated from the contest and sent back to Britain. The series was presented by Davina McCall and the eventual winner was ex-Spandau Ballet lead singer Tony Hadley, who was awarded with the prize of a recording contract.

Page 85 – Chelsea Under the Bridge

Under the Bridge is a purpose-built West London live music venue.

Page 110 – Vincent Price

Vincent Leonard Price Jr. was an American actor best known for his performances in horror films, although his career spanned other genres, including film noir, drama, mystery, thriller, and comedy. He appeared on stage, television, and radio, and in more than 100 films. In 1982, Price provided the spoken-word sequence to the end of the Michael Jackson song 'Thriller'.

Page 112 – plastic jock cup

A protective undergarment used for cycling, football, cricket and other contact sport or vigorous activity.

Page 115 – Sardi's

Sardi's is a continental restaurant located at 234 West 44th Street (between Broadway and Eighth Avenue) in the Theater District in Manhattan, in New York City. Known for the hundreds of caricatures of show-business celebrities that adorn its walls and as a theatre people hangout. Sardi's opened at its current location on March 5, 1927.

Page 124 – 5 After Midnight

5 After Midnight, also known as 5AM, are a British boy group formed in 2016 during the thirteenth series of *The X Factor*, finishing in third place.

Page 130 – Ola Ray

Ola Ray is an American model and actress most notable for her role as 'the girlfriend' of Michael Jackson in the short film *Thriller*.

Page 135 – Costa

Costa Coffee is a British multinational coffeehouse company founded in London in 1971 by the Costa family supplying roasted coffee to caterers and specialist Italian coffee shops.

Page 146 Bom Dia Brasil

Bom Dia Brasil – Portuguese for 'Good Morning Brazil' is a Brazilian breakfast television programme produced and broadcast by Rede Globo. The show premiered on 3 January 1983, and includes segments from studios around Brazil, moderated by the main presenters in the home studio. The show includes Brazilian political and economic news.

Page 176 – Capoeira

Capoeira is an Afro-Brazilian martial art that combines elements of dance, acrobatics, and music.

It is known for its acrobatic and complex maneuvers, often involving hands on the ground and inverted kicks. Capoeira emphasizes flowing movements rather than fixed stances, the *ginga*, a rocking step, is usually the focal point of the technique.

Page 178 B-Boy / Breakers

Breaking, also called breakdancing or b-boying/b-girling, is an athletic style of street dance. While diverse in the amount of variation available in the dance, breakdancing mainly consists of four kinds of movement: toprock, downrock, power moves and freezes. Breakdancing is typically set to songs containing drum breaks, especially in hip-hop, funk, soul music and breakbeat music, although modern trends allow for much wider varieties of music along certain ranges of tempo and beat patterns.

Page 192 – Choreographic clean ups

A term used for re-rehearsing dance routines to ensure each of the dancers are doing the same as one another. These rehearsals usually take place before opening a show and regularly within the run.

Page 203 – Priscilla

Referring to the west end musical 'Priscilla – Queen of the Desert'.

Page 213 – 'a string of one nighters'

A term used for a series of shows that only spend one night in each city.

Page 213 – 'the pit'

The area where the band are situated is commonly known as 'The Pit' or 'The Band Pit'.

Page 215 – 're-blocking'

A show term used to describe changing the formations of certain routines or sections when members of the company are sick, injured or off.

Re-blocking also takes place in touring shows when certain venues present problems such as restricted stage space or unusual obstacles.

Page 233 – Kenrick Sandy

Kenrick 'H2O' Sandy MBE is co-founder and co-Artistic Director of Boy Blue Entertainment, Associate Artist at the Barbican London and is one of the most renowned choreographers in the UK urban and commercial scenes.

Page 247 – Larry O'Keefe

Laurence 'Larry' O'Keefe is an American composer and lyricist for Broadway musicals, film and television. Larry co-wrote Bat Boy and Legally Blonde and with co-author Kevin Murphy, O'Keefe co-wrote *Heathers: The Musical*, directed by Andy Fickman and choreographed in the UK by Gary Lloyd.

'2,4,6,8' Words and Music by Gloria Jones / Pamela Joan Sawyer © Sony/ATV Music Publishing LLC

'ABC' Words and Music by Berry Gordy / Freddie Perren / Dennis Lussier / Alphonzo Mizell

© S.I.A.E. Direzione Generale, Jobete Music Co. Inc., Emi Music Publishing France, Sony, Jobete Music Co Inc

'All Revved Up' Words and Music by Giorgio Moroder / Tom Whitlock © Arista Records

'Another Part Of Me' Words and Music by Michael Jackson © Sony/ATV Music Publishing

LLC, Warner Chappell Music, Inc

'Bad' Words and Music by Michael Jackson © Sony/ATV Music Publishing LLC, Warner

Chappell Music, Inc, Songtrust Ave

'Beat It' Words and Music by Michael Jackson © Sony/ATV Music Publishing LLC

'Ben' Words and Music by Don Black / Walter Scharf © Sony/ATV Music Publishing LLC

'Billie Jean' Words and Music by Michael Jackson © Sony/ATV Music Publishing LLC

'Black or White' Words and Music by Michael Jackson © Sony/ATV Music Publishing LLC

'Blame It On The Boogie' Words and Music by David John Jackson Rich / Elmar Krohn / Hans Kampschroer / Michael George Jackson Clark / Thomas Meyer © Peermusic Publishing, BMG Rights Management

'Blood On The Dance Floor' Words and Music by Michael Jackson / Teddy Riley © Sony/ATV Music Publishing LLC

'Can You Feel It' Words and Music by Sigmund Esco Jackson / Michael Jackson © Sony/ATV Music Publishing LLC, Warner Chappell Music, Inc, Kobalt Music Publishing Ltd.

'Copacabana' Words and Music by Barry Manilow / Bruce H. Sussman / Jack A. Feldman © Universal Music Publishing Group, Peermusic Publishing, BMG Rights Management

'Dancing Machine' Words and Music by Davis Hal / Parks Weldon Dean / Fletcher Donald E © S.I.A.E. Direzione Generale, Bust It Publishing, Sony, Jobete Music Co Inc, Publisher(S) Unknown, Stone Diamond Music Corp

'Dangerous' Words and Music by Bill Bottrell / Michael Joseph Jackson / Edward Theodore Riley

© Kobalt Music Publishing Ltd., Sony/ATV Music Publishing LLC, Warner Chappell Music Inc, Downtown Music Publishing, BMG Rights Management

'Defender' Words and Music Peter Andre / Dantae Johnson / Nait Rawknait Masuku

'Dirty Diana' Words and Music by Michael Jackson © Sony/ATV Music Publishing LLC

'Don't Stop Til You Get Enough' Words and Music by Michael Joe Jackson © Sony/ATV Music Publishing LLC, Warner Chappell Music, Inc

'Earth Song' Words and Music by Michael Jackson © Sony/ATV Music Publishing LLC, Warner Chappell Music, Inc, Universal Music Publishing Group, Songtrust Ave

'Ease On Down The Road' Words and Music by Charles Emanuel Smalls © Sony/ATV Music Publishing LLC, Warner Chappell Music, Inc

'Farewell My Summer Love' Words and Music by Keni Lewis © Sony/ATV Music Publishing LLC

'Flava' Words and Music by Peter James Andrea / Waheed Olalekan Cole / Wayne Anthony Hector / Andrew David Whitmore © Warner Chappell Music, Inc, Universal Music Publishing Group, BMG Rights Management

'Ghosts' Words and Music by Michael Jackson / Teddy Riley © Sony/ATV Music Publishing LLC, Warner Chappell Music, Inc, Global Talent Publishing, Spirit /Global Talent Music, BMG Rights Management, Songtrust Ave

'Girl You're So Together' Words and Music by Keni Lewis © Sony/ATV Music Publishing LLC

'Give In To Me' Words and Music by Bill Bottrell / Michael Joe Jackson © Kobalt Music

Publishing Ltd., Sony/ATV Music Publishing LLC, Downtown Music Publishing

'Gone Too Soon' Words and Music by Larry Grossman / Alan "buz" Kohan © Warner Chappell Music, Inc, Spirit Music Group

'Happy Birthday' Words and Music by Patty Hill / Mildred J Hill (disputed)

'HIStory' Words and Music by Michael Jackson James Harris III Terry Lewis © Sony/ATV Music Publishing LLC

'Heal The World' Words and Music by Michael Joe Jackson © Sony/ATV Music Publishing

LLC, Warner Chappell Music, Inc, Kobalt Music Publishing Ltd.

'Heart Of Glass' Words and Music by Chris Stein / Deborah Harry © BMG Rights Management

'Human Nature' Words and Music by Steve Porcaro / John Bettis © Sony/ATV Music

Publishing LLC, Warner Chappell Music, Inc

'I Don't Want To Miss A Thing' Words and Music by Diane Warren © Universal Music Publishing Group

'If I Were Your Woman' Words and Music by Gloria Richetta Jones / Pamela Joan Sawyer/ Clarence Mc Murray © S.I.A.E. Direzione Generale, Brown Babies Music, Emi Music Publishing France, Copyright Control (Non-Hfa), Jobete Music Co Inc, Polygram Int. Publishing, Inc., Music Sales Corp Obo New Hidden Valley Music

'I Haven't Stopped Dancing Yet' Words and Music by Gloria Richetta Jones Universal Music Group (on behalf of EMI); Spirit Music Publishing, The Royalty Network © Spirit Music Group

'I'll Be There' Words and Music by Davis Hal / Gordy Berry / Hutchison Willie M / West Bob © S.I.A.E. Direzione Generale, Jobete Music Co. Inc., Universal Music-careers, Emi Music Publishing France, Copyright Control (Non-Hfa), Jobete Music Co Inc, Sony/Atv Songs Llc (Non-Rep) Mijac Music, Bug Music Obo Martin Page Music

'I Just Can't Stop Loving You' Words and Music by Michael Jackson © Sony/ATV Music Publishing LLC, Warner Chappell Music, Inc

'In The Closet' Words and Music by Michael Joe Jackson / Edward Theodore Riley ©

Sony/ATV Music Publishing LLC, Warner Chappell Music, Inc, BMG Rights Management

'Imagine' Words and Music by John Winston Lennon © Sony/ATV Music Publishing LLC

'Is It Scary' Words and Music by Michael Jackson / James Harris Iii / Terry Lewis © Sony/ATV Music Publishing LLC, Warner Chappell Music, Inc, Kobalt Music Publishing Ltd.

'I Want You Back' Words and Music by Freddie Perren / Alphonso Mizell / Deke Richards / Berry Gordy Jr © Sony/ATV Music Publishing LLC

'Jam' Words and Music by Michael Jackson / Rene Moore / Teddy Riley / Bruce Swedien © Sony/ATV Music Publishing LLC, Universal Music Publishing Group, Spirit Music Group, Music

& Media Int'l, Inc

'Just Good Friends' Words and Music by Songwriters: Graham Hamilton Lyle / Terry Britten

© Warner Chappell Music, Inc, BMG Rights Management

'Liberian Girl' Words and Music by Michael Jackson © Sony/ATV Music Publishing LLC, Warner Chappell Music, Inc

'Love Never Felt So Good' Words and Music by Michael Jackson / Paul Anka © Sony/ATV Music Publishing LLC, Warner Chappell Music, Inc

'Maggie May' Words and Music by Martin Quittenton / Roderick Stewart © Sony/ATV Music Publishing LLC, Warner Chappell Music, Inc

'Man In The Mirror' Words and Music by Glen Ballard / Siedah Garrett © Warner Chappell Music, Inc, Universal Music Publishing Group, BMG Rights Management, Songtrust Ave

'Music and Me' Words and Music by Don Fenceton / Jerry Marcellino / Mel Larson / Michael R. Cannon © Sony/ATV Music Publishing LLC

'My Bad Boys Coming Home' Words and Music by Ed Cobb © Sony/ATV Music Publishing LLC

'Natural' Words and Music by Catherine Roseanne Dennis / Jean Francois Fredenucci / Sylvie N'doumbe / Andrew Todd © BMG Rights Management

'Off The Wall' Songwriters: Words and Music by Rodney Lynn Temperton © Warner Chappell Music, Inc

'Outta Control' Words and Music by Burrell / McPherson / Martinez / Christina Nassar

'PYT (Pretty Young Thing)' Words and Music by James Ingram / Quincy Jones © Warner Chappell Music, Inc, BMG Rights Management

'This Is How We Do It' Words and Music by Montell Du'Sean Jordan / Oji Pierce / Ricky M L Walters © Sony/ATV Music Publishing LLC, Warner Chappell Music, Inc, Universal Music Publishing Group, Kobalt Music Publishing Ltd., The Bicycle Music Company

'This Place Hotel' Words and Music by Michael Jackson © Sony/ATV Music Publishing LLC, Warner Chappell Music, Inc

'Thriller' Words and Music by Rodney Lynn Temperton © Warner Chappell Music, Inc

'Two Can Play That Game' Words and Music by Bernard Belle / Teddy Riley / David "redhead" Guppy / Thomas Reyes / Bobby Brown © Sony/ATV Music Publishing LLC, Warner Chappell Music, Inc, Universal Music Publishing Group, BMG Rights Management

'Wanna Be Startin' Something' Words and Music by Michael Jackson © Sony/ATV Music Publishing LLC

'Who's Lovin' You' Words and music by William Robinson Jr. © Sony/ATV Music Publishing LLC

'Who Wants To Live Forever' Words and Music by Brian May © Sony/ATV Music Publishing LLC

'Will You Be There' Words and Music by Michael Jackson © Sony/ATV Music Publishing LLC

'Working Day and Night' Words and Music by Michael Jackson © Sony/ATV Music Publishing LLC

'You Rock My World' Words and Music by Fred Jerkins / Lashawn Ameen Daniels / Michael Jackson / Michael Joe Jackson / Nora Shena Payne / Rodney Jerkins © Sony/ATV Music Publishing LLC, Warner Chappell Music, Inc, Kobalt Music Publishing Ltd., Songtrust Ave.